T0294003

APPLAUDING THE KOP

APPLAUDING THE KOP

THE STORY OF
LIVERPOOL FOOTBALL CLUB'S
GOALKEEPERS

PAUL WILKES

First published by Pitch Publishing, 2020

Pitch Publishing
A2 Yeoman Gate
Yeoman Way
Worthing
Sussex
BN13 3QZ
www.pitchpublishing.co.uk
info@pitchpublishing.co.uk

A CIP catalogue record is available for this book
from the British Library.

ISBN 978-1-78531-651-7

Typesetting and origination by Pitch Publishing

Printed and bound by TJ International, Padstow, UK

Contents

For Gemma, Owen, Liam
and Joshua x

Acknowledgements

MY WRITING career has been a rollercoaster over the last ten years, and I have certainly come a long way since I started a blog on Spanish football. I would like to thank those who helped me from the very start and gave me the confidence to pursue writing as a feasible option. From Elisa and the late Armando for giving my first opportunity to write on their website (albeit for free) to Ben Cove at Unibet for giving me my first paid writing gig. I would like to express gratitude to my father-in-law Rob Billington, his then business partner Paul Kemshell and others at WRM Media for listening to my vision and then implementing it for my website.

I have worked with numerous editors and sub-editors through the years, and I appreciate all of their advice and tips. It's at *FourFourTwo* where I have freelanced for the longest, and where I continue to provide content. The staff has changed a lot over time but I'm particularly beholden to Gary Parkinson and Joe Brewin. They have listened to my countless ideas and pitches, while also allowing me to represent the company at some of the biggest matches in the Premier League.

I would also like to praise Jane Camillin at Pitch Publishing for giving me the platform to write this book and for her understanding when I was forced to juggle multiple balls during the latter stages. Alex Daley for his attention to detail and support, Duncan Olner for making the cover look so extraordinary, Graham Hales for making it more readable and correcting my grammar, and anyone else behind the scenes at Pitch.

The two best Manchester United authors in the business have been exceptionally helpful. Andy Mitten has been brilliant with me since we first met in the press room at Anfield before Liverpool versus Borussia Dortmund. He has given me guidance and information that isn't available in manuals. Wayne Barton has also been extremely supportive and given me belief. Ryan Baldi is another that has offered me some assistance, while Jason Pettigrove has been meaningful with his direction at various times that I have worked in this profession.

The interviews that I conducted for the book have all been invaluable and worthwhile. From the legends I heard stories about to those I watched play on TV and within stadiums: Jamie Carragher, Ronnie Whelan, David Fairclough, Mick Halsall, Paul Stewart, David Thompson, Jean-Paul van Gastel, Stephen Wright, Stephen Warnock, Markus Babbel, Tony Warner, Michael Stensgaard, Sander Westerveld, Pegguy Arphexad, Scott Carson, Martin Hansen, Peter Gulacsi, Danny Ward and John Achterberg.

The media staff at Manchester City, Leicester City, Huddersfield Town, Derby County, RB Leipzig, Ingolstadt and Basel for allowing me to speak to their players about the subjects covered. The lads at Aldridge White Watch for the constant badgering in order to motivate me to finish this book.

I'm also grateful to my mum and dad for their support in my life and for bestowing me with the principles that have meant I can be trusted with information from strangers.

My three children, Owen, Liam and Joshua, for their patience with me during this time and for their understanding. I hope this will set an example that dreams are there to be achieved.

Finally, my wife Gemma, who has been supportive of me throughout the process. She has read through chapters for me, despite a blatant dislike of all things football. I know it has been difficult at times, but I hope you can now see the full benefit.

Foreword

GROWING UP in the mid-1980s, Neville Southall was probably the best in Europe, maybe even the world. I always knew that we had a better goalkeeper than Liverpool.

The first thing that springs to mind regarding goalkeepers is the 1986 season when both Liverpool and Everton were going for the title and the FA Cup. Liverpool came out on top, although I think everyone thought that Everton would win the league. Bruce Grobbelaar made a mistake in the Merseyside derby, when Kevin Ratcliffe hit a shot from about 30 yards at the Kop end and it snuck underneath the Liverpool man.

Bruce was always remembered for things like that; he was a little unorthodox, although he had his good moments as well. He was so agile and athletic, probably ahead of his time, in terms of coming out and using his feet. It would put your heart in your mouth, but we see this a lot from goalkeepers now.

Roy Naylor was my goalkeeper when we won the FA Youth Cup at Liverpool a decade later. The team contained Michael Owen, David Thompson, Jon Newby and a keeper who looked like Eddie the Eagle. I don't think any of us thought that Roy was going to go on and play for Liverpool, but I always remember the Manchester United game in the quarter-final.

He was brilliant and kept us in it. They totally out-played us in the first half and had a few one-on-ones. His Eddie the Eagle features helped him that day, as everything seemed to hit his chin.

That game was famous for Michael's hat-trick, but without Roy Naylor we would have really struggled. Roy was a massive part of that Youth Cup win.

He was one of the lads that was quite shy and used to get a bit of stick, but he always took it quite well. That United game was a massive moment for him because he got a lot of attention afterwards from the lads.

David James was my first goalkeeper when I was promoted to the seniors. He was a great person to have around was Jamo. He's mad, really! He's hyperactive! A big character and a very funny lad. I had him at England as well throughout my international career. I sometimes look at Jamo and think that you couldn't get a better possible physique for a goalkeeper. Normally, someone of that size isn't that agile, but he was unbelievable. So quick and robust, although he just probably lacked concentration and focus. That made him make bad decisions at times.

That was the biggest thing with Jamo. His decision-making stopped him from becoming a world-class goalkeeper. He was a top Premier League goalkeeper and had over 50 caps for England, but he just couldn't quite get up to that level of your Peter Schmeichels, Edwin van der Sars and Petr Cechs. He was probably a level below those guys because he just didn't have the concentration. It meant that, at times, he would make poor choices like coming out for a cross or when he had long spells not doing anything.

I always remember Jamo in a cup game he played for Watford against Everton. He was coming for everything and punching everything. He always seemed like a goalkeeper who wanted to be involved in the action all the time. I used to sometimes think, 'Is that always the best thing for a goalkeeper?' He always wanted to make his mark in a game, whereas a goalkeeper who isn't involved or isn't in the firing line normally shows that the match has gone well for the team. That was just his style.

Without a doubt this improved as he got older. Jamo was very dedicated and he employed sports psychologists. He wanted to do everything he could. He had that maturity when he went on in his career. That shows in the fact he has the record for the most clean sheets in the Premier League and also the fourth-highest amount of appearances. Jamo had a long and very good career, but he will probably be a bit disappointed how it finished at Liverpool and then not getting back to a club of that level again.

Tony 'Bonus' Warner was the back-up keeper. He was called that because he never played but always got the win bonus when the team won. He's a big character in Liverpool.

As a 17-year-old, I was playing for the reserves at Notts County and it was snowing. We were warming up and this ball came flying towards me. I half-volleyed it and I couldn't have connected with it any better. It was heading straight for his head. I couldn't even shout him; it was going that quick. It hit him right on the ear. He turned to look and saw it was me. He came marching over. Honest to God, I thought the goalkeeper was going to kill me in the warm-up!

It's brilliant to see him around the city when I'm out. It was always going to be difficult for him at Liverpool. I think it's hard for any top club to bring a goalkeeper through. It very rarely happens because there's so much pressure on that position, and it was best for him that he did move away.

Brad Friedel was a great personality and character also. He probably caused a few problems when he came in because we had two recognised number ones, in him and David James. Roy Evans made that decision. In some people's eyes, Brad is rated a better keeper than David James because of his career in England and at Blackburn, but it didn't quite happen for him at Liverpool. He was coming from America to a big club and it was difficult with David James still there. There were issues over who had which goalkeeper number and little things like that.

It's very difficult to have two top-class goalkeepers. With goalkeepers, everybody needs to know who the number one is and for 12–18 months that was a problem at Liverpool. Evans had brought Friedel in, but Gérard Houllier returned to David James when he took over. It was after an away performance at Manchester United, when Brad wasn't at his best. It was almost like Jamo won that battle in the end in some ways.

Sander Westerveld came in on the back of people saying that the keepers weren't good enough and I think it was right to make a change in 1999. I don't think Sander ever surpassed the goalkeepers who had gone before him in Jamo and Brad though. The team was a lot better, so there were better defenders and the clean sheet record was better. We added defensive strength in Sami Hyypia and Stephane Henchoz, so that was a strong period for us, in terms of turning the team around.

Sander seemed to have something in his head that said he needed to score a goal in every game he played. I always felt that he was trying to beat the opposition goalkeeper and kick the ball as far as he could. He had some kick on him as well; it was almost like Ederson these days. I don't think he was a massive success, but he just did all right. Don't get me wrong, Sander played his part in the treble success in 2001. It was only a couple of years before Houllier changed it. It was probably very ruthless, and some people may say unfair, that we signed two goalkeepers in one day. It can't have been a nice situation for Sander to be in; it certainly wouldn't have been easy.

Jerzy Dudek was one of those who arrived. He wasn't as big a frame as other goalkeepers, so he wasn't as dominant off his line. Many say that Jerzy was a great shot-stopper, but it makes me laugh when people say that because every goalkeeper is a good shot-stopper; if he's not then what's he doing in goal! It's the basic requirement of any goalkeeper when he starts at ten years old that they can save a few shots. Jerzy maybe made more of saves than other goalkeepers, as if he was doing it for the cameras.

When my headed back pass went through his legs and Diego Forlan scored in a game with Manchester United, I was just glad Diego got a touch on the ball or otherwise it would have been another own goal for me. It was never going to be easy after that mistake and against one of your biggest rivals as well. I don't think Forlan had scored for United before that game, then he got two goals in a huge match. When you come under huge pressure it's how you react! How you can then go on and have a big Liverpool career! Jerzy showed great character and was the man of the match when we played United again in the League Cup Final a couple of months later. He made some wonderful saves in the second half. He is a legend now because of Istanbul and definitely finished really strongly.

All the goalkeepers I played with were very good, but I don't think until Pepe Reina came that we played with a great one. It was always a difficult position for us. Was it their ability that made managers change goalkeepers so quickly or was it the actual pressure of playing for Liverpool? The scrutiny and level of intrusion was higher than many of the places they had been before!

Pepe was a big personality in the dressing room, very similar to David James in some ways. He was very strong off his line, very aggressive. That team needed to be more combative under Rafa Benitez as it was a little bit weak in 2005. Rafa made changes with the goalkeeper, Peter Crouch at 6ft 7in up front and Momo Sissoko in midfield; he had great energy as well. You could see how the team was going.

Pepe was the best goalkeeper I played with in a Liverpool shirt by a long way. I think distribution-wise, he was what you see now in a goalkeeper. Pepe was quick and agile. He probably fell just a bit short of Schmeichel, Van der Sar and Cech of that era, but there was very little in it. He was a big upgrade in what we had before. It was the closest we came to winning the league and we lost the European Cup Final, so he was unfortunate that he only came away with an FA Cup winner's medal.

Some of the other goalkeepers in my time can count themselves lucky to have ever come to the club. Charles Itandje was awful. He was a joke of a signing really. It's always difficult getting substitute goalkeepers. What kind of character accepts being sub? Straight away you think there's something wrong with his character and how good can he be? It was a revolving door for the number two goalkeeper. I used to just pray that the first choice never got injured. We were quite lucky in that with Pepe. Itandje was a disaster for us, so it was good when he moved on. Diego Cavalieri didn't play too often; I can always remember that he was a bit stiff and very left-footed. I think for a lot of them it's a dream to come to Liverpool. They accept being sub for a couple of years, make a few quid and then move on! They can also put they played for Liverpool on the CV.

From the goalkeepers in recent years, I don't think me and Loris Karius would have got on particularly well! That's nothing to do with his ability. He is very cocksure and confident in himself and if someone isn't at the required level, then that's not ideal. Sometimes you feel sorry for someone and you want them to do well. You can see how much it hurts them when things go wrong.

In the aftermath of the Champions League Final in Kiev, I wanted to give him a hug; I was working on the side of the pitch and I felt really sorry for him. You can say that he cost Liverpool the game, but as footballers we have all had games where it hasn't gone well, and you have cost the team. It was just unfortunate for him that it was in the biggest game of his life. I did feel sorry for him, but it was only probably a couple of weeks before he was back to his normal self. He is confident in himself, shall we say! That's not a trait that I particularly like in someone that I'm playing alongside who is not at the top of his game. I'm not quite sure how well it would have gone with me and Loris.

I think Alisson has the edge on Pepe. He is the top goalkeeper in the world right now. Virgil van Dijk was huge when he signed, but I think the goalkeeper was equally as important. Don't forget that when Van Dijk first came, Liverpool were involved in some high-scoring games. They won a Champions League semi-final

7-6 over two legs against Roma with Karius in goal. That tells you all you need to know.

The difference with Alisson has been unbelievable. Liverpool have gone from a 75-to-80-point team to a 95-to-100-point team. Yes, other people have improved, but for me the goalkeeper has added ten to 15 points there, no doubt about it. At the end of his time at Liverpool, if he continues to be successful, then the big debate over who was the best ever will be between him and Ray Clemence.

As a defender, I liked goalkeepers who didn't create panic. A cool head makes everyone else feel relaxed. I think that's very important. You could see that in the difference between Simon Mignolet and Alisson. It has an effect on the crowd as well; the fans get really jittery when there's no confidence in a goalkeeper. That can then go right through the team. A top goalkeeper spreads calm through the stadium.

It's fairly obvious, but I wanted them to make big saves. I never wanted goalkeepers to do anything outrageous. I just didn't want them to do stupid things. I don't mind if you don't pull off a worldly save, just don't make silly mistakes or bad decisions. Almost be a seven out of ten every time. That will do me. In Alisson and Ederson, you see nine out of tens now.

Jamie Carragher

'As a goalkeeper you make a
mistake and the ball is in the goal,
that is the life of a goalkeeper.'

Jürgen Klopp, January 2020

Introduction

ANDREAS SCHRANZ came running towards the Kop end at Anfield, when the supporters began to serenade him with applause. I was pretty sure he had never played for Liverpool, but he responded in kind with his own clapping anyway. Maybe it was just a friendly gesture for a goalkeeper who would likely see numerous goals fly past him under the floodlights of a European night. Grazer AK were already two goals down from the first leg after a Steven Gerrard brace in Austria, so it was certainly plausible that Liverpool would add more at home. It was also likely to be Schranz's biggest match of his career, so it was highly possible that the welcoming Scousers were simply taking pity on the onslaught about to delivered by Gerrard, Harry Kewell and Milan Baros.

Grazer AK surprisingly won the game 1-0 in August 2004 and, while it wasn't the most shocking thing to happen to Liverpool in the Champions League that season, it did make new boss Rafael Benitez a little concerned. I was still a little perplexed by the premonition of Schranz's performance, but I just presumed as an Austrian international he was headed for a bigger club. That move never materialised for Schranz, but I did find out why the Liverpool fans were so accepting.

The term 'Applauding the Kop' comes from the act of the away team's goalkeeper receiving applause from Liverpool's Kop stand either before the game or as the team returns from half-time. If the goalkeeper reciprocates the clapping to acknowledge the olive branch handed to him by the home supporters, then it will be gladly received. However, if he ignores this kind act of appreciation, he is routinely booed for the remainder of the match. Manchester United and Everton stoppers are naturally less likely to retort the gesture and will often receive a barrage of abuse. It's believed that Gordon Banks was the first recipient of the tradition, when he visited Merseyside for the first time since England won the World Cup in 1966.

It was far from the first time that I had watched a match at Anfield, but it was the earliest that I had noticed this situation. Perhaps I was too caught up in the emotion and moment of previous visits not to have noticed this tradition. Liverpool's goalkeepers would be thankful of the support they received from the supporters inside the stadium. The same can't always be said of those on social media, although the toxicity of the platform is never a true reflection. Throughout the years we have witnessed the sublime to the ridiculous and often from the same player. For every outstanding save, there has been an error of equal proportions in terms of extraordinariness.

Everyone makes mistakes, but when those mistakes become frequent and start to outweigh the good, then it's certainly not unreasonable to expect better from those involved. Imagine if you continually messed up at work, the likelihood is that your boss and co-workers would demand more and if you couldn't provide that after numerous warnings, you would likely find yourself looking for a new job. If those mistakes were watched in person by 55,000 people and a further few million on television cameras, then the scrutiny is naturally much more severe. When that person is also paid significantly, then the expectation becomes even higher still. Among all the anger and frustration from the fans, it's important to remember that goalkeepers are human. They may act mentally strong and they forge resilience throughout their lives, but their feelings and emotional state are visible.

Liverpool have certainly had their fair share of characters wearing the goalkeeping gloves, whether that has been high-profile signings getting criticism for errors in career-defining games or the lesser-known back-up keepers who have gone on to prove themselves elsewhere. The capacity to find a trusted lieutenant between the sticks has been the source of much frustration for many managers at Anfield.

Technically, the goalkeeper role is different to any other on the football pitch. Each player has to have unique skillsets for each position, but for the goalkeeper that extends even further. They may now be required to be better with their feet than ever before, while they still have to fundamentally ensure that they stop the ball going past them into their goal. The multiple substitutes in the modern game mean that it's rare to get an outfield player looking rather uncomfortable between the posts due to an injury or sending off anymore. We are often told that goalkeepers are 'crazy', 'different' and 'rare breeds'. That generalisation certainly does them a huge injustice, although the majority have interesting personalities. It's arguable that no position is under greater scrutiny due to the increase in matches, television exposure, articles and social media.

My own fascination with goalkeepers comes from my experiences of playing for teams as a kid. I was a decent enough shot-stopper, but I didn't command the area, catch crosses or have a significant presence due to my diminutive frame. It goes without saying that I was never going to make it professionally, but in my first game in the position as a 12-year-old we only lost 1-0. This was a massive improvement on previous games, where we had been beaten by seven or eight goals. It didn't take long before normal business was resumed, and I touched the ball more times from picking it out of the net than I did in open play. It was also made much more difficult by the use of full-sized nets, where I couldn't even touch the crossbar when jumping. This small insight into the world of goalkeeping did allow me to feel the pain and suffering of making mistakes that cost the team. It was never anything that anyone ever said, but the look of disappointment on the faces of those that had been chasing round after a football for 90 minutes.

It was not possible to cover every single goalkeeper who has worn the Liver Bird on his chest either in a match shirt or training jersey. I hope that every chapter teaches you something new, makes you smile or laugh and gives you a better understanding of either the player or the period. I know there will be some who expect more coverage of the earlier legends such as Elisha Scott and Tommy Lawrence, but there's naturally less information from those eras and I felt that the modern-day struggles of others were just as prevalent. I also didn't want this book to be solely about Liverpool; I think the paths trodden by those on the way to Liverpool and then their experiences afterwards told a bigger story than just sitting on the bench at Anfield. I think that it illustrates the conflict and sacrifices made by those that came to the club and shows a human side to their fight. As more foreign players arrived in the 1990s, their stories and experiences naturally differed from those of their British counterparts. I hope fans of European football get just as much from this book, as you gain an insight into some unique teams on the continent.

I approached every major goalkeeper of the last 40 years regarding an interview, whether that was directly to them or through people working for them. Those who haven't been interviewed either have a book of their own, a book planned or simply weren't comfortable with divulging their life story. The original plan when I conducted the first interview in November 2016 was to use the same framework as Simon Hughes's book *Ring of Fire* where he interviewed individual players about their own story, which is what I have done in the latter chapters. However, to tell the complete story through Liverpool's history was not possible. It would have been nice to have conducted long-form interviews with Ray Clemence or David James, but I hope you will find that by speaking to their former team-mates it gives an alternative viewpoint. There are some that don't have their own chapters but were among the best to feature for the club.

Their absence isn't to downplay their importance; it all depended on who I interviewed. Pepe Reina for instance is spoken about by many of the goalkeepers. I felt that he has been covered sufficiently through the stories of others in various chapters. I also would have liked to have spoken with some of the more recent custodians such as Simon Mignolet and Loris Karius, but for whatever reason it didn't happen. Alisson could now become the greatest ever at Anfield if he maintains this level, but I didn't feel at this time that an interview with him would have been worthwhile. It's also difficult to get access to those who are playing with him, but I'm sure that you will agree the John Achterberg chapter will give insight into the club that is rarely seen and is a nice way to conclude this book.

How goalkeepers are remembered is always quite interesting. Many will think of specific moments such as winning trophies or massive clangers, as each of us has our own very different consciousness. The media's perception will also play a huge factor in that retrospective feeling, rightly or wrongly. It's impossible not to talk about the politics at the club when discussing each of the goalkeepers, as like many of the managers, their futures were linked to results. I thought it was important to set the scene when appropriate and discuss not just the keeper, but the other factors that ultimately affected their environment. The Liverpool that Bruce Grobbelaar arrived at in 1981 was much more favourable than the one he left in 1994, while the opposite could certainly be said of David James. Hopefully, this book will go some way to understanding the individual circumstances of each player and how things could have been different had they not joined the club when they did.

Chapter 1

The First Custodians,
Paving the Way

THE FORMATION of Liverpool Football Club in 1892 saw John Houlding, who owned Anfield, task John McKenna with the search for players. McKenna was acting as both recruiter and manager, in pursuit of talent that could operate in the shadow of league champions Everton. His main area of expertise proved to be Glasgow, although they naturally took players from their old club that had now moved to Goodison Park.

Sydney Ross became the first goalkeeper, or 'custodian' – as they were known in the 1890s – to play a competitive game for Liverpool. He was born to parents Alexander and Elizabeth on 8 June 1869 in Edinburgh. Ross signed from Scottish club Cambuslang, on the south-east outskirts of Glasgow. The 23-year-old was only 5ft 7in tall but that didn't mean he was easy to beat. 'The position of goalkeeper is perfectly safe in the hands of Sydney Ross,' pronounced local sports paper *Field Sport* before an official ball had been kicked. 'His display in the practice matches stamps him as one of the finest custodians who ever appeared in a team.' His agility and communication skills seemed to be his greatest asset.

Aided by an impressive defence, he kept nine clean sheets in 18 matches as they won the Lancashire League. Their opening match of the 1892/93 season saw them thrash Higher Walton 8-0. Ross broke his leg in March 1893 in a Lancashire Cup second-round game with Bootle. It meant that his contract wasn't renewed, and he transferred back to his former side in the May. Billy McOwen took his place in the team and the Blackburn-born goalkeeper was instrumental in the Second Division. Liverpool collected 50 points from a possible 56 and were unbeaten. McOwen saved an incredible 11 of the 12 penalties that he faced and only conceded 13 goals as the Reds were promoted to the top flight. He decided to retire from the professional game and concentrate on his job as a dentist.

William McCann joined from Abercorn FC and played in Liverpool's first season in the First Division. He wasn't the only new signing that didn't hit the ground running, as they took ten matches to get their first victory and were relegated. An incredible 39 goals conceded in 15 league games ensured that his stay lasted just eight months. Matt McQueen was next, and he was arguably the most versatile player ever to play for Liverpool. McQueen started his career as a forward before moving to full-back and then goalkeeper. He played in every position and was part of two Second Division-winning squads, making a total of 150 appearances. His adaptability wasn't only confined to the pitch though, as he later became a linesman and then a director and manager at the club.

Harry Storer was the first goalkeeper to hold down the position at Liverpool for a sustained period, when he signed in December 1895 from Arsenal for £100. Storer was also flexible in sport, having played six games of cricket for his home county of Derbyshire. The stopper would be number one for the next three seasons on the football field, with Tom Watson as manager from the summer of 1896. In September 1897, Storer had a particularly good game as they recorded their first win over Everton. Watson's tactical approach saw Liverpool become more defensively solid, which enabled Storer to concede fewer goals. Liverpool cemented their position as a top-tier side in those years, even finishing second in 1898/99.

The next season started badly when the Reds lost their first eight matches and Storer was replaced by Bill Perkins between the posts. Perkins had joined from Luton Town in the March and made his debut a week later in a 3-2 win over Newcastle United. He was the first Liverpool goalkeeper to win a league title, as Watson's men secured the trophy in 1901. Only Perkins, Tom Robertson and Bill Goldie started all 34 games in the league that term, as they lined up in a 2-3-5 formation. In 1902/03, Perkins shared the goalkeeping duties with Peter Platt before the new signing from Blackburn Rovers eventually made the position his own. Platt started the next year as first choice with Perkins leaving for Northampton Town, but it was disastrous for the club as they were relegated to the Second Division.

The experienced Ned Doig joined from Watson's old side Sunderland, who were known as the 'Team of all the Talents'. Liverpool paid £150 for him in the summer of 1904. The 37-year-old instantly became a fan favourite, with his ability to punch the ball clear due to his boxing credentials. 'The veteran has displayed all his old ability, and although he has seen so many years' service he is as agile and clever as ever,' read the club programme in November 1904. Liverpool were promoted back to the top division at the first attempt.

However, their move back into the big time didn't start well for the team or Doig. They lost five of their first eight games including heavy defeats to Everton and Aston Villa, with Doig conceding 20 goals. Watson had no time for sentimentalism, and he sent a postcard to Doig's address informing him he was no longer required. The promising Sam Hardy was signed from Chesterfield. The defensive improvement was immediate, and Liverpool saw only 26 goals against them in the following 30 league matches. This enabled them to win their second league title in five years.

Hardy grew in stature and, in 1907, he made his England debut at Goodison Park. 'To me his intuition seemed extraordinary,' remarked his eventual successor Kenneth Campbell. 'He seemed to place himself right in the spot where a shot was to come in, and by doing so was able to clear his lines with the least possible fuss. Frankly, my ideas of goalkeeping underwent a change, and, although I had a fairly respectable reputation as a keeper at that time, my own feelings were that I was but a tyro. And right here just let me say that I was indebted to Sam for many valuable tips during his term at Anfield while I was there.' Hardy earned himself the nickname 'Safe and Steady Sam' and he was their first goalkeeper to make over 200 appearances for the club. He stayed at Watson's Liverpool until he left for Aston Villa in 1912.

William Scott had been the goalkeeper across Stanley Park for the last eight years and his brother Elisha was given a trial at Everton off the back of his recommendation. However, after they deemed he was too small, Liverpool spotted his capability and signed him as a replacement for Hardy. 'I don't think Scott ever weighed more than ten stone odd,' read one column in the *Liverpool Echo*. 'The story goes he wore an extra jersey to make him look bigger and more formidable.' It seemed to work.

The rules changed that year for goalkeepers, which meant they were only allowed to handle the ball inside of their own penalty area. For the next three seasons, Scottish international Campbell was Liverpool's goalkeeper, with Scott as back-up. The club's results were less than spectacular, although they did remain in the First Division and finished runners-up to Crystal Palace in the 1914 FA Cup Final.

Scott made his debut on New Year's Day in 1913, when he kept Newcastle United at bay in a 0-0 draw. The Geordies were so impressed that they tried to buy him afterwards, while it was reported that he had played with an injured arm. 'His debut was brilliant and a pleasing augury,' read the review of his performance in the *Liverpool Echo*. A year later William joined Elisha at Anfield after he made the transfer from Leeds United. The First World War interrupted football between 1915 and 1919, with Liverpool competing in the Lancashire Section for two of those years. When normal proceedings resumed, Liverpool were much better, and Campbell had a fight to keep his place. He initially played while Scott recovered from an operation, but the Irishman impressed in February 1920 and a month later Campbell had asked for a transfer.

Elisha Scott's return after the war heralded a new era for the number one jersey, with David Ashworth now manager following the death of Watson. Ashworth's approach was based on a solid defence that conceded few goals and Scott was a huge factor. Liverpool won back-to-back league titles in 1922 and 1923, with Scott missing just three games. 'To prove successful, the goalkeeper must learn the art of always being in the right place at the right moment,' wrote Scott in an article about his two decades at Liverpool. 'He has to keep his eyes on the ball all the time, but he cannot afford to ignore any opponents, who come within shooting range of the net. In guarding the net, you must not be too obvious in your methods. Forwards practice all kinds of tricks to disguise their real intentions, and goalkeepers must be just as cunning.'

Arthur Riley began to give Scott competition at the end of the 1920s and he eventually replaced the legend on a full-time basis in 1934, when Scott joined Belfast Celtic as player-manager. In Scott's final home match against Chelsea, he took to the microphone to articulate his feelings towards the supporters. 'We have always been the best of friends and shall always remain so,' he said. 'I have finished with English association football. Last but not least, my friends of the Kop. I cannot thank them sufficiently. They have inspired me. God bless you all!' When Anfield was redeveloped in December 2014, the club placed granite benches in front of the new Main Stand. Scott's is one of the seven in a special project called 'The Men who Built Anfield' along with

Billy Liddell, Bill Shankly, Bob Paisley, Kenny Dalglish, John Barnes and Steven Gerrard.

On Scott's bench reads a quote from Everton's legendary striker Dixie Dean, 'The greatest I've ever seen.' The forward used to send a tube of aspirins to Scott the night before a game with a note that told him to sleep well ahead of the goals he was going to score against him the following day. They shared a friendship and unique footballing battle throughout their careers.

Liverpool continued to struggle over the next few years as they finished in the top half of the league just once in six seasons. The Second World War started in 1939 with Riley and fellow South African goalkeeper Dirk Kemp made sergeants in the 9th King's Liverpool Battalion. Top-level football was lost for another seven campaigns, but when it restarted Liverpool profited.

Cyril Sidlow joined George Kay's side in February 1946 from Wolverhampton Wanderers. He was described as a good shot-stopper and was also among the first to throw the ball to his defenders in order to retain possession. He played in 34 of the 42 games of the 1946/47 season, with stiff competition coming in the form of Charlie Ashcroft and Ray Minshull. Liverpool, with a team that contained Paisley, Liddell and Albert Stubbins, won the league title in the first year back following the war. It went right to the wire though, with Kay's men winning an infamous encounter with Wolves, but having to wait two weeks for Stoke City to play their final fixture. Liverpool were beating Everton in the Lancashire Cup Final when it was announced over the PA at Anfield that Stoke had lost at Sheffield United and scuppered their own title chance. Unfortunately, this wasn't the sign of things to come, as Liverpool struggled in the subsequent seasons. They lost the FA Cup Final in 1950 to Arsenal and their league positions were no better than eighth. Their decline continued when Kay left in 1951 for health reasons and Don Welsh took the managerial mantle. Sidlow departed the club in 1953 and Liverpool were relegated in 1954 with Ashcroft now in the number one jersey.

It was a difficult start to life in the second tier, with Liverpool in serious danger of dropping down a further division. Dave Underwood started six out of the first seven league games in goal, which resulted in just one win. Ashcroft regained his place for the next couple of months, but a 3-2 defeat to Luton Town prompted another change. Liverpool's third South African goalkeeper, Doug Rudham, was now tasked with the role having just signed from Johannesburg Rangers, while Welsh also made changes to the defence. He kept the club's first clean sheet of the season in a 1-0 win over Nottingham Forest, but it did little to stop the onslaught upon their backline in subsequent matches. They had lost 12 times on the road before the end of the calendar year including a record 9-1 defeat at Birmingham City. Liverpool didn't get relegated and saw some improvement the following season when Underwood and Rudham shared the responsibilities. The club finished third, but Welsh's inability to gain promotion saw him resign in 1956 and former Liverpool wing-half Phil Taylor was given the task of managing the club.

He immediately signed Tommy Younger from Hibernian, who had won two Scottish league titles with the custodian. Younger missed just six matches over the next three seasons.. However, the Reds narrowly missed out on regaining their top-flight status during this period. Younger left for a player-manager role at Falkirk in 1959 and in turn they sent Bert Slater in the opposite direction. Slater's small demeanour saw him earn the nickname 'Shorty'. He lasted only three matches as Taylor's first choice, even though they won two of them. The defence were still leaking goals and he conceded seven goals in games with Cardiff City, Bristol City and Hull City, so Rudham came back into the side.

Taylor left in the November and a month later he was replaced by Bill Shankly. The Scotsman restored Slater to the line-up and, although Liverpool finished just outside the promotion places in the next two years, they were laying the foundations for the future. Off the pitch, Shankly constructed the now infamous

'Boot Room' personnel with Bob Paisley bolstered to first-team coach and Joe Fagan given reserve manager duties. On the field, the established captain Ronnie Moran was assisted by Ron Yeats and Gerry Byrne in defence, a young Ian Callaghan was given an opportunity and Ian St John and Roger Hunt formed a solid strike force. Training sessions were now systematic and no longer had the relaxed atmosphere of previous eras. Shankly installed many of the principles that we come to expect of the modern-day football club. He was also perhaps the first Liverpool manager to have complete control over his own team selection, with the directors often interfering in the past. That possibly explains why so few goalkeepers were able to get a consistent run in the team.

Slater lost his place at the end of the 1961/62 term and Jim Furnell played in the final 13 games as Liverpool were finally promoted back among the elite of the country. Furnell began the next season in goal, but then he broke his finger in training. 'I went down to collect the ball in a five-a-side and caught the finger on the ground,' said Furnell to the *Lancashire Telegraph* in 1998. 'Shanks took me out of goal and made me complete the match up front. He wouldn't believe that it was broken, but Bob Paisley insisted I should go along to have it checked out by the doctors. I spent a week in hospital, needed a bone graft and didn't play again for months. Didn't realise it at the time, but it was the end for me at Anfield. That's when I saw another side to Shankly. If you were injured it was as though you stopped existing. He didn't come to visit me and more or less ignored me when I reported in at the club for daily treatment.' A 22-year-old Tommy Lawrence seized his opportunity and never looked back.

Chapter 2

Tommy Lawrence,
The Flying Pig

'THE GREATEST quality Tommy Lawrence brought to the team was calmness,' said Ian St John. Lawrence was just 17 when he joined Liverpool, although he had to wait five years before he made his first-team debut. Furnell's injury just 13 games into the 1962/63 season gave him an opportunity that he seized. Liverpool's new goalkeeper didn't particularly look the part, as he weighed over 89kg and wasn't that tall. 'He was a bulky keeper,' said Ian Callaghan. 'But Tommy was remarkably agile for his size and had a wonderful, philosophical temperament.' The rather unflattering nickname of 'The Flying Pig' was born.

Lawrence had played as a midfielder for Warrington Schoolboys, which meant he was unusually good with the ball at his feet once he was converted to keeper. It also ensured that he read the game well and his positioning enabled him to close down opposition forwards. Under Bill Shankly's instructions, he now needed to be on the 18-yard line when the ball was at the halfway line rather than the usual six-yard area. 'At first I was frightened to death,' admitted Lawrence to *Matchday* magazine. 'We did it at Melwood a few times, then we tried it at Anfield. Well, I'm standing there, and the Kop is giving me some stick. "Get back on your line!" they're all yelling. No goalkeeper did that in those days. I thought, "Oh my God." But it worked. I'd come out and do like they do today. You didn't get sent off in those days either. So, I used to bring them down. If they pushed it past me, I'd just hit them.'

His surprising speed when moving forward combined with his imposing frame made it difficult for opposition forwards in one-on-one situations, while his ball-playing ability saw him labelled as a pioneer for the modern-day sweeper-keeper. The Reds lost the first three matches Lawrence played, but then won the next nine as he conceded only five goals. They faded badly in the final quarter of the campaign, but the early form and FA Cup semi-final was a sign of things to come.

Bill Shankly signed a contract for the first time in the summer of 1963 having spent the previous five years on a rolling deal. Liverpool had finished eighth in the league and Everton were champions, but there was a feeling that this youthful side were ready to make an impact. It didn't start well though, with back-to-back defeats at Anfield against Nottingham Forest and Blackpool leaving Liverpool with just nine points from their opening nine games. They managed to overturn their run and wins during the Easter period against Tottenham (twice), Leicester City and Manchester United were definitive, as Lawrence conceded just two goals.

Two matches with Arsenal had a profound influence on both Lawrence and Liverpool's title hopes. The first encounter at Highbury in December 1963 saw Liverpool winning 1-0 with just 20 minutes left, when a shot from Joe Baker trickled towards Lawrence. Defender Ron Yeats shouted to his goalkeeper to collect it, but Lawrence opened his legs and allowed the ball to roll into the net. The Reds held on for a 1-1 draw, but all of the players knew that Shankly wouldn't be happy. They shot off into the dressing room in order to get in the bath before their manager could give them any verbal retribution. However, they weren't fast enough and Shankly burst into the room. 'Where is he?' he boomed. 'I am here, boss,' came the feeble reply from the goalkeeper. 'Before you say anything, boss, I want to apologise to you and the lads. I should have never opened my legs to that ball.' Shankly replied, 'It's not your fault. It's your fucking mother who should have never opened her legs.'

In the final game of the 1963/64 campaign, the Gunners travelled to Anfield. Liverpool had to win in order to collect the championship. Arsenal were awarded an early penalty and George Eastham was tasked with converting from 12 yards. Roger Hunt had told Lawrence before the match that he had noticed Eastham normally takes his penalties to the right-hand side. The keeper followed his striker's advice and saved the spot kick. Liverpool went on to win the match 5-0 and claimed the league title after a 17-year hiatus.

The combination of St John, Hunt and Alf Arrowsmith scored 67 goals and the team as a whole managed a club-record 92 goals in total, while Lawrence played in 40 of the 42 league games. He had now firmly established himself in the team and he missed only a further two matches in the next five seasons. The next year wasn't as successful in the league, but their prosperity in the cups meant that they were still on an upward trajectory. In the space of just three days in August 1964, they drew 2-2 in the FA Charity Shield against a West Ham side that contained Bobby Moore and Geoff Hirst, then tasted European Cup football for the first time, beating KR Reykjavik 5-0 in the Icelandic capital. They dropped down to seventh domestically at the end of the campaign, but their 2-1 victory over Don Revie's Leeds United to claim their first FA Cup showed that they had certainly matured.

The crowds gathered to witness Liverpool parade the trophy that had eluded them for so many years and had become an obsession at the club. They also felt that they had a good chance of winning the European Cup for the first timel, when they beat Internazionale 3-1 in the semi-final first leg at Anfield. However, the return in the San Siro became one of the most contentious games in Liverpool's history. The players felt that Spanish referee Jose Maria Ortiz de Mendibil wasn't even trying to hide his bias, as he gave the Italians everything. Football in the country during the 1960s was rife with scandal over bribing officials. There was more than a little bit of bemusement over Inter's first goal, but their second enraged the normally mild-mannered Lawrence. When the goalkeeper beat Joaquin Peiro to the ball, he carried it across his area, bouncing it on his travels. Peiro hooked the ball back and put it into the net. George Best would do a similar thing six years later in an international game between England and Northern Ireland, but the Manchester United attacker's version was disallowed. Some observers felt that Lawrence was complacent in not knowing that Peiro was in the vicinity. Inter won the encounter 3-0 and went to the final.

The only other time Lawrence got as riled was when Shankly blamed him at half-time in a game for his part in conceding a goal. He shocked his team-mates when he took off his jersey and told the manager, 'If you can do better, do fucking better!' It took vital interference from coaches Bob Paisley and Reuben Bennett to ensure that Lawrence returned to the pitch after the break. For once, Shankly was speechless.

Mick Halsall was born in Bootle and later became an academy player at the Reds. He was only four when he went to Anfield for the first time for a match under the floodlights, but he will never forget the imposing figure in front of him. 'You always thought how's he a keeper because of his frame,' says Halsall about Lawrence. 'He wasn't as big as people thought, until you saw him in real life. What a goalkeeper he was!'

Liverpool won the league for the second time in three years in 1966 and reached the final of Europe's third competition, the European Cup Winners' Cup. Once again Lawrence was pivotal with his fearlessness and courage that were vital in an uncompromising era. In the 0-0 draw with Newcastle United, he had to have three stitches and a tetanus injection at half-time following a collision with Billy Thompson when he dived at the feet of the forward. After the game, he could barely walk and he told waiting reporters, 'I think I'll be all right for the next match!' He did indeed play in the 1-0 defeat to Leeds in the following game, although that was their only league loss in 17 games. Strangely, Liverpool beat Leeds the very next day and ended the Yorkshire club's unbeaten home record for the season.

'He was invaluable,' said Shankly. 'Sometimes I would advise Tommy that I thought he was getting a bit too heavy, but it was natural for him to carry weight.' Shankly would put Lawrence under pressure in training by having four or five players take shots straight after one another. He may have been a big lad, but Lawrence would jump back to his feet and make save after save. Sometimes he was busier in practice than in the matches. 'They could have 80 minutes when nothing was happening and be frozen near to death,' admitted Shankly, such was their dominance over the opposition. 'I'd say to Tommy, "Keep alive, son, keep warm. I'll give you some hot water bottles to tie to your legs!"'

The Reds won the Charity Shield against Everton at the start of 1966/67, as Hunt was among the players to parade the World Cup before kick-off. But it proved to be a disappointing season for Liverpool as they not only dropped down to fifth in the table but were heavily beaten by Ajax in the European Cup semi-final. Rinus Michels's side were just beginning to show their potential, with Johan Cruyff pulling the strings. They won 5-1 in Amsterdam, although the game should never have been played due to the amount of fog. Shankly claimed that it was that bad, he walked on to the pitch to give instructions to his full-backs at 2-0 and the referee never even noticed. Lawrence complained afterwards that he couldn't see the ball, in what was probably his worst display.

Hunt and Lawrence were good friends and would often play golf together much to the annoyance of Shankly. In December 1967, they were both almost late for a home match with

Manchester City. As they both drove in separate cars down the East Lancashire Road to the ground, they were stopped in their tracks by an accident ahead. The players had to run to the game, which was then delayed by eight minutes on the insistence of the Liverpool boss. The match finished 1-1 with Hunt grabbing the equaliser.

The emergence of Manchester United and Manchester City as credible forces at that time combined with Liverpool's ageing team meant that they suffered a trophy drought. They did finish runners-up to Leeds in 1969, but many of the new signings failed to make the next step that they required.

Lawrence played in every league fixture between 1967 and 1969 but then midway through the 1969/70 term, he was removed from the first 11. A 1-0 defeat to Watford in the FA Cup was seen as a disaster due to Liverpool's poorly organised defence and Lawrence's inability to save Barry Endean's header after getting a hand to it. That game was too much for Shankly and Lawrence was one of three changes to the team for the next game with Brian Clough's Derby County. Liverpool may have also lost that fixture but debutant Ray Clemence had still performed well, while Shankly had decided to use the rest of the season to give young players their opportunity. The now 29-year-old Lawrence played just once more for Liverpool before leaving for Tranmere Rovers with St John in 1971.

Lawrence became an internet sensation in 2015 when he was stopped by a BBC journalist on Liverpool's Church Street. He was asked if he remembered the Merseyside derby cup tie of 1967. When he replied that he was the goalkeeper for Liverpool, the clip went viral. He sadly passed away in January 2018.

Chapter 3

Ray Clemence, *Mr Reliable*

LIVERPOOL'S BUDGET in the late 1960s meant that they were always planning for the future rather than buying the biggest stars of the time. Another huge factor in this approach was the vision and consistency that their long-serving manager Bill Shankly provided them. The profile he desired were teenagers from the lower divisions that could be used in the reserves to learn their trade.

Ray Clemence was one who fitted this policy, but Shankly certainly didn't rush into a decision. 'I watched Ray more than any other player I bought, because he was a goalkeeper,' explained the boss in his book, *Shankly*. 'I used to travel to see him at Scunthorpe, where they kicked off at a quarter to seven on Friday night every fortnight, and I spoke to other managers about him.'

Chief scout Geoff Twentyman initially spotted Clemence and told Shankly to take a closer view. The manager believed there were more aspects to a goalkeeper's game than an outfield player, which meant he wanted to observe him in a variety of scenarios. 'Scunthorpe were struggling a bit, so I suppose that helped me,' said Clemence in the *Secret Diary of a Liverpool Scout*. 'Maybe if we were doing well, I wouldn't have played or had less to deal with in games, so Geoff could scrutinise me a little bit more.'

Shankly was suitably impressed by his overall ability, while he was also endeared to the fact that Clemence was left-footed and right-handed, as he felt that gave him more balance. He signed him for £18,000 in 1967.

Clemence didn't make his first-team debut until a year later, as he began to refine his trade. In early 1970 he was given a run in the side, starting with matches against Derby County and Coventry City. He played in the final 13 league games of that season, which included three consecutive clean sheets against Wolverhampton Wanderers, Crystal Palace and Sunderland. 'To take over from Tommy Lawrence, who was a legend in his own right,' says former academy player Mick Halsall. 'The way the club went about it was absolutely outstanding. They brought them in, put them in the reserves, made them develop, made them understand the philosophy of the club and when they were ready, they went in.'

Liverpool had the best defensive record in the league in Clemence's first full season with the senior side. They drew an incredible 17 matches, which stopped them finishing higher than fifth place in the table. The FA Cup Final did offer them some hope of silverware when they faced Arsenal. Clemence, who was wearing a cap that would fall off on several occasions, illustrated maturity beyond his years to keep the league champions at bay inside 90 minutes and Liverpool even looked like creating an upset, when they scored first through Steve Heighway in extra time. Arsenal responded though with two goals in ten minutes through Eddie Kelly and Charlie George.

In 1971/72, youngsters Kevin Keegan and Phil Thompson began to get more game time, the former quickly creating an exciting partnership with John Toshack. There was an improvement from previous seasons, but their lack of experience cost them in certain games. However, the foundations had been laid and a year later saw an even further advancement in their ability. Clemence had little goalmouth action, as the Reds won three of their opening four games. A defeat against Leicester City saw Clemence described as 'far from his best' by *The Guardian* reporter Albert Barham, as Keith Waller scored a hat-trick. He was then left out of the subsequent match with Derby County, but debutant Frank Lane carried the ball over his own line and Clemence was restored to the line-up in subsequent games. Liverpool found their groove and lost just once in their next 20 league games.

In the 0-0 draw with Arsenal, he had to be on form in order to thwart John Radford, Peter Marinello and Bob McNab on several occasions. 'That sequence of saves was a supreme example of the goalkeeping art,' wrote Alan Pinch in the *Liverpool Echo*, while Barham in *The Guardian* noted, 'Fourteen minutes of scintillating football dominated by Clemence with feline grace in his goal.'

With Tommy Smith and Emlyn Hughes in central defence, Ian Callaghan and Heighway operating out wide supplying the crosses for Keegan and Toshack, Clemence was firmly cemented in place. 'They always talk about how good the defence was,' says former Liverpool striker David Fairclough. 'There was an awful lot of times when he didn't have to do a lot. But then in the last minute, he would make a world-class save. They could have been winning 1-0, Liverpool, just hanging on, then Clem's concentration levels right to the end were just unbelievable.'

Liverpool won the league that season and it was the start of an era of dominance. They would claim 11 league titles and four European Cups in the next 18 years. The UEFA Cup (now Europa League) was also collected that year after they beat a Borussia Monchengladbach team containing Berti Vogts and Juup Heynckes in the two-legged affair. The Germans became regular opponents for the next few years in European competition. Shankly wasn't to get the European Cup, the prize he most coveted, as he left the club at the end of the following year, when they finished runners-up to Leeds United. He did win the FA Cup for a second time though, when Liverpool completely overwhelmed Newcastle

United in a 3-0 victory. Clemence was faultless in taking high balls, although he didn't have a save to make.

New boss Bob Paisley inherited a squad that had plenty of character and Clemence was at the forefront. 'Clem was a huge personality,' admits Fairclough. 'He was very vocal. I came into contact with the first team as an apprentice. Ray was someone you very much knew about. He was larger than life. I didn't mix with Ray so much because of the age difference at the time. But obviously there was never any doubt in the quality. I kind of looked up to the likes of him and Keegan, who were the England internationals and regulars at that time.'

Paisley's first season was 1974/75 and the young ginger-haired striker Fairclough began to be involved with the seniors. 'He was loud,' says Fairclough about his goalkeeper. 'He could be a little bit moody at times, in a training sense. You hear all the time these days that you have to be 100 per cent all the time in training. I never felt that was always the case at Liverpool at the time. It was more about being ready for the games and Clem was one of those that on occasions, he might be in goal for shooting for example and if he wasn't ready for it, then you might as well have had anybody in goal because the ball would be flying in. The next moment, he might have got a telling off or whatever and his attitude would change. And once his attitude changed, he was just unbelievable. Even in training moments, he could just flip the switch. He wasn't one of those that was always working meticulously at his game – not to me anyway – he did it when he felt he needed to.'

Phil Thompson also observed similar, 'Clem was majestic, acting as my eyes and ears in the box. He could be unemployed for 80 minutes and then pull off a world-class save. What was amazing was that he was the worst trainer in the world. Shooting practice was a complete waste of time. I might as well have gone in goal.'

Training sessions consisted of plenty of five-a-side games, as the bulk of their technical work came from small-sided drills.

'He was one of those players that they didn't let play with the first team most of the time because he was too dangerous,' adds Fairclough. 'He was liable to be a bit temperamental and slip. He was known for making the odd rash challenge.'

Clemence was your typical over-zealous goalkeeper when he played outfield and would charge around the pitch taking out the opposition, particularly the younger players if they happened to get past him. 'Like a lot of keepers, Clem always fancied himself as an outfield player in training,' Ian Callaghan wrote in his autobiography. 'His enthusiasm sometimes ranaway with him and Bill Shankly had to rein him in because his tackling on the training ground could have injured one of us!'

On the occasions he was allowed to participate it would assist his overall game. 'If it was a Monday morning, they might go and do a little bit of individual goalkeeper work, but invariably they joined in the games,' Halsall says. 'One for the fitness and two to tidy their feet. It helped them to distribute the ball a little bit more accurately.' Lawrence has been heralded in the football world for the early stages of developing the sweeper-keeper role. 'Clem continued that after Tommy,' says Fairclough. 'He was always on his toes, he stood high in his penalty area to give the likes of Thommo and Emlyn Hughes that support right behind them.'

The 1975/76 season saw Liverpool back on top as they completed another league and UEFA Cup double. They were the first trophies of Paisley's era and Fairclough played a vital role towards the end. He scored seven goals in the final eight league games while Liverpool conceded just four times in that period. Clemence's control over his back four was another key ingredient to that title success.

'He made positive decisions,' recalls Fairclough. 'He used to always turn around and say, "If I have shouted mine and you don't get out the way, then I'm going to take you, I'm going to take them and I'm going to take the ball." If Clem says, "Keeper's!" Well, you knew anything in his way was in danger. That's a great attribute to have. That you can control your penalty area. For me, the only keeper who did that after Clem for the next few years was [Pepe] Reina. He was very dominant in the way that Clemence was I felt.'

Ronnie Whelan played with Clemence in the latter part of his time at Anfield, and feels the way he orchestrated those in front of him definitely stood out. 'He was the first real goalkeeper that I heard shouting so much in football,' says Whelan. 'When I made my debut, honestly, he was telling everybody – midfield, full-backs, centre-backs, telling everybody that there was someone coming on your left or someone coming on the outside. I had never experienced that with goalkeepers before. Yes, they shouted and screamed, but this was all really … It was a great help to all the players that he played with. He could organise everybody in front of him, which was very good.'

Clemence was very much the boss of his penalty area and errors were extremely rare. 'I can remember seeing him making a couple of mistakes when he was finding his feet as a young goalkeeper,' Fairclough says. 'Once he became established, there was only the mistake he made against Kenny in the international that I can ever remember, when you felt he was at fault.'

For England, Don Revie opted for the Liverpool keeper in this period, but it wasn't always that way. 'People around that time would have the argument about [Peter] Shilton and Clemence,' says Fairclough. It was the Gerrard versus Lampard debate of that era for England, without the added caveat of whether they could actually play together. In goalkeeper terms, the modern-day equivalent would certainly be Ederson against Alisson, which must be a regular source of topic in bars across Rio de Janeiro and Sao Paulo. 'They were different in some ways,' says Halsall on the battle for the national team pole position. 'Shilts would never really come off his line in terms of coming to collect it. I think Clem had everything.'

Sir Alf Ramsey chose Shilton at the end of his time as England manager, then Revie preferred Clemence in the period between

1974 and 1977, with Shilton back in the fold under Ron Greenwood once he had transferred to Nottingham Forest. 'Shilton was a great goalkeeper, but I have to say that we would all come down in the Ray Clemence camp,' adds Fairclough. 'It's amazing to think how many caps Shilton got and Clem got 61 caps. To think how many caps Clemence should have got really. In our eyes, he was the number one. There's no question! I respected Shilton and if you scored a goal against him you felt it was an achievement, but Clem was every bit the goalkeeper that Shilton was.'

It was an intense rivalry within the media and general public, but the two were incredibly good friends. Clemence would talk fondly about Shilton to his Liverpool team-mates and they would room together on international duty.

Liverpool had a number of back-up keepers during Clemence's tenure, but the probability of them overtaking him remained low. Frankie Lane, Grahame Lloyd and Peter McDonnell all acted as understudy, with Lane managing only three appearances. 'Clem was helpful to all the goalkeepers who were behind him,' says Fairclough. 'I think they would all turn around and say they were grateful to him for all the help they had.'

Steve Ogrizovic had the role for five years and played in as many games. 'The likes of Oggy would have been hugely influenced by Clem, but equally grateful of the support that he had given them,' Fairclough thinks. 'I'm sure he was never anything other than a team player in that sense.' Ogrizovic had a short career as a police officer before he became a professional footballer, he was just 20 when he joined from Chesterfield. 'He was terrific Ogg, a real character,' says Halsall.

On Fridays, the squad would get split into groups. The first team would go and prepare for their upcoming match and the reserves would play a five-side which was led by Roy Evans. 'Oggy would play out, there wouldn't be any shape to the games. He quite enjoyed doing the Cruyff turn which he said he invented. We had to put him straight and say, "Ogg, I think a certain gentleman in the World Cup was first to present that technique and it certainly wasn't you." There was an awkwardness about him, but he was great. It was a great crack on a Friday morning trying to see how many Cruyff turns he could get in. I think his record was something like 23 in one session.'

Halsall played at full-back in the reserves. In one of his first games he was standing near the post, when Ogrizovic called for the ball and Halsall decided to duck. Coventry City's young striker Mark Hateley got between them and headed into the goal. At half-time there was a debate between Evans and Ogrizovic in the dressing room. The two were arguing over Halsall's role in Hateley's goal, while the youngster sat silently in the corner. Ogrizovic never aimed his displeasure at Halsall but was defending his own actions, while Evans felt the goalkeeper shouldn't have confused the situation. 'It just so happened that at the end of the game, Roy pulled me and said, "You will never duck again Mick, will you?" I said, "No chance Roy, I will just head the ball away!" He said, "And if he punches you in the back of the head, that's all right isn't it?" I said, "Yeah, without doubt!" It was a massive learning curve.'

Ogrizovic made over 500 appearances for Coventry City after he left Merseyside. He became firm friends with Halsall from their time together in Liverpool's reserves and from working for the coaching staff at Coventry in later years. 'Oggy just had to keep waiting on his chance,' says Whelan. 'He was a good goalkeeper, he went to Coventry and played for years. The two goalkeepers he had in front of him were Clem and then Bruce [Grobbelaar], so it was a hard deal to get into the Liverpool team with those two that won so many trophies over the years. He was a good goalkeeper, but I don't think he was the standard of Clem or Bruce. Unfortunately for Oggy, because he was a great lad.'

Liverpool's success continued in the late 1970s with back-to-back European Cups in 1977 and 1978 along with league championships in 1976, 1977 and 1979. The red machine was demolishing all comers in an attacking sense, with the top keeper on the continent making crucial saves. The 1977 European campaign witnessed a quarter-final match with St Etienne that would go down in Liverpool folklore. Paisley's men had to overturn a 1-0 away defeat from the first leg in France. The Kop was bouncing when Keegan lobbed keeper Ivan Curkovic to draw the score level on aggregate. Clemence then had to make an acrobatic save off a header from midfielder Christian Synaeghel and push away a stinging shot by winger Dominique Rocheteau, who now works as the club's sporting director.

St Etienne scored the all-important away goal just six minutes after half-time when Dominique Bathenay hit a swerving effort from distance. Liverpool struck back almost immediately through Ray Kennedy, after he latched on to Toshack's lay-off. Liverpool still needed another goal to progress to the semi-finals so enter super-sub Fairclough to race clear of the St Etienne defenders and confidently finish to send Anfield into hysterics. That's where the story of this epic encounter normally ends, but Fairclough remembers that Clemence still had an important contribution to ensure a final-four date with FC Zurich. 'He made a save late on after my goal,' says Fairclough. 'He made a save to his right side. It was a comfortable height for him. I don't think he was ever vulnerable to anything in particular.'

Clemence's footwork and positioning meant he rarely had to make extraordinary stops. 'The number of times he made saves at crucial times in the game and what he achieved,' says Halsall. 'He was phenomenal, Clem.' His ability to keep the ball out of the net with what appeared like minimal exertion was possibly what his team-mates admired about him the most. 'He didn't make a fuss out of making saves,' confesses Fairclough. 'There were one or two goalkeepers that you could say once they got to it, threw in a couple of rolls for the cameras. I don't think you could ever level that at Ray Clemence. He was always one who everyone had the most confidence in. You never felt vulnerable with him there. He did dominate his penalty area. He must have given the centre-halves massive confidence.'

The final saw Liverpool beat Borussia Monchengladbach 3-1 in Rome. It came just days after they had lost to Manchester United in the FA Cup Final, when a fluky Jimmy Greenwood goal sailed over Clemence's head. The players were feeling down after the game, but Clemence lightened the mood. 'We have a great day coming on Wednesday in Rome,' he said according to Phil Thompson. 'There is no way now that we are going to be beaten in the European Cup Final. Let's enjoy ourselves.' Terry McDermott recalls that he broke out in singing and dancing, which saw others join in.

The Reds picked themselves back up and the drinks began to flow. It was perhaps not the ideal preparation, although it relaxed the team enough to produce a brilliant display. McDermott's goal was cancelled out by Allan Simonsen shortly after the break. At 1-1, Monchengladbach began to govern the game and were close to going ahead. 'Uli Stielike broke away on his own, it was him versus me,' said Clemence in the ITV documentary *European Cup Winners*. 'If he had have scored with that, then I'm not sure what would have happened.' Tommy Smith headed Liverpool in front in what was meant to be his final game for the club and then Phil Neal converted a penalty after Kevin Keegan was sent tumbling. 'To win the European Cup for the very first time, not only for you personally but for the football club was very special,' admitted Clemence. The keeper certainly had to be at his best, as he illustrated bravery in commanding moments and for many of his team-mates that defined his legacy.

Monchengladbach's Rainer Bonhoff hit the post in that game and scored a sublime free kick the year afterwards in the semi-final. He was known across European football for his ferocious shot and you could have forgiven the Liverpool goalkeeper if he was unnerved when facing him from another set piece. 'I can remember Clem making a save from him off a free kick,' recalls Fairclough.

'It thundered right down Clem's neck; it was directly at him. He never had any fear. He had massive courage. There were never any question marks over Clemence. He was as brave as a lion.'

Despite the greatest success in the club's history, changes were made to the team. Keegan left for Hamburg, but the fans needn't have worried as his replacement Kenny Dalglish went on to surpass even the highest of expectations. Graeme Souness and Alan Hansen arrived, and they would also be heralded for the impact that they would have on the club. Hansen made his debut in September 1977 and Clemence was so convinced by his new centre-back that he felt the Scotsman could help prolong his time at the top level. His performance in the subsequent 2-0 defeat to Manchester United caused the goalkeeper to have a rethink. He told Hansen afterwards, 'I thought that, far from putting six years on to my career, playing with you would take six years off it!'

Club Brugge were another familiar foe in European competition. Liverpool beat them 4-3 on aggregate over two legs in the UEFA Cup Final in 1976. Then, two years later they had a comfortable 1-0 win in the European Cup Final, with the only real scare coming late on when Clemence had to save from Jan Sorensen and Phil Thompson needed to clear off the line.

Liverpool's defence was impeccable throughout the 1970s, but the 1978/79 term was absurd even by their standards. 'I remember him making saves in that season, when we only conceded 16 goals all season – four at home, 12 away,' says Fairclough. 'There was a game at Norwich, he made incredible saves. I'm not saying he was faultless, but he had some amazing years.' Clemence had natural agility and a presence that made him such a success. 'These days goalkeepers are monsters, they are 6ft 5in and 6ft 6in,' Fairclough continues. 'Clem wasn't massive in that sense, he was probably just 6ft 1in, but he struck you as having a big personality.'

When Clemence retired from the game he worked in the international set-up and he realised the extent that the goalkeeper position had evolved. 'I can understand somebody sat in the stand thinking, "It was straight at him, what's he doing?" But until you're behind it and you see how much it moves and how late it moves you don't understand it,' said Clemence to the FA's official website. 'That's why a goalkeeper's position has changed again since I played and a bit after I played. When people were shooting from 18–20 yards you would certainly see me, and goalkeepers after me, close to the six-yard line, narrow the angle and make the goal as small as we possibly could. These days, goalkeepers tend to make those saves midway in the six-yard box and occasionally only a yard off the line. The reason for this is it gives them more reaction time; it just gives them a split second more to move their body to try and make the save.'

Liverpool's training at the turn of the decade would see the squad participate in a long run on a Saturday morning, with a minute's rest in between intervals. Clemence would just keep jogging around without stopping as he was so far behind the outfield players. The week was structured so that the apprentices would have to do crossing and shooting drills for the first-team goalkeepers. 'The big thing that stood out for me with Ray was how demanding he was,' says Halsall. 'The quality that was asked for us to produce, even though we were apprentices. It certainly taught us to concentrate in by-areas.'

Clemence would ask for crosses that were driven across his penalty area and others that hung up to the back post. 'He would ask for variations of crosses,' confirms Halsall. 'Especially in those days, where you had a different type of centre-forward to modern-day football. It was getting it wide and get it into the box. If we were shooting, we had to be exact. There was never any thought of trying to chip him because if you did and he caught it, then he would volley the ball away. In his eyes, it was like, "Who are you to try and chip me?" We had to hit the target, we had to make sure we were working him. What's the use of doing it if he wasn't getting any work? If they went in, they went in, but very few did because of his athleticism.'

Eddie Niedzwiecki from Wrexham would occasionally come over for training. He later played for Chelsea and worked with former Manchester United striker Mark Hughes at a variety of clubs, as part of his backroom staff. He said, 'For whatever reason it stays in my mind, I can remember them doing a triangle. The goalkeeper would stand at one of the markers, and you had to work from the point up across to the left. The goalkeeper would have to serve a ball across the floor, and they would work across the triangle. I thought, "Bloody hell! That's hard." He [Clemence] was very professional in all aspects of his work.'

Clemence had everything and there weren't any notable weaknesses in his all-round game. 'His overall ability to come and collect crosses to distributing the play,' says Halsall. 'He was just exceptional. He looked after himself really well.' Clemence won 12 major honours in his ten years on Merseyside and even though he had immense quality around him, his general contribution shouldn't be underestimated. 'Ray Clemence was as much a legend as a Liddell, a Hunt or a Keegan in my book,' said Thompson, funnily enough in his book. 'He was immense as a goalkeeper and got on with his day-to-day routine without any fuss.' Fairclough agrees with that assessment, 'He was mega! When people turn around to me and say, "Who was the best player you ever played with?" Obviously, I always say Dalglish for example, but I played with Ray Clemence and I thought of him at the time as the best goalkeeper in the world. We obviously didn't see as much of the likes of [Dino] Zoff on a regular basis, but Clemence was absolutely crucial. He was a massive mainstay of Liverpool.'

Clemence and Liverpool won the European Cup in 1981 for a third time at the Parc des Princes in Paris. They defeated Real Madrid on a pitch that Clemence described as like a 'cow field', when Alan Kennedy was the unlikely hero in an unspectacular match. Just a few months earlier, a new man had arrived on the scene that was confident he was not just there to make up the numbers. Clemence conducted a joint interview for the *Daily Star* with this mysterious arrival, which didn't exactly endear him to his new understudy. When asked how long it would be before he surpassed the England international, the new fella replied, 'I'll probably take his place next season.' Clemence immediately walked out.

Chapter 4

Bruce Grobbelaar,
Handstands, Trophies and Trauma

'IT WAS strange because we kind of knew that Ray was considering leaving for certain reasons that he had,' says David Fairclough on the transition from Ray Clemence to Bruce Grobbelaar. 'I can remember Bruce just showing up as a signing for the reserves. His character was one that was obvious. He wasn't shy and full of life. It was novel in terms of his accent. He was immediately there in your face.'

Bob Paisley and then chief scout Tom Saunders took a trip to Belle Vue in April 1980, where Doncaster Rovers used to play their matches. Grobbelaar was playing for Crewe Alexandra in the Fourth Division, on loan from Vancouver Whitecaps in Canada. 'Before the game, he had three of his team-mates lined up on the penalty area firing in shots at him,' explains Paisley. 'Bruce was dancing around like a cartoon character stopping every attempt. I turned to Tom, who was sitting next to me and said, "We can go, I've seen enough."'

Paisley and Saunders did stay longer to assess his all-round capability and made him their new signing just 12 months later. They even had a £1 bet over whether he had the initiative to find his way to the Adelphi Hotel. Saunders may have had an incredible eye for a talented player, but he underestimated the determination of his latest purchase as he came bowling through the door.

Grobbelaar's new team-mates knew even less about their new 23-year-old shot-stopper. 'You could see straight away his ability and agility,' says former captain Ronnie Whelan. 'He was so agile it was unbelievable. He was plucking balls out of top corners and things like that. It was impressive when he come. He was very fit, even at the end.' In his second game for the reserves against Bolton Wanderers, he began to attract attention not just from his team-mates and reserve manager Roy Evans, but from the opposition. 'Somebody hit a shot that was angling for the top corner, it wasn't like today, when you get there and push it over,' explains Whelan. 'He leapt into the top corner and came down with the ball. One of their midfielder's come up to me and said, "Where the friggin' hell did you sign the monkey from?" He had unbelievable agility to get to balls that no other keeper could ever get to.'

Mick Halsall also played in that reserve team and he played with Grobbelaar for the first time against Manchester United's second string. 'We went to Old Trafford on a Saturday afternoon, I never really thought anything at the time,' says Halsall. 'But as it went on you could see the personality and character in the man.' They weren't the only characteristics that were notable from an early stage. In pre-season, Grobbelaar would be among the top runners which was certainly a shift in dynamic from previous generations. 'He was a great athlete,' continues Halsall. 'It was the first time I had seen a goalkeeper of that nature. With all due respect to Ray, who I think could run a little bit, but it was never something that he was overly keen to do. Big Ogg was a different frame and stature. But Bruce could run.' Whelan also confirms his friend's fitness levels, 'He was always up there with the running. Year in, year out, Bruce was at the front. Fit as a fiddle.'

Liverpool won the European Cup just two months after Grobbelaar joined the club, when they beat Real Madrid in France. They were at the peak of their powers and destined for further success. The players expected that their new unknown goalkeeper was there to learn for the next couple of seasons before progressing to the first team, as Liverpool had done so seemingly in the past. However, it didn't work out that way and Grobbelaar was the new number one for the 1981/82 campaign.

'Probably Clem left sooner than we thought,' confesses Fairclough. 'One minute he was there, the next he was going, and Grobbelaar was in the first team. Brave decision really to think you were going from England's top keeper and now you're bringing someone in who had only been playing in the NASL. We never had discussions about these things, but I'm sure in people's minds they were thinking, "Oh God! Clem's gone!" When goalkeepers come in, they invariably take a little time to settle down.' The squad expected Clemence to stay at Liverpool for the remainder of his career, so it was certainly a shock to now have someone new in his place. 'He was certainly confident in his ability, but very much unknown,' adds Fairclough.

Grobbelaar made his debut at Molineux against Wolverhampton Wanderers alongside Mark Lawrenson and Craig Johnston. It was to be the first of 318 consecutive appearances for the club, although a goal from Mike Matthews meant they lost 1-0 and it was far from the best of starts. It got harder for the new keeper, and Liverpool won just two of their first eight league fixtures. The press began to pile pressure on Paisley and rumours circulated around his long-term future. Liverpool's defenders were used to Clemence orchestrating them, whereas Grobbelaar didn't initially communicate his ideas. When he left his area there was little warning and his enthusiasm saw him make numerous errors in his first six months.

'We were expecting that type of thing because it naturally happens,' admits Fairclough. 'At that point, it's down to the goalkeeper's overall personality, it's up to them to work it out. It's a strange position and in those days more so than it is today.' After the keeper's mistakes in the European Cup game with Bulgarian champions CSKA Sofia cost the holders the tie, Liverpool's players were deafly silent towards their new recruit. They wouldn't pass to him in training, with centre-back Alan Hansen the worst culprit. Grobbelaar was convinced that he needed to entertain and wasn't prepared to listen to his new team-mates' advice. 'He did make mistakes in those early times and a few later on,' Fairclough says. 'I think it was always in his make-up that he was liable to do something unexpected. For the manager, he was probably pulling his hair out never knowing when the next incident might occur.'

Paisley persisted with Grobbelaar and the goalkeeper knew he owed his manager a huge debt of gratitude. 'Liverpool's strength was that they believed in the people that they put in the team,' continues Fairclough. 'They weren't the type to make jumpy decisions and swap from one thing to another. They had confidence in their choice and then gave them the opportunity to prove if they could sink or swim.' Luckily for Paisley, Grobbelaar was like a duck to water once he found his rhythm. The manager requested that the player he called 'Grobble-de-jack' should come to his office. 'In North America they entertain,' said Paisley. 'Here, we win. If you don't play better, you will find yourself back at Crewe. Now eff off and think about it.' Grobbelaar started to take heed of the guidance that was offered to him by not just his boss, but the senior players, and as a result he became respectful of the club's traditions and what he needed to do in order to succeed. Liverpool's productivity improved a lot after the Christmas period, and they won 20 of their final 25 league games to reclaim the title.

The connection between the new keeper and his back four continued to grow the next season as he kept four clean sheets in a row including the Charity Shield game with Clemence's Tottenham Hotspur. 'People knew that he was going to come, so the top players that they were, decided that they were going to start protecting the goals a little bit,' says Halsall. 'His defence had a real understanding of what they needed to do around Bruce.' He also became more accepted for his personality off the pitch. 'Bruce was a good laugh, a great people person,' Fairclough says. 'He had great dexterity, he could throw a ball a million miles and throw a ball up into the air, all these daft things. How can you throw a cricket ball 100 yards into the sky! He endeared himself because he was like, "Can you do this?" or "Can you do that?" He seemed to be able to do everything because he was incredibly versatile in his athleticism.'

Grobbelaar would stage competitions where you hold your hands behind your back and fall forwards to see how far you can drop before you got your hands out to stop your nose from landing on the floor. 'There was no way I was doing that,' says Halsall. 'Especially with this nose, I wasn't going to risk that getting bent again. He was just a total character.' Liverpool would hold their Monday morning five-a-side sessions, which were designed for the players to get the weekend out of their system. Grobbelaar had a different approach to Clemence in the small-sided games and if he scored, he would conduct his theatrical handstands in celebration. 'I'm not sure too many of us tried to copy him because we would have broken our backs,' Halsall admits.

Liverpool won the league again in 1983, which turned out to be Paisley's last title before he retired. Joe Fagan was appointed to replace him as the Reds promoted from the Boot Room once again. Fagan bolstered his defence with the signings of Gary Gillespie and Jim Beglin, but they featured very little to begin with. It was business as usual. Liverpool did have a few notable exceptions though, such as the 4-0 defeat to Coventry City, after Grobbelaar's error in the opening minute, which is regarded as one of the worst defeats in the club's history. A 2-2 draw in the League Cup semi-final with Walsall was another cause for concern, but ultimately, they continued to brush teams aside and won the league championship for the third successive season.

The league title wasn't the only trophy that Liverpool were collecting with unbelievable frequency as the League Cup became a common resident of the Anfield trophy room. They won the competition for four consecutive seasons between 1980 and 1984. Grobbelaar came face-to-face with the man he superseded in his first League Cup Final in 1982 when Liverpool beat Tottenham Hotspur 3-1 after extra time with two goals from Whelan, and the picture of Grobbelaar walking around the pitch on his hands during the lap of honour became a famous image across the world.

The following year, Liverpool defeated Manchester United 2-1, although Grobbelaar was lucky not to have been sent off after he took out Gordon McQueen when he was racing towards the goal. It's perhaps the latter of the quartet of finals that was the most acclaimed or certainly the most iconic of the decade. The match with Everton was the first time that the final had been broadcast live on British television, while it was also historic as the intense rivalry had never before been played out in a major final. The armchair fans were treated to a quality game with Howard Kendall beginning to assemble a strong side, although it did end goalless after extra time. It was perhaps the 100,000 inside the stadium that had the most fun, as chants of 'Merseyside, Merseyside, Merseyside' could be heard in cohesion from all the travelling support. This was particularly poetic given that it was the generation of hooliganism in England. The 0-0 stalemate set up a derby game in Manchester for the replay. Graeme Souness scored the only goal of the game at Maine Road.

Liverpool had done a double for the third consecutive season, but they still had the chance to go one better. A trip to the Stadio Olimpico was on the itinerary as they faced Roma in the Italian club's own stadium. Phil Neal gave Fagan's men an early lead but Roberto Pruzzo equalised before half-time. Grobbelaar made a number of saves in the hostile atmosphere inside the 90 minutes, with extra time not providing much goalmouth action, so the final was to be decided on penalties.

In Liverpool's final training session before they flew out to Italy, Fagan had the team practise penalties in preparation for this outcome. However, it didn't go exactly to plan. Five of the reserves took penalties against Grobbelaar and he failed to save a single one. Then, to make matters worse, five of Liverpool's first team took penalties against back-up keeper Bob Bolder and none of them scored.

The players were determined to stay positive, but there must have been a sense of panic when Steve Nicol's opening kick of the shoot-out flew over the crossbar and Roma captain Agostino Di Bartolomei converted his. Regular taker Phil Neal pulled it level when he sent Franco Tancredi the wrong way, then Bruno Conti stepped up. Fagan had told Grobbelaar to put them off before the shoot-out had started, but it took the keeper a little while to evaluate what his manager meant. He walked slowly up to the goal and initially faced the wrong way before turning around. The confident Conti suddenly became fazed and his effort followed Nicol's over the upright. Souness, who had played one of his finest games in a red shirt, scored next and centre-back Ubaldo Righetti followed to make it 2-2. Ian Rush's penalty was his first in a competitive match for the club, despite his impressive scoring record in open play. It was far from convincing but once again Tancredi had guessed the opposite side. Grobbelaar was swaying from side to side in the manner of a drunk man when Francesco Graziani had his turn. The unsteady legs distracted the forward and he missed. When Ray Kennedy scored afterwards, Liverpool had won the European Cup for the fourth time in seven years.

'The wobbly legs?' says Whelan, who was also playing that night. 'We didn't see it coming, but it definitely put two World Cup winners off. He never saved a penalty either. The two of them blasted it over the bar. The handstands after League Cup finals! They were just these things that we got with Bruce. Something was always going to happen when he was there.' Whelan believes that everyone played a vital role in that treble-winning season. 'You can't go all season without not all putting something in,' he says. 'Bruce was as influential as anyone else that season. It's hard to say that Bruce was the man because there were so many. You had to have everybody really flying and on top of their game. We were always told, "If two aren't playing well, then we can carry two and get through it! If it starts to get any more than that, then we are going to struggle!" We didn't have many games where more than two players struggled, there would always be nine of us there ready to go.'

It was virtually impossible for Fagan's Liverpool to repeat that size of trophy haul, but in his second season they were still very much on the verge. The first match of the 1984/85 campaign was for the Charity Shield against Everton. Grobbelaar made a save from Graeme Sharp at close range, but the ball fell kindly for the Everton attacker once more. His second attempt was blocked by Hansen and then it hit Grobbelaar on his foot, diverting it into the goal as he was making his way back. It was a very unfortunate own goal to concede and certainly not an error. Everton were deserved winners, but Grobbelaar had made countless saves to keep the score down. 'If it wasn't for Bruce it could have been a lot worse,' Fagan commented in the press conference, when questions were critical of his keeper. 'What I saw out there today was a collective failure.'

That season they ultimately fell short due to their results against the other best sides in England. Everton, Manchester United and Tottenham Hotspur joined them in the top four at the end of the campaign and Liverpool beat only one of them in 11 attempts across all competitions. None of it could be blamed on Grobbelaar though, who was consistent throughout. They finished runners-up to Everton in the league, were beaten in a semi-final replay of the FA Cup to eventual winners Manchester United and lost in the European Cup Final to Juventus after 39 fans horrifically died in the stadium. It could have been a different story, although ultimately this was the first season in which that Liverpool hadn't won anything for a decade.

Grobbelaar was the undisputed number one, although there admittedly wasn't much competition at the club. 'It always seemed that Liverpool weren't ever looking for another top goalkeeper,' adds Whelan. 'That these were back-up and they would do. Then, hope that the goalkeeper wouldn't be out for too long. With Bob Wardle or Bob Bolder, they weren't a Bruce or a Clem. It was difficult for them. It's very hard. We had times when Bruce was making mistakes, but we had times when he was making world-class saves.'

Huyton-born Chris Pile had come through the ranks of the club and he even made the bench for Heysel after Bob Bolder broke his leg a month before the game. Pile had only turned 18 a month before, so was the youngest player at the time to ever be involved in a European Cup Final. Bolder left to join Charlton, which made Pile the reserve for Grobbelaar. A slipped disc put him out of action for two months and Mike Hooper was almost instantly signed. Pile left Liverpool after four years in 1987.

There was still the occasional mishap from Grobbelaar, but the team bond that had been created meant they rarely criticised each other after mistakes and they were more forgiving than previously. It helped that he would respond instantaneously and that they were often much better than their opponents. 'He would laugh it off fairly quickly,' says Whelan. 'Then, he would go out and play a blinder the next game. I'm sure it's not something that he lay in bed thinking about many nights. It's unfortunate for goalkeepers that when they do make a mistake, it's really highlighted. Bruce had one or two blunders in his time, but no more than any other goalkeeper. He was a tremendous goalkeeper, Bruce.'

His position as Liverpool's first choice would be called into question several times the next season. Kenny Dalglish had been tasked to lead Liverpool both on and off the pitch as player-manager, after Fagan retired following the Heysel Stadium disaster. Dalglish's side lost just one of their opening ten league games to a Newcastle team that contained Peter Beardsley and an 18-year-old Paul Gascoigne. However, it was the 2-2 draw with West Ham United that gave him the more worriment. Grobbelaar was at fault for both of Frank McAvennie's goals. 'Poor Bruce Grobbelaar,' wrote Roy Hayes in the *Liverpool Daily Post*. 'You either laugh or cry at him and unfortunately the latter far outnumbered the former on Saturday. The man who has mixed slapstick with magic ended up with a face as long as a clown's pocket at Upton Park after two costly clangers.'

Two games later, it was another 2-2 that would see questions start to be asked about Dalglish's team. A mix-up between Ray Kennedy and Grobbelaar led to one of the goals and the manager had to wait a little longer for their first away win. 'I'm not going to criticise individual players,' he said afterwards. 'They're all giving 100 per cent – so I can forgive mistakes. I've made plenty of them out there.' Liverpool continued to concede goals, but they did win eight of their next ten league matches. The Merseyside derby in the February threatened to undermine Grobbelaar once again. Kevin Ratcliffe's goal in the 74th minute was followed by Gary Lineker's strike just three minutes later. When Dalglish was asked if Ratcliffe's shot had taken a deflection, he replied, 'So he [Grobbelaar] says.'

Liverpool won at Tottenham for the first time in ten years in the following match, but it took an Ian Rush strike after another Grobbelaar error. 'Bruce was the most relieved man in the ground when I scored the goal,' said Rush directly after the game. 'I'm glad for him that I got the winner.' That week Grobbelaar was accused by the BBC of costing Liverpool 15 points across the season. 'After all the publicity I've been getting it was a poor show to make a mistake like that,' he admitted to the press. 'Fortunately, the lads pulled it round for me. In the past I've made mistakes and they haven't been able to do that but this time it might be quickly forgotten.'

Grobbelaar's next howler was a little less obvious, although it was a save that he should have made nevertheless. George Lawrence's effort for Southampton not only drew an immediate response from Liverpool – as John Wark and Rush reversed the scoreline within ten minutes – it also had a lasting impact. They were just two points behind Everton in the league at this stage, after they were 13 behind following the derby defeat. Liverpool won eight of their remaining nine games and Grobbelaar conceded just one goal. Dalglish scored the decisive winner at Stamford Bridge to become the first player-manager to win the league. The FA Cup Final just seven days later against Everton gave Grobbelaar a further chance for redemption. He took it. Just after the hour mark, with the scores at 1-1 following goals from Lineker and Rush, Grobbelaar was needed. Hansen's attempted back pass was intercepted by Graeme Sharp and the striker's header was destined to put the Toffees ahead until Grobbelaar miraculously pushed the ball over the bar. 'I got back as quick as I could and made a real kangaroo leap to reach the ball,' said the goalkeeper at the final whistle. He credited his Australian team-mate with teaching him the technique, but the forward was equally as complimentary. 'Perhaps this will convince people what a great goalkeeper Bruce really is and stop them getting on his back so much,' added Johnston. Liverpool scored just moments later through Johnston and then Rush added a third to give Dalglish the double.

The two Merseyside giants were among the best teams in Europe, but due to the ban on English sides competing on the continent they could only demonstrate it on a domestic level. They were more than familiar with one another and Rush was a constant scorer against the arch rivals in this period. He netted again in the 1-1 draw for the Charity Shield, which was Liverpool's ninth appearance in the season opener in 15 years. Grobbelaar picked up an injury to his stomach muscle just ten minutes into the second half and he was replaced by Hooper, who made his Liverpool debut. 'Hooper, a novice in league football but a 22-year-old well-versed in Shakespeare as a former university student, is set to maintain the Liverpool tradition of fielding interesting goalkeepers,' read *The Guardian*. The opening league game with Newcastle was the first time that Grobbelaar hadn't started for five years. Hooper would deputise for the next eight matches, but a mistake in the 2-1 defeat to Southampton meant the now fit Grobbelaar was ready to reclaim his spot. Not that Dalglish was willing to publicly condemn the youngster. 'Are you blaming the lad?' he snapped back at the press. 'Why do you mention Mike Hooper? If I blame him, it will be privately!'

Grobbelaar's return couldn't have been any easier as Liverpool beat Fulham 10-0 in the League Cup. A crazy 3-3 draw with Aston Villa came next, when Grobbelaar misjudged a high cross and Gary Thompson headed past him. The Zimbabwean maintained his position though as Liverpool won four of the next five games. The Luton Town defeat was the worst team performance under Dalglish to date, although Grobbelaar could certainly have done better in the final two goals of the 4-1 loss. Liverpool recovered well and lost just twice in their next 20 matches. They were, however, haunted by Kenilworth Road for a second time when they had to play Luton in a second FA Cup replay. The plastic pitch was a source of frustration for many away teams in Bedfordshire, and Luton clearly took advantage of their own familiarity with the surface. 'The players had enough time to prepare mentally, but I still believe that if you have an artificial surface, you have an artificial game,' said Dalglish.

Five successive victories put them top of the league, but they followed it with four consecutive defeats in the February and March of 1987. After a 3-1 win over Nottingham Forest they travelled to Manchester United confident they could still overhaul Everton in the title race. Grobbelaar gathered a header from Norman Whiteside, but as he landed, he came down on Johnston and injured his arm in the process. 'I think I have broken my elbow,' said Grobbelaar to Roy Evans who was treating him with his sponge. 'Let me have a feel,' replied the under-qualified physiotherapist. 'Oh shit, try not to let the opposition know that you've broken it!'

There were just under 20 minutes remaining of the game and the keeper was called into action on two occasions. In the closing stages, Hansen chose not to leave the ball to run out like Grobbelaar shouted, but instead hooked it into the path of Peter Davenport. The forward lobbed a stranded Grobbelaar, who attempted to reach it with his left hand because of the discomfort in his opposite arm. Grobbelaar had an operation that evening and missed the final four games of the season. Everton's victory over Newcastle meant they were out of reach, even though Liverpool beat them the week after.

The squad was transformed in the attacking areas that summer with Rush leaving for Juventus and Peter Beardsley, John Barnes, John Aldridge and Ray Houghton all arriving at Melwood. They gelled almost instantly and, although Grobbelaar was back in the team, all the focus was on the flair of this new-look side. The keeper kept five continuous clean sheets as they overcame the hoodoo of the artificial surface at Kenilworth Road with a 1-0 victory. The run of ten shut-outs between December and February showed that Grobbelaar was back to his best. 'He was very outspoken,' says Halsall on the goalkeeper's occasional discussions with Hansen. 'He had great command of the 18-yard box, and he was very deliberate over what he wanted.'

Liverpool set a 29-game unbeaten record in the league and even the loss to Everton in the League Cup couldn't dampen spirits. It was, inevitably, the Toffees who also ended the sequence of unbeaten league matches. Grobbelaar dropped a cross that allowed Wayne Clarke a simple finish, but the watching media were a little more sympathetic due to his form earlier that year.

Liverpool then played Nottingham Forest three times in 12 days. They lost the first encounter before winning the second to set up an FA Cup Final with Wimbledon. The final instalment of that trilogy would be recalled fondly years later as Dalglish's team played scintillating football to beat Brian Clough's men 5-0. Liverpool claimed the title with just two league defeats that year, but a Lawrie Sanchez goal at Wembley meant that they were denied the double. The final, from a Liverpool viewpoint, became known for Aldridge's missed penalty and 'The Anfield Rap', the song they recorded in the build-up.

As Liverpool and Grobbelaar profited more on the field, his antics grew behind the scenes. 'Honestly, he was just a one-off, you didn't know what he was going to do!' says his good friend Whelan. 'We would be in a pub having a laugh, then he would be doing a handstand on the bar. It would be something out of the ordinary or something that he wanted to do.' Whelan attended a supporters' club in New York a few years ago and went to watch the Reds play in a bar in the early hours of the morning. They showed him pictures of the year before, when Grobbelaar was doing handstands on the bar. 'Considering this was late evening time and the kick-off had been at eight in the morning! Bruce had been in the pub all day and was still able to do handstands that night. He had a remarkable capacity for drinking, but then still first in the running the next day.' Had Grobbelaar ever drunk a pint of beer while doing one of his infamous handstands? 'I can't remember him doing that one, but he will tell you he did! He will tell you I was there as well!'

Fairclough also has fond memories of the crazier side of Grobbelaar, 'You remember Bruce for doing daft things like the handstand after the League Cup win at Wembley. He got the nickname "The Clown" because he just did things that endeared him to you. He was like your mad mate at school that would just do things, Bruce was like that. Because you are loved by the lads, they kind of see through your shortcomings at times. They don't seem to matter because everyone thinks you are a great laugh. He was a great social guy, he still is, loves to get out and have fun. That was a big part of Liverpool life.'

Hooper was back in goal from the September of 1988, just three league games into the new season. Grobbelaar had fallen ill with meningitis before the Tottenham match and had to be hospitalised. He missed the next four months with the illness. It was at this point that perhaps his reputation grew in his absence as Liverpool won just ten of the 26 games in all competitions that he was out. His return to the team coincided with 19 wins in the next 21 matches. 'He was very professional and very committed,' says Halsall. 'Like all of them at the club, he was a total winner.'

In April 1989, Liverpool played Nottingham Forest in the semi-final of the FA Cup at Hillsborough and 96 supporters sadly lost their lives. Out of all the players, Grobbelaar was the nearest bystander to the incident with events taking place in the Leppings Lane stand behind his goal. His involvement in trying to help the fans saw him shouting to a policewoman to open the gates when he began to realise the severity. It was an incredibly difficult moment for the club and everyone involved. Dalglish and the players particularly took it badly as they not only witnessed the trauma unfold in front of them, but they also attended the funerals of the deceased. In a time when men rarely talked about their feelings, it would have a lasting effect on those on and off the pitch.

However, the shared experience of adversity can at times pull people together, especially as it was the second significant horror in four years for many of them. 'It's difficult to say, there was a bit, if there hadn't been a unique bond before that,' reflects Whelan. 'When I signed for Liverpool in 1979, the team that was there of Dalglish and Souness, they had a really strong bond, they were really close. When I started coming in, a lot of them players were going the likes of Jimmy Case, Ray Kennedy, Clem, but the bond that the new group had as well along with Souey and Kenny. We come in with Thommo, Nealy, Alan Kennedy. There was me, Rushy, Bruce, Craig Johnston Lawro … There was five or six of us that came into such a successful group of lads that had a great bond before us but carried on the great bond with the younger lads coming through as well. I'm sure if you have never had a great bond, then some tragedies like Heysel and Hillsborough would bring you closer together, but we were as close as you could be. That went right through more or less until the end of my career. When we played, we had a great rapport!'

At that time, Grobbelaar had a newspaper column in *The Sun* newspaper but following their slanderous headline a few days after Hillsborough, the keeper quit on the spot. He would later have a more personal ordeal after the newspaper wrongly accused him of match fixing in 1994. The result of numerous court cases saw him forced to pay the legal costs, which left him bankrupt.

After beating Nottingham Forest in the rearranged semi-final, Liverpool defeated Everton in an emotional game at Wembley when the recently returned Ian Rush scored a brace. With the events of Hillsborough still etched at the forefront of the players' minds, Liverpool had to play a league game with fellow title challengers Arsenal on the final day of the season. It had been moved as a result of the tragedy and subsequent match rearrangements. George Graham's side hadn't won at Anfield in the previous 15 years, while Liverpool were unbeaten in the league for the last five months. The only real threat from the away team in the opening 45 minutes came when Grobbelaar failed to take a cross from Michael Thomas and Steve Bould's header was directed off target by Nicol. Liverpool exerted their influence as the half progressed and never really looked in danger.

However, seven minutes after the interval Alan Smith guided a header past Grobbelaar. It meant that Arsenal needed just one more goal to snatch the league away from Liverpool's grasp and they promptly increased the tempo. Grobbelaar had to make a save from Thomas, but as the clock ticked down it looked more likely that Liverpool were going to score. The keeper looked assured and comfortable in possession as his experience shone. Then, in stoppage time the unthinkable happened. A long ball from Lee Dixon down the flank was controlled and then flicked on by

Smith. Thomas's first touch ricocheted off Nicol and back into the midfielder's path, putting him through on goal. He coolly lifted the ball over the advancing Grobbelaar to give Arsenal their ninth league title.

Grobbelaar wasn't particularly known as one of football's hard men, but there was no doubting he was much steelier than his jokey exterior suggested. 'Believe me, yeah!' says Whelan. 'Nobody messed with him! If Bruce was upset, you just left him alone and just moved away. You could see that he had been through a lot more different things to us. If you are going to war, then he is a great one to have in your team. He was always going to be there, first up. He was also one that would look after players as well. You could tell he had been through a little bit more than us.'

Before his loan move to Crewe, Grobbelaar had a trial at West Bromwich Albion. One evening he was out with Mark McCarrick when a group of lads decided to chase them around Handsworth. After a while, Grobbelaar's athleticism saw him begin to pull away from the former Birmingham City full-back. All of sudden, Grobbelaar stopped and said to McCarrick, 'Hold on, what are we running for? I'm not running!' He instantly turned around and confronted the chasers.

In Grobbelaar's teenage years, he had to fight for his country in the Rhodesian Bush War where he would witness death. This ordeal set him out from his footballing counterparts, although he was known to embellish the truth a little. 'The army stuff sounds horrendous, but he could be prone to a little bit of exaggeration from time to time,' says Fairclough. 'If you had done something, then Bruce was like, "I done that, but I was upside down!" or "I was hanging off a tree from one leg!" It was kind of always a little bit better than everyone else and everyone saw through it. It was nothing that was detrimental. He's a good lad. I like his company; you can't not like it he's great!'

Paul Stewart didn't arrive at Liverpool until the 1990s, but he recalls that Grobbelaar was still telling tales of his time fighting with guns. 'He always had an anecdote about what he was doing when he was in the Guerrillas in Zimbabwe,' says Stewart. 'The players would laugh about it because it always got extended and every time, he told it, then it would get exaggerated a little bit more. He was undoubtedly a character that could hold an audience. His stories – irrespective of how much he exaggerated them – were just great to listen to.'

Liverpool were keen to make amends in August 1989 following Arsenal's dramatic championship win in the May. The victory over the Gunners in the Charity Shield was the first of 11 matches unbeaten including a 9-0 thrashing of Crystal Palace. It came as a real shock when they lost four games in the autumn period, but they recovered well to go a further 19 games without a loss.

They then faced Manchester United away, which could have been a home game for Dalglish's men such was their dominance. John Barnes converted a penalty after just 15 minutes and then added a second only ten minutes into the second half. There was very little danger until Whelan scored one of the most bizarre own goals as his back pass sailed over the head of Grobbelaar from a considerable distance. 'I just lobbed him from 40 yards or whatever,' confesses Whelan. 'I told him, "He should have been on his line!" We were battered for eight minutes, but we held on. I just walked into the dressing room and held my hands up and said, "I'm sorry about that!" We were cruising, we were 2-0 up! I did that and I just looked around the dressing room and said, "Sorry!" But only for putting them under pressure for eight minutes, not the 82 minutes when I was man of the match before that.'

Liverpool did lose the next game, against Tottenham, but it would be their last defeat in the league as they went on to win the title. This one was extra special due to the heartbreak of Hillsborough 13 months previously. They couldn't add the FA Cup to the celebrations, though, after an error-ridden 4-3 semi-final defeat to Crystal Palace had the players arguing afterwards in the changing rooms.

The 1990/91 campaign started well with Liverpool winning ten games in a row. They were fortunate not to lose against Norwich City in the next matcvh, when they managed to attain a draw when Grobbelaar had to be in fine form; he was at fault 11 days later in the tie with Manchester United in the League Cup, but it didn't stop their supremacy in the league. Liverpool were top of the table at the end of the calendar year and looking like firm favourites to retain their crown.

An improbable five draws in the first eight games of 1991 came next before three successive Merseyside derbies. Howard Kendall's Everton were a shadow of their late-1980s side but the encounters were still forcefully contested. David Speedie's two goals made him an instant cult hero in the league encounter as Liverpool won 3-1. The FA Cup game at Anfield finished 0-0 with Grobbelaar performing well and ensuring a replay at Goodison Park. This one had no shortage of entertainment and goalmouth action as every time Liverpool took the lead, Everton equalised and the night ended 4-4.

Rush's perseverance enabled Beardsley to capitalise for the opener, but then Grobbelaar beat the ground in frustration after he failed to push Sharp's header around the post. Beardsley showed Dalglish why he should have been in the team in recent games with an excellent solo goal, only for a misunderstanding between Nicol and Grobbelaar to give Sharp an easy tap-in. Rush's clever header was then undone as Gary Ablett allowed the ball to run behind him and Tony Cottee duly obliged. Barnes's curler was the pick of the bunch before Liverpool's soft centre allowed Cottee to equalise yet again.

'I can see a save that he [Grobbelaar] made against Everton in the 4-4,' says Fairclough. 'You just see him flying through the air, he was incredibly agile.'

Manager Kenny Dalglish resigned the following day in a moment that shocked football.

Chapter 5

David James, *Mistakes, Madness and Maturity*

GRAEME SOUNESS arrived as Liverpool manager in April 1991, two months after Kenny Dalglish had departed. There were just five games left of the season and the Reds went on to finish as runners-up to Arsenal. Souness had won three league titles in five years as manager of Glasgow Rangers and it was expected that his knowledge of Liverpool would make him the perfect successor to Dalglish. He immediately made alterations to his squad and then in his second season he signed a new goalkeeper.

David James joined from Watford for £1m just one month short of his 22nd birthday. 'I think Souness tried to change everything so quick,' says Paul Stewart, who joined Liverpool a few weeks after James. 'It wasn't just me and Jamo, the season before he bought Mark Wright and Dean Saunders, it was almost like he was trying to turn it around in such a short time and change everything that Liverpool were about. I think that was part of the issue that he had.'

Liverpool had gone from a team that had seamlessly transitioned into each era to a side that were in crisis. Souness had to get the balance of freshening up the squad, while simultaneously preserving the elements that still worked. He failed to do so, which naturally led to some displeasure from those he was seeking to oust. 'I think that's always the case and not just Liverpool, in truth that's football,' adds Stewart. 'Players get to an age where they have to be replaced. It's just evolution and you can't get away from the fact that it's how the game works. There were some fractions of the players and some perhaps did resent some of the new ones coming in.'

Ronnie Whelan and Bruce Grobbelaar were two established players who found themselves on the periphery and although Whelan never had any personal issues with the new arrivals, he could see a shift in the dynamic of the dressing room from the years prior. 'That was when it was difficult,' he admits. 'Everybody got on well when we played together talking about Bruce and Souey. He had different ideas, when he came back. That's it! Those different ideas didn't include me or Bruce. That's football!'

It wasn't just personnel that was overhauled by Souness; training habits and diets were altered. They weren't unreasonable suggestions although the way he implemented his plan was a little more controversial. Souness was also given the task of negotiating contracts which wasn't a shrewd move. 'That caused some bad feeling and it was the beginning of a downward spiral in my relations with some of the players,' said Souness. 'Eventually I fell out with most of the guys who were at Anfield when I returned.' Injuries certainly hampered his team selection and the interview with *The Sun* on the anniversary of Hillsborough was a huge factor in losing many of the fans. It wasn't the ideal scenario for youngsters coming into the first team, let alone a relatively inexperienced goalkeeper.

James was now at a team that had won league titles and was looking to supplant Grobbelaar, but like the man he was seeking to emulate, he wasn't exactly short of confidence. 'He was another one that was off the wall, David,' says Whelan. 'He wasn't shy. He was of a new generation. He was in and about the dressing room chatting to everyone.' In this situation, there's always an element of the new pretender arriving to claim the throne and Grobbelaar wasn't interested in stepping aside, due to his testimonial aspirations. However, he was always receptive towards James and it was Souness that he took issue with.

'He would put any sort of differences aside and train as they always did,' Stewart says on Grobbelaar's relationship with James. 'I never saw any resentment.' Grobbelaar's place was now under threat, but he was still his usual self. 'It didn't seem to affect him when I was there,' confesses Stewart. 'He trained with Jamo and knew he was brought into replace him, but he never showed it. They were all professional. You went into that club and could see why they had won so much because they trained as professionals and did the job that they were paid to do.'

The two goalkeepers were both huge characters, but they maintained a close connection throughout. Grobbelaar was James's idol after he watched Luton Town play Liverpool when he was younger. The senior man was initially picked for the Charity Shield game against Leeds United. 'It was a game that we weren't really in to be honest,' admits Stewart. '[Eric] Cantona was his usual mercurial self and dominated the game, even though he was linked [with Manchester United] at the time. It was more than a 4-3 defeat; we were lucky to get that.' Grobbelaar misjudged a cross and Cantona completed his hat-trick when he headed into an empty net. 'Souness had brought a few players in and we hadn't played together,' says Stewart about his debut. 'I don't think we were too worried about the result and it was nice to play at Wembley.'

Souness had told Grobbelaar that he was still his first choice, but when their opening-day fixture against Nottingham Forest was switched to a Sunday for television, a problem arose. Grobbelaar wanted to play for his country against South Africa in an historical fixture but Souness wasn't willing to negotiate the terms. James was thrust into action for the next nine league games, where Liverpool managed just two wins and no clean sheets. Saunders scored twice for his new club Aston Villa in a 4-2 defeat for Liverpool, while the match later became infamous for Ronny Rosenthal's crossbar miss. James could have done better on at least two of the goals, although he was hardly shielded by debutant centre-back Torben Piechnik. Liverpool then conceded four goals to Chesterfield in the League Cup, which meant a reprieve for Grobbelaar. 'David James had all the attributes to become a fantastic goalkeeper but plunging him into the side at that time when the team was in transition was not the right decision,' said Grobbelaar in his autobiography.

The Zimbabwe international played in the next four matches, with James then used for the Tottenham Hotspur game afterwards. It was at that stage that Mike Hooper was brought into the frame. Hooper conceded just one goal in three appearances, but then a Merseyside derby defeat and 5-1 drubbing at the hands of Coventry City saw James restored. 'David James is not everyone's favourite goalkeeper, but I believe he has been unfairly blamed for some of Liverpool's defensive frailties over the last few years,' said Souness in 1999. 'I can remember when Bruce Grobbelaar was the first choice and he made some horrendous errors. And David did not have the benefit of playing behind men of the calibre of Phil Neal, Alan Hansen and Mark Lawrenson. I cannot help wondering how Bruce would have coped with the defenders who were supposed to be protecting James.' Souness certainly has a point, although that comment is perhaps tinged with how his relationship with Grobbelaar soured, while also conveniently forgetting that he was initially responsible for signing some of the players in those defences.

Grobbelaar left on loan to Stoke City in March 1993 after further issues with Souness regarding playing for Zimbabwe. James continued to play for the remainder of the campaign, although he was certainly learning on the job. 'Calamity James sees red' was the headline in *The Independent* after the then 22-year-old was sent off for kicking Norwich City's captain John

Polston in a 1-0 defeat. 'The game hinged on that incident,' said Souness to the press afterwards.

Liverpool finished the season in sixth and performed poorly in the cup competitions. 'I probably had a year with him and most of that year I was injured,' says Whelan. 'I didn't have a lot of dealings with David. I saw him on the training pitch, but not many games.' Whelan observed the new keeper from a distance and, like most, it was the early mistakes that seemed to stick in the memory but, watching old footage recently, he was surprised at how good some of the saves were that James made when he was at Liverpool. 'I must have missed most of it when I was there,' he confesses. 'It seemed David's mistakes were a lack of discipline and concentration. At times, he seemed to lack the mental ability to be able to deal with it. I had seen Bruce and Clem make mistakes, but they were able to come out of it. I thought that he would get carried away with wanting to do things when he didn't need to get involved – as Bruce did a lot as well. Bruce and David wanted to be involved all the time. Because they had good defenders in front of them and they didn't get as much of the ball. They would run out to the wing to try to do something or try a back-flick.'

Stewart felt that perhaps James's move to Liverpool happened a little too early. 'He had all the attributes that a goalkeeper needed size-wise,' he says. 'He did drop a few clangers, as we know. We brought him in young and goalkeepers don't mature until they are about 30. That's when their best seasons tend to happen.' Injury to James and Hooper's transfer to Newcastle United meant that Grobbelaar played for the majority of the 1993/94 term. The season had started brightly for the Reds, but then Souness's men won just six league games from 19 between September and the middle of January. The match with Everton included the notorious bust-up between the keeper and a young Steve McManaman, who did well to hold his own. Wins over Oldham Athletic and Manchester City briefly kept the manager in position, but then defeat to Bristol City in the FA Cup saw Souness leave of his own accord.

Stewart was certainly not the only player glad to see the back of the former midfielder. 'I don't think many people got on with him because of his arrogance and the way he managed the club,' admits Stewart. 'It wasn't just me, there were bigger players than me that didn't get on with him. I didn't succeed at Liverpool as I would have liked to have done. I didn't get on with the manager, but as I have publicly said it wasn't Graeme Souness's fault or anyone else, but my own.' Souness did enable a number of youngsters to come through the ranks including McManaman, Robbie Fowler and Jamie Redknapp, although the latter was far from his biggest fan, even though he now works with him as a pundit on Sky Sports. Souness certainly appears a little humbler in recent years and he has lost an edge in his personality, which perhaps makes him a little more open-minded.

Roy Evans was then appointed and after no wins in his first three games, James was back between the sticks until the end of the season. Grobbelaar left that summer and then there was no longer the uncertainty around the position. James played in every game of the 1994/95 season, which he regards as his favourite in his time on Merseyside. Liverpool climbed back up to fourth in the table and the foundations of a new team began to emerge. The atmosphere in the dressing room was a lot more laid-back and perhaps that eased the pressure a little on the goalkeeper. 'Football was changing, and I chose to embrace it freely rather than take a tight rein,' Evans explained in *Men in White Suits*. 'They were young lads; Christ, they were young lads with a life to live. I wanted them to self-govern.'

However, James will be the first to admit that he allowed himself to be distracted by life outside of football at times. In the summer of 1995, Stan Collymore joined the club and he struck up an early friendship with his keeper. The pair would be among the players that travelled down to London after games for a night out, while they would go fishing together in Ireland. Collymore initially stayed with his new team-mate before commuting from his home in Cannock. Their relationship cooled a little after a short period and many of the squad were unhappy with the way Collymore spoke about James in the aftermath.

That season also saw another young player given the opportunity to spend more time with the first team. David Thompson was making an impression in the youth set-up and after a few injuries Evans was keen for him to gain some experience. As he walked on to the bus, the first thing that the 17-year-old heard was, 'Oh, for fuck's sake, we must be struggling, we are scraping the bottom of the barrel now!' That comment came from James and it was his way of teaching the new lad about the mentality and camaraderie at the club. 'I knew he was only joking, but deep down I was thinking, "Is he fucking serious though?"' admits Thompson. 'He had so much energy, he couldn't keep still. I found that he was almost like a child with ADHD. His mind was like a 100mph. He is a very intelligent guy. He is a great artist; I think at times the drawing must have been a great release for him to actually sit down and be still.'

James certainly shows traits of Attention Deficit Hyperactivity Disorder, although like many adults of his generation, he has never been formally diagnosed with it or any other disorders. It would perhaps explain some of the concentration issues when he was younger and how he learnt as he progressed through his career to curb sudden urges. He openly admits that he likes structure and said he would have been in the army had he not made it in football.

It wasn't just his inability to keep still that he had to deal with, as he also has Obsessive Compulsive Disorder tendencies. 'My match preparation at Liverpool used to be at least 24 hours long,' said James in an interview with *FourFourTwo* in 2007. 'I'd go through a routine from Friday afternoon onwards. Meals, bed – everything had to be done at the same time, in order. It pretty much worked as well. It wasn't superstition so I didn't have to wear the same suit or shoes or anything like that. I just had to know things were ready and if someone disrupted my preparation, I wasn't happy. But I never told anyone what I was doing. Then I became more and more into it and the more into it you are, the more you have to do things yourself.'

James was a very popular character in the dressing room throughout his time at Liverpool. He was regarded as infectious and generous, although his casualness with money was one of the reasons why he was forced into bankruptcy when he divorced the mother of his children in 2014. 'Jamo was just lively,' says Thompson. 'He did train very hard; he was always in the gym and he was an extremely strong man. He was a natural athlete. He never once shut up. He had a really active mind; he could just talk and talk. He is hilarious.' The keeper used to smoke 20 a day when he was at Liverpool. 'He was just one of those guys that needed to be on the move and couldn't keep still. He would have about two dozen coffees a day, double expressos as well. So, not only was he charged up with what I would say is ADHD, but he had charged himself up with caffeine as well,' laughs Thompson. 'He really is a funny, funny man. A great guy.'

James's charisma would have the team laughing as he mulled over life, while asking himself questions and then answering them simultaneously. He was always extremely inquisitive and much cleverer than many give him credit for. At Watford, he would mull over statistics and he was keen to break records. 'He was absolutely unreal,' confesses Thompson. 'He got a lot of stick at Liverpool, which some of it may have been right, but most of the time his performance level was off the chart. He could kick it miles. He could throw it from one length of the pitch to the other. His agility for such a big man was amazing and his shot-stopping – I have never seen a goalkeeper like him to be honest. His reading and anticipation of where people were going to shoot. Sometimes he was there before they had connected with the ball. I found it very frustrating actually. In training, I would be hitting good shots with an extremely high force going right in the top corner and there was Jamo tipping it off the crossbar.'

The first 4-3 encounter with Newcastle United, in 1996, was voted the best Premier League game ever, due to the talent and ability on display providing pure drama right to the end. However, as neither side won the league it illustrated that both teams were lacking the discipline, professionalism, structure and nous that was greater over at Manchester United. It was still an extraordinary game though. 'That Keegan-esque style of football was entertaining but non-profitable,' said James to *The Chronicle* in 2014. 'It didn't have the silverware to show for it in the end.' The same could certainly be said about the Liverpool side. The FA Cup Final defeat to Manchester United that season became more known for the pre-match clothing attire beforehand from a Liverpool standpoint, although James wrongly had to take the brunt of the criticism. He had done some modelling work with Armani, but he didn't choose the suits or arrange it, he simply passed on a telephone number.

The next season Liverpool finished just seven points behind United in the title race, although they felt that they should have done better. The goalkeeper showed a run of consistency when he conceded just four goals in ten matches over the Christmas period and into the start of March. He was rewarded with his international debut against Mexico, when he became the only black goalkeeper ever to play for England. 'Obviously, he was unfortunate to have the likes of David Seaman around at the same time,' thinks Thompson. 'Otherwise, he would have been without doubt England's number one.'

It was also at this time that James was in the headlines again for the wrong reasons following a few high-profile errors and due to his honesty. After an erratic display in the second 4-3 victory over Newcastle, he admitted that he got 'carried away playing [video games] *Tekken 2* and *Tomb Raider* for hours on end' the night before. 'I was quite honest in my assessment of the game afterwards, saying that I should have saved two or three of the goals and from that got barraged for about three months!' admitted James. He described the first encounter as 'magical' but the second as 'nearly ruining my career'. From those looking in it seemed that he lacked maturity, but the reality was he was misunderstood. His use of computer games has helped him channel his hyperactivity and he has used it in a therapeutic way. It's of course not ideal to overdo it and lack sleep, but these are lessons that he has had to acquire through the years which may have been more obvious to others.

A month later, Liverpool faced United at Anfield, with the two clubs separated by just two points at the top of the table. A mix-up between Bjorn Tore Kvarme and James almost handed Andy Cole the opening goal, but it just proved to be a sign of things to come. With the score at 1-1 Gary Pallister headed United in front when James unconvincingly tried to punch the ball away. The keeper was never going to get there first as the cross was delivered perfectly into the defender. Then he completely misjudged a cross from Gary Neville to give Cole the simplest of tap-ins. Sky commentator Andy Gray described the moment as 'the mistake that has handed the title to Manchester United'. James was under fire once more.

'He got a lot of criticism for coming for crosses because maybe he would drop a few,' says Thompson. 'But I never saw a goalkeeper come for as many crosses as he did and catch a high percentage. Imagine the pressure he would take off the defence by coming for the crosses.' Another condition of James's potential OCD was that he would keep persevering in adversity. Goalkeepers with lesser resolve would have stopped leaving their line, but he continued with the approach until he mastered it. 'He was a very mentally strong guy,' continues Thompson. 'He was very confident and that served him well throughout his career. He didn't really adjust his game too much, he just improved.'

Liverpool required more experience in the quest to close the gap, so signed Paul Ince and Karl-Heinz Riedle in 1997. They also purchased American international Brad Friedel to give James competition, but they had to wait until the December before he could join up with the squad due to problems acquiring a work permit. After a difficult start, Liverpool won 13 out of 18 matches in all competitions between November and January. James kept a further clean sheet against Blackburn at the end of the first month of 1998, his fifth in six games. A rush of blood to the head saw him concede a penalty in the next game against Southampton, and Liverpool lost 3-2, although James wasn't the only one not at the necessary level that day. His poor clearance against Sheffield Wednesday gave them a 3-1 lead with just 20 minutes remaining, but Michael Owen completed his hat-trick to give Evans's men a 3-3 draw. Defeat to Middlesbrough in the League Cup semi-final and then an indifferent performance in the derby saw Friedel take James's place. There was little contrast still, as goals continued to be leaked by Liverpool's defence and their once-promising campaign petered out.

James didn't let the criticism get to him, although that's not to say underneath that muscular exterior, he isn't thoughtful and concise. He set up the David James Foundation after a trip to Malawi to raise awareness for AIDS research. He is also a global ambassador for the Special Olympics and extremely aware of the environmental factors that the world faces. 'I think he was scared to let people in, but the more you got to know him and the more you scratched the surface, then he was a caring guy,' adds Thompson. 'He could cut you down with a comment or a shrewd remark, but deep down he was a sensitive guy.'

Friedel continued as first choice in the next term, with Gérard Houllier now alongside Evans as joint manager in the dugout. The American held down the role until his two mistakes against Manchester United in October cost him. 'Liverpool's need for a goalkeeper of championship-winning potential was again embarrassingly obvious at Old Trafford last night,' read *The Guardian*'s match report. James was back in the team, where he remained when Houllier took full control in the November. It seemed that the Frenchman, though, wanted to break up Evans's team and that a new goalkeeper would be a good way to start. James didn't get on particularly well with new assistant manager Phil Thompson and he was frequently arguing with him and Houllier. There's no doubting that he doesn't get the credit he deserves for his overall time at Anfield, but a move to Aston Villa was perhaps the best outcome for all involved when he left in the summer of 1999.

James spent two seasons at Villa Park as John Gregory's men finished in the top eight in both years. He was at fault in the FA Cup Final in 2000, when Roberto Di Matteo's goal gave Chelsea a 1-0 win, although he had been the hero in the penalty shoot-out win over Bolton Wanderers in the semi-final. 'Penalties are paradoxical things,' wrote James in *The Guardian* in 2008. 'If you give away a penalty and don't save it, it's your own terrible mistake, but at least it's you that everyone is blaming rather than someone else. If a defender concedes one and you don't save it, you feel even worse. You picture their face as the guy lines up to take it, full of expectation. And then disappointment. I would rather it was all in my hands. I know that sounds mad, but at least then it's my responsibility and no one else's.'

James moved on to West Ham, who initially did well in his first season and finished seventh. However, they were relegated in his second year with one of the most talented squads to have dropped out of the top flight. Manchester City was his next stop, where Stuart Pearce even used him as a striker late in the final game of the 2004/05 season when they desperately needed a goal against Middlesbrough.

Thompson was reunited with James in the south of England in 2006. 'When I signed for Portsmouth, he was the goalkeeper there at the time,' says Thompson. 'I know he had a couple of knee injuries, but nothing had left him. In fact, he had got even better. You could not beat him in training in shooting practice. He was so dynamic. The experience of life meant that he had settled down a bit. He was just an amazing goalkeeper. Jamo was key to the success we were having on the pitch.' Portsmouth had acquired a number of former Liverpool players at this point with Djimi Traore and Glen Johnson also in that squad. James would play a pivotal role in helping the club win the FA Cup in 2008.

When he left Pompey in 2010, he still made another 100 appearances in England with Bristol City and Bournemouth. He had short spells in Iceland and India before his playing days were over. 'For as long as I'm not letting either side down, I'll continue,' said James to *The Independent* in 2013, when he was at Íþróttabandalag Vestmannaeyja. 'I won't retire until the game retires me. Yes, there are moments where I've thought, maybe now's the time. But then something good happens, and you think, no, not yet. So, until I can't actually do it anymore, I'll never retire. Maybe I'll fade away.'

His longevity means that only Gareth Barry, Ryan Giggs and Frank Lampard have played in more Premier League games than him, while he won over 50 caps for England. 'He looked after himself,' explains Thompson. 'He was a natural athlete. He could have played Basketball or gone into any other sporting industry. It was a hell of an achievement.'

Chapter 6

Tony Warner, *Merseyside, Millwall, Malta and Mimms*

TONY WARNER didn't particularly like watching football when growing up. The only child, from south Liverpool, would see his life change, though, due to the influence of his father and uncle. His dad would observe the Reds in great detail, while his brother played as a goalkeeper for Tranmere and at youth level for England before leaving for college football in America. 'I can always remember my first goalkeeper session, in Court Hey Park in Childwall,' recalls Warner. 'The casey balls that really stunk of leather and were dead light. We played between two trees.' His uncle would just throw balls at him to test out his reflexes.

He went to play for local pub side The Cat's Whiskers. Warner continued, 'They had a manager called Reggie Smith and he was really big in the area for football. We were terrible, we would get caned every week. We would just get battered. Funnily enough, there was another team in our league called Mersey Bus and they used to get battered every week as well. Their keeper was the other keeper at Liverpool [when we grew up]. He was in the A team and I was in the B team. We were at them clubs from nine, ten, 11 and 12, then at Liverpool he was probably 17, so there's a few years in between but I often think was there a correlation there between getting lots of pressure and having to deal with things.'

At this point I decided to tell Warner of my own story of playing as a young goalkeeper and conceding large amounts of goals. In one match, Burntwood Youth Club played Elford Town and we lost 13-0 with me conceding the 13 goals and former Wolverhampton Wanderers goalkeeper Matt Murray at the opposite end for the team from Lichfield. 'It's not an exact science then is it to get battered all the time,' replies Warner.

At 14 years old, he started to go to matches. However, it was the blue half of Merseyside that grabbed his attention. 'I never used to go to any away games, I just went to the home games,' he says. 'I was a big fan of Neville Southall, I still am. In my eyes he was the best in the world at that point. He was phenomenal. Looking back now, I have been lucky enough to have been in the game, you talk to players who were around Southall and everyone just says the same thing – he was just unbeatable. I spoke to Mike Stowell – when I was at Leicester, he was the goalkeeping coach – and he said, "It was demoralising being second to Southall. When there were shooting drills, Southall would go in and concede none, then you would concede two, Southall none, you none, Southall none, you four, Southall none. He would just never concede; it was impossible to get it passed him."

'He would find it really easy saving, so he would start doing different things like not using his hands and heading it out. Off the shoulder and stuff like that. I have heard it off Stowell, Paul Wilkinson and a few players, who just said he was amazing. He was my first hero, Southall. As an Everton fan, I was lucky enough to have the world's best goalie on my doorstep. It was superb. He always had a big brand-new Volvo estate and you would just see it going past. You could just see this big muzzy [moustache] over the steering wheel. He would drive past you.

'He was a character and he is different. At Everton there was a walk through to the car park for the fans and it's an opportunity to get autographs. Everyone would stop, but Southall never stopped. If you kept up with him, you might get two autographs out of him by the time he got to the door. He would knock you over and walk straight through you. I couldn't get in the right position. You always had to be in the perfect spot, and I could never get close to him. I got the matchday programme one day and the centre spread was this picture of Southall and I thought, "Right, he is not fucking getting away today." He come through with his big muzzy, bowling people over and I just got in there and put my arm across him, as much as I could. He just signed it without even looking. I think it's at my mom's now, his autograph and it was a boss picture.'

Warner played for Merseyside when he was at school, but when he got too old, he started playing open age Sunday league football at Sefton Park in the Liverpool District League. The 18-year-old was playing every Sunday and then working for an accountancy firm during the week. He was sitting at home one day off sick when he received a phone call from Steve Heighway. The former winger was now working at Liverpool as head of youth development. He asked Warner if he was interested in playing in a game the following day, so they could observe him.

'I was genuinely sick; I was sick as a dog,' confesses Warner. 'My dad took me down the next day and I took another day off work. I walked in and he said, "Do you recognise anyone?" And I recognised [Robbie] Fowler, I must have played against him in a youth game or something back in the day. I recognised his face. I recognised another lad, Paul Morris, who I used to play against at school. I recognised them two. I played the game and he [Heighway] said, "We would like you to come in and play for us on a Saturday, if you're not doing anything." I was working by Alder Hey, which isn't too far from Melwood. On a Tuesday and a Thursday, I would walk down after work and train with the academy goalkeeper coach. I played for Liverpool on a Saturday, you had an A and a B team, I was playing in their B team. We would play against Manchester United and Burnley, all good games and I was really happy with it. There was nothing in the offering, it was all on a non-contract.

'The contrast between playing against Gary Neville on a Saturday or [David] Beckham or [Nicky] Butt in these games and then on a Sunday you were playing against madness. You would be putting your own goals up and there was dog shit on the floor. Fellas on the ale, fellas not turning up and others still in their going-out gear from the night before. All wired and pissed or whatever. The contrast was amazing, but they both helped each other. The stuff at Liverpool was obviously fantastic because technically it was great, so that helped in Sunday league for you to develop. But the Sunday league helped because it was men's football and there were certain things you had to kind of take and you had to suffer. The physicality of it and people just not caring about you in as far as challenges.

'I was 18, a young lad and people would just come and flatten you. You would be on the floor rolling round and when you got up no one would care about it. I wouldn't exactly say it was dangerous, but there were some dangerous tackles going around. There were threats of violence and loads of fights. In fights at football clubs, there are a few fisticuffs and it gets dragged apart. Here, people were getting strangled and others just standing and watching. People were getting seriously injured. In that way, in terms of going to Liverpool, the physicality and not being scared of certain things. They both kind of dovetailed each other quite well. I think that helped my development in a strange kind of way. The tackles are horrendous, but it is what it is. It's Sunday league football and it's probably the lowest you can get in football, but it opens your eyes.'

That situation continued for a year and the B team won the league. Warner thought that would be the end, but he phoned Heighway in the summer and was happy to hear that he wanted him back. Warner said, 'They stepped me up to the A team and it was the same situation again, I was still working. At this point,

I pulled Heighway and said, "Is there any chance? I have been here for a whole year and I am playing with lads who are on relatively half-decent contracts. I am not embarrassing myself and I'm playing every week. Is there are chance of me coming in full time?"

'He said, "Well, we have got Mike Hooper, we have got Bruce Grobbelaar and David James. We can't really fit anymore pros in but stick with it and we will see how we go." At no point was I ever going to walk away from it because I thought, why? It's such an opportunity. I had seen a lot of lads come and go in the 18 months that I was there. Maybe they were told they weren't good enough, I don't know! But nobody was there for 18 months like I was without a contract, they just weren't. Then, just before Christmas, Steve Heighway said, "Can you come in for a two-week trial?" On Christmas Eve, he called me in and said, "We are going to give you 18 months!" So, it was a good Christmas. I can remember driving home in my dad's car, it was before we had phones and I couldn't wait to tell him.'

This was at the time when clubs were beginning to develop large-scale academies. 'Liverpool started it all off, but everyone has got one now,' adds Warner. 'If you invest in those academies, then you have to fill them with players and that includes goalkeepers as well. I was at Liverpool when the academy got developed, I think it was 98. That's when it started, a lot of players and bodies. I got brought in four years earlier in 94, when I first signed. If it had gone on any longer, then the opportunity would have passed me by. I was in the right place, at the right time. You just don't get lads coming in from Sunday league to top level Premier League clubs. That's not to say it can't happen, but it's very rare because you need so much development to get to that level now. If I was any older, then I would have missed the opportunity. If I was 20, then I would have been too old. I just got in on the last chance saloon.'

Warner initially dealt with Heighway, but due to his position he began to operate with the specialists. 'The goalkeeping coach when

I first arrived was a fella called Vic Johnson,' explains Warner. 'I was really happy with that because I had never had a goalkeeping coach before.' He then worked with Joe Corrigan. 'Celtic would fly him up for one day, then we would have him for two days and then he would go to Middlesbrough. So, Joe was like travelling around the country as a goalkeeping coach. Then, he came into us full-time, so when I stepped up into the first-team squad, Joe was my main coach. I trained with Joe for about five years.'

It was at this stage that Warner started to have regular communication with some of the established names who now formed the coaching staff. 'Ronnie Moran was the first-team coach and Sammy Lee was the reserve coach; I dealt with Sammy a lot because I played a lot of reserve games. It was a good environment and they were good people, knowledgeable and humble as well. There was nothing that those men hadn't done. There are teams now where kit men have got assistants. There are teams now with like five assistants. Ronnie Moran was the kit man at Liverpool. There was a laundry woman, but when you got to the ground, it was Ronnie Moran that would push the skips in, put the kit out and put it back. He had been around for European Cup wins. He had won how many medals and been around for how many league campaigns. That's how the club was back in the day.'

Graeme Souness was in the last few weeks of his tenure as manager when Warner began full-time. It didn't work out for Souness or the club, but he was still one of the best midfielders ever to wear a red shirt. 'I think I spoke to him once or twice in the gym, but I didn't have much interaction with him,' confesses Warner. 'I have probably spoken to him more since I left the club. Souness as a player, was one of those that I really admired because he was good at the time. He might not get away with what he did now, but as a player he was phenomenal. He would take on all comers. He was very hard, no one would mess with him, but he could also play as well. He was a top player. He went away to Italy and he improved over there as well.'

Roy Evans replaced Souness at the helm in January 1994 and then, when Bruce Grobbelaar left in the summer, an opportunity arose for Warner. 'I can remember going in to Roy Evans and I might have asked for a new contract. I can remember being cheeky and asking for something. He said, "We will look into it, anything else?" There had been an injury with the first team, so I had been on the bench for a little bit, but I was still training with the other team. I said, "How about you get me in there in the first-team changing room?" Looking back now I was a right cheeky bastard. I said, "How about you get me in there?" He said, "You're right, you have been in the squad a little bit, go and get your stuff." I walked back into the changing rooms and I was like, "See you lads, I'm off!" I walked in, got my peg and that was it. There were the likes of Jamie Redknapp, Mark Kennedy on my right, we were sitting on the end. John Barnes and Julian Dicks.'

Having played in Sunday league football – where everyone is friends and would socialise together – the dynamic of the new dressing room initially surprised Warner. 'I can remember standing there with Julian Dicks and Torben Piechnik and they were caning each other,' remonstrates Warner. 'Julian was trying to line him up, so if they took it too far, they could start fighting. I can remember thinking, "Fucking hell! You guys are all on fortunes how come you all hate each other?" The penny dropped pretty quickly. Julian would be saying, "You're fucking shit, you!" and things like that. Torben had won the Euros with Denmark after they got through the back door. He would say in his Danish accent, "Get your medals on the table." Julian would be like, "Your medals are shit, you're shit." They were face-to-face. I was like, "Why are they arguing? I can't believe it!" I'd never seen this before. From then on, I saw lots of arguments and realised that's just the way it is: full of egos.'

This introduction was tough but character-building for many players within that era. 'There were some hard people there. What you would find is that when players were out the team that's when they would start. There were some big personalities. Paul Stewart gave me some terrible stick; we were playing a reserve game and we got beat. He was savage, caning everyone, "You're not doing this and you're not doing that." He said, "What chance have you got with a goalie that can't even fucking kick the ball," aimed at me. I was like, "Ah!" My head's hanging down. Someone said, "All right then fucking big lips, get out and help him then. When do you ever help anybody? Tomorrow?" He said, "All right then, I will." I remember finishing training and Stewie walking over with a big bag of balls, saying, "Come on!" I was like, "All right." My kicking was everywhere and all over the place. You could see that he didn't want to be there, but he had to make the point. He never came back the next day, he was probably knackered.

'There were some big characters, but they were brilliant; I couldn't have been involved in a better dressing room. They were great. There was some grounding and you had to take some stick. I weren't too bad with all that kind of stuff because I never got offended. The more offended you got, then the more stick you got, which I worked out quickly. Either give it back with a laugh or swallow it.'

Did anyone help him to adapt to this new environment or was it every man for himself? 'No one would really put their arm around you, but they would [help],' says Warner. 'I can remember speaking to Mark Wright a couple of times just in games. I would maybe ask him to do something and he would be like, "I can't do that because of X,Y and Z." I would think, "Okay, I won't say that again." The penny drops. There weren't many that were like arses that were being nasty to you. Everyone had a good solid character. If you show willing, show effort, you're developing and you're not a bad player in your position, then people will have you. If you're fucking shit, then people don't like playing with you. Here's me, they are probably saying, "That Warner, he was fucking shite!" You might be better off asking someone else that one,' he smiles.

'They want to get on with their business and if you're not up to scratch, they will kind of give you a few pointers, but you have to fucking learn because they have their own job to do. David James helped me a fair bit because me and him were pretty much together for the five years that I was there. Jason McAteer was a good mate of mine, me and him were room partners for a couple of years. They were a knowledgeable firm; they knew football inside out.'

Ian Rush and John Barnes were the senior professionals in the squad at that time. 'It was strange for me looking back because I was never involved as much with the first team, so you don't see yourself on the same level,' admits Warner. 'So, you kind of have a voyeur on the outside looking in. It's Ian Rush, fucking hell! I can remember my dad going on about Ian Rush and John Barnes when I was a kid. They would just terrorise everything all the time. Rush was coming towards the end, but he was still a top finisher. John Barnes was a good organiser. Jamo would mess around a bit in training and Barnes didn't like that so much. So, when we got brought across for games, Barnes would always say to me, "Get in there," and point at his goal. Any team with Barnes in a five-a-side would always win because he would organise so well, he would pull all the strings. He was constantly talking. His knowledge, and he would tell you to do things and you would be like, "Why do I want to do that?" Then, you would realise. He was so ahead of the game.'

In his prime, Barnes would beat opposition full-backs for fun and create goalscoring opportunities for himself and others. In his early 30s he no longer had the same speed or acceleration, so he adapted his game to become more of a deep-lying playmaker in the style of Xabi Alonso or Jan Molby. 'He had an Achilles injury, I think, which put paid to his pace. At the time that I went in there, he was that midfielder. He was just brilliant. He wouldn't be getting smashed, he would just be playing and moving. He was brilliant to be around. He was a really great character as well such a nice fella. He had a lot of time for everyone. He was just a top fella.'

Fowler finished as top scorer for the Reds in the next three seasons. 'People ask me now who was the best striker that I played with or been around. I never actually played with him for the first team, but I trained with him for years,' Warner says. 'I've seen the sharp end of his tools enough times in training. For me, he is the most natural striker I have ever seen, and I think a lot of people would say that. I was talking to my mates about this a while ago. People have opinions on players and every time you mention Fowler everybody is like, "Yeah, top level." You talk to fellow pros and those that have faced him, he was unreal. The thing about Fowler was once he got within range, and he had a long range as well, you were just always in danger. It could be anywhere on the pitch; left foot, right foot, with his head, very quick and no back lift. Intelligent, he was just brilliant.

'Fowler was fast, but everything about him was great. Michael Owen was lightning quick and an absolute phenomenal player, but for me Fowler was more dangerous from different areas. Once Owen was away from someone there was no stopping him and he could finish. Fowler would terrorise you. His speed of thought was just brilliant. I went on a tour with him about six years ago to Barbados and we had all been there a few days on the ale. We walked out on to the pitch and everyone is a little portlier these days. He just hit this ball and it would have beaten most keepers now, it was phenomenal. He is about two stone heavier and he just laces this ball, with the dip and whip. You're like, "Yeah, he has still got it!" Top draw!'

Jamie Redknapp was in midfield and as shown on the Sky One programme *A League of Their Own* he certainly enjoys the banter. 'He wasn't getting taken advantage of. He was one of the main characters. The likes of [Steve] McManaman, Fowler and Phil Babb. John Scales was a bit quieter. [Oyvind] Leonhardsen was a bit quiet, he would get terrorised a little bit. He wouldn't care, but no one got bullied.'

Stan Collymore arrived in the summer of 1995 for a British record fee of £8.5m. 'Stan would rare up now and again. I remember once, Jamo was giving him a bit of stick and he had just signed. Stan just stood up in the dressing room with no shame and said, "Jamo, you were one of the reasons why I came to this club and you're giving me stick, what's going on?" Jamo was like, "Fuck off Stan! Put up or shut up that's the way it is!" Stan has been around at Southend and Palace, but that was just Stan. You could never get to the bottom of Stan. The thing with Stan was he was a good character and among it the vast majority of the time. Then, he would just flip, and anything would send him. He would just go berserk.

'There would be no rationale to what he had just done. Then, something weird would happen and he would be all right again. I've said it before, if someone is an absolute prick all the time, then you would just have nothing to do with them because they are a prick. But Stan would be sound for big periods and then he would just do something really weird. You would just be like, "Why have you done that?" or "Why have you said that for?" He let himself down. Then, he would draw you in and do it again. He has had some problems. I had a lot of trouble with Stan when I was first at the club, but I talk to him now. I wasn't talking to Stan for about seven years, but we had a charity football match. I thought, "Life's changed, and I'm not bothered anymore."'

Warner spent a lot of time with David James and he believes that he was certainly not given the full credit that he deserves. 'He used to have parties at his house, so we would go back there. I got on really well with him. He was a phenomenal goalkeeper, for all the criticism that he gets, he was a top goalkeeper. He made mistakes in vital games and then after that every mistake he made was magnified. You would see [Peter] Schmeichel and [David] Seaman making mistakes, but they wouldn't get the coverage that Jamo got. It was really unfair.'

Steve Harkness was Liverpool's first-choice left-back that season and Warner confirms that he had a fondness for excrement. 'No one likes shit do they,' proclaims Warner. 'If someone's scared of spiders, then you throw a spider at them. If they don't like clowns, then you throw a clown at them. Harkness would always have shite everywhere on handles and that. You would be like, "Ah fuck! I've got shite on my hands!" and you would have to go and wash it off. The big one was shitting in wash bags. Everyone had Louis Vuitton wash bags that were all brown and they would have to go and wash their aftershaves off because you wouldn't want to throw it away. The toothbrush would have to go. Give it a good swill out and then throw it all back in. It was a laugh. I would never go berserk over stuff like that because I enjoyed the laugh. I'm a bit like that myself, I've done that plenty of times. If you really didn't like someone, then you wouldn't shit in their wash bag because a fight would start. It's probably a sign of affection. It means they like you.'

The high-jinks were commonplace in the dressing room but nowadays you wouldn't get away with it. When Warner was coaching at Bolton, he worked alongside fellow coach David Lee. The former right-winger was an apprentice at Bury and his team-mates would put him in an old wicker basket. 'They would say, "Get in that basket," and he said, "I had to do it!" He got in, they used a leather strap to tie it down and then put it in a bath and turned it on. It would be like a James Bond film, where at the top of the basket, there's just enough air to breathe. They would be all rolling around laughing at him. But now, you would go to jail. You would get two years for that, but he loved every minute of it.'

In those days, players would be seen out regularly in bars and nightclubs. They would finish the game on a Saturday afternoon and then either get the train down to London or have a night out in Liverpool. 'Cream was the big one,' recalls Warner. 'There was this bar in town that was the best by far called Retro. It was on

Mathew Street on the corner. It was always full of great people, good music. A few of the chaps from town would always be in there and it had a back door that you could always go into. You just gave a little knock on the back door and he would let you in. It was just brilliant. It hasn't been surpassed since the 90s. It was just perfect. Duncan Ferguson would be in there and all he ever used to drink was Crystal, worth a fortune. He would just stand there in his Everton trackie and his flip-flops on. The fellas behind the bar knew him really well and he would just walk in, flip-flops, Crystal, legend. It was superb.'

The celebrity lifestyle and good looks saw the Liverpool team of that era given the 'Spice Boys' tag. Warner said, 'It was that Britpop culture and going out gave more exposure. Footy players have always gone out with celebrity birds, but it all became more apparent. Giggs was going out with a few like Dani Behr and obviously Beckham with Posh Spice. The lads would be seen out in London a fair amount of the time. We would come out of bars late and get photographed. Robbie Williams was knocking around at this time and I remember seeing him in a few hotels. So, we got tagged with it, the white suits especially.'

In the 1996 FA Cup Final, Liverpool's players wore white Armani suits. Has Warner kept the now infamous apparel? 'Yeah, I've still got it,' he says. 'It was actually a nice suit. If we had won the game, the suits would have been heralded. The result killed the suits. The game was terrible.'

Eric Cantona's strike five minutes from time saw Liverpool lose to arch rivals Manchester United and Alex Ferguson. 'I think we got that [Spice Boys] tag because the only team that were our main competitors were United. Arsenal were obviously very good, but I think we were definitely the best team, bar United. We were just unfortunate that they were around at the time. United were just a bit better than us and we were seen as the pretenders. We had the capability, but we weren't getting the results, whereas United had the perfect formula.

'They had Ferguson, who had been there a long time and evolved, developing his own system. He was the task master that got the best out of his players, where we were just a bit shy of it. People would think they can't do it because of outside influences, and I think that's what gave us the Spice Boys tag. It was a bit unfair, but it stuck. We are talking about it now 24 years after the event. It was a bit unfair because we had a good solid side, a superb side. That team would have been a good side in today's environment, but it gets seen as a failure which is a shame.'

Some of the scenes around Melwood were a million miles away from today's culture. Warner said, 'Training started at 10.30am. If you could dive out of your car at 10.25am, get your boots and kit on and get on the training ground for 10.30am, then that was fine. You would see lads sprinting [across the car park]. There was no problem with that at all. You would have your breakfast, which would be bacon, sausage, eggs and toast. The canteen was right next to the meeting point and there would be lads standing there eating bacon and sausage butties. I can always remember Razor [Neil Ruddock] standing there, with a bit of tomato sauce dripping down his top. There was no problem with it. If you did that now, they would kick you out the door.'

The emergence of David Thompson, Jamie Carragher and Michael Owen from the youth team in 1996/97 added more to the squad, but they were still a little short of wisdom. Liverpool finished fourth in that campaign but they did have the same points totals as Newcastle United and Arsenal just above them. Evans then signed Paul Ince and Karl-Heinz Riedle the next summer.

Warner said, 'Incey is Incey. I guess some people wouldn't like all that, but I can't think of one particular instance. I remember him getting some stick, when someone was saying, "You have played for United and Inter? How come they got rid of you and you have ended up here?" That was a bit of a laugh and a joke. I think him and John Barnes had a bit of needle. They weren't very vocal, and you could tell that there was something between them.'

And the World Cup-winning striker? 'He took my number 13 [shirt], the bastard,' jokes Warner. 'He always had it throughout his career. I went into Roy Evans's office and he said, "We have signed Karl-Heinz Riedle," I was like, "Okay!" "But he wants number 13." I was like, "That's my number, Gaff!" He said, "Well! We have given it to him." Was I that arsed? I don't even know if I was that bothered, I just didn't want to get mugged off. No one says fine and then just walks out, you have to fight your corner a bit. He said, "If you had made your debut in it or played in number 13, then I wouldn't have given it to him. But you haven't actually played in it yet, so for that reason. He wants it, is really strong on it and he has worn it throughout his career."

'He was a good player. One thing I remember about him was that he could head a ball from anywhere. He was very average height, but he had incredible hang time. Once he got his head on the ball his technique was flawless. One thing he would do you with – if you were at an angle and he couldn't beat you there – he would head it right over you. It would be yards above you and then it would just drop in at the far post. Heidar Helguson was the same when I was at Fulham. They had similar technique and were very good at spotting what everyone else had closed off to. He was a really nice fella.

'He always had a boss motor. A black convertible Porsche 911 on a left-hook. He would always rock in, dead stylish. He would always tell us about this hotel he had bought. These would be the things you would hear. I'm standing next to fellas that own hotels. I was like, "You own a hotel Karl?" He was like, "Yeah! I own a hotel!" I was like, "Fucking hell!" He said, "Yeah, it's in the Alps, there's loads of snow in the winter, perfect. Then, in the summer it's all nice and green, loads of walking, so I get business all year round." There were lads walking in saying they are buying a new BMW and Karl's got a hotel. He would get out of his Porsche with his lovely European gear on. He would wear those shoes Toggs. He was ahead of his time.'

The young Carragher was unsurprisingly unafraid to voice his opinions. Warner continued, 'He was very much as he is now. He hasn't changed at all. He was tough tackling and mouthy, but in the right way. He was focused and determined. He was a really good lad; a good character and he was really funny. There was him and his cousins that would play with us, they were like a little crew and they would just terrorise every one of their age. Really funny characters, but it was Carragher that stepped forward and went on. I can always remember him in the gym and challenging Paul Ince to a shoulder press contest with 20kg dumbbells. Incey was quite good at it, but what they would do is every day they would be in there having a go. That was a by-product of Jamie's personality. He would always call Incey, Don. He would say, "Come on Don, let's get in the gym!" He would be throwing tackles in during training and he wouldn't care about reputations. He would get stuck in and I think that the lads liked that. It's the way he is now. He didn't care, if someone squared up to him, then he squared back up to them. He was a good player.

'[Steven] Gerrard was the same. They were very similar. Good quality. To be honest with you, if you had said to me now, if I thought the two would be the players that they were, then I would probably say no! But that's more fool me. When I was 23, I wasn't looking to see how good other players would be. Could anyone say that a player was going to be that good? Especially Gerrard! He has had a phenomenal career and he is Mr Liverpool.

'I was speaking to Heighway a few years ago and we were talking about players of that age group. He said, "Thommo was the best technical player that I have ever brought on." Thommo was amazing. He keeps himself in good nick. Nowadays, when we go to tournaments, he just runs riot, no one can get the ball off him. He is dead entertaining and funny. We were in Hong Kong and he chipped someone from the halfway line. He got player of the tournament and he is a really infectious character.'

In November 1997, Warner and Thompson went on loan to Swindon Town, who were managed by former Liverpool midfielder Steve McMahon. 'I loved being a Liverpool player, it was nice, you can't knock it,' says Warner. 'But now it was time to play. I was 22 or 23 then and I hadn't played a game, so how old do you get before you are seen as a bit of a fraud? So, the opportunity arose. Roy Evans said to me, "This is it mate! Macca's all right, get yourself down there." I can remember going down there, having a few doubts and thinking am I ready. I was in the hotel and I can remember thinking to myself, "If you want to be a footy player, you have got to play." Mark Wright phoned me the night before and said, "Good luck mate! If you want to be a player, then this is it!" David James and Joe Corrigan phoned me as well. "Making your debut is superb and we have all had to do it!" I was ready for the challenge and I really enjoyed it. I didn't have that much to do to be honest with you, but I done okay. I played the game and we won 1-0.'

However, the excitement quickly faded and Warner understood the ruthlessness of football. 'The next game was Stockport away and I had a really bad game. Paul Cook banged a free kick in against me and I just remember making bad decisions. The left-back played the ball to me and I gave it him back, he was like, "What the fuck are you doing mate?" I realised it wasn't as easy as you think, it's difficult. We got caned about 4-1 and then the other kid came back in then. My one-month loan spell finished. Thommo done really well. He was a revelation, as Thommo would do. He was superb. I thought to myself I have played professional footy now and I want a bit more of this. Then I got an opportunity to go to Celtic.'

Jonathan Gould and Stewart Kerr were both injured in November 1998 and Celtic needed a goalkeeper. 'Brad Friedel come in on the Friday and said, "The manager is going to pull you in a minute, as an offer has come from Celtic, do you want to go?" I was like, "Of course, yeah!" He said, "There's an Old

Firm derby next week and if you go you will be playing!" I just sat my arse down on the bench and I got the shout to go to Roy Evans's office. "I've just got off the phone to Celtic and everything is agreed," he said. That was the Friday, so I went up the M6 to Glasgow and I can remember getting met at Parkhead by Eric Black. It was about two o'clock, but it was wintertime, so it was a bit dark. They put me through my paces to see what I had got. They were volleying balls at me. He said, "We are going to meet at the ground tomorrow, and we will get you a lift," and all that. I got picked up and took to the ground. I recognised Alan Stubbs, as he was a Scouser. We went and played St Johnstone and I thought this is a gimme. We got beat 2-1! I thought, "Fucking hell! This wasn't supposed to happen." They scored early on and then [Henrik] Larsson [equalised] 1-1.'

Celtic's goalkeeper coach was Peter Latchford and he gave Warner a step-by-step guide to his new team-mates before the match. On French full-back Stephane Mahe, he said, 'Watch him. He will give you a back pass around your neck.' With Warner calling for the ball to be played back to him, Vidar Riseth, in the left-back position, tried to switch the play to the right, but it hit another defender and flew into an empty net.

'I think we were seven points behind Rangers, it might have been ten,' recalls Warner. 'We were going into the Old Firm derby the next week and the pressure was right on us. I can remember looking at the papers on the Monday and Tuesday. It said, "Celtic have got Liverpool's fourth-choice goalkeeper in!" I was like, "I'm THIRD choice, the bastards." I was sitting in the hotel room and I made the conscious decision to not read any more papers because I'm not going to get any joy out of them. I just put them in the bin and decided not to read them. You could see the tension in the city. If they beat us, then they would have been miles ahead.

'I was in the gym. There was a fitness coach, he used to be at [Aston] Villa, called Jim. He was a karate expert, he used to work on the doors, he was hard as nails. I would walk in and say,

"Come on Jim, get your six-pack out!" He would be like, "No! No!" I would say, "Go on!" and he would be like, "Go on then!" He would pull out this washboard, then go straight into character, "You don't get them from picking grapes lad!" He was a right hard case. Me and him were sitting there and he said, "You know these Old Firm games? I have seen them make or break people." I'm like, "I can imagine, yeah!" He goes, "You'll be all right though." He was just saying this is a game and you need to be on it.'

Celtic travelled up to the hotel in Loch Lomond before the match. Warner says, 'I'm on the coach and Mark Wright phones me; him and Rob Jones were always together. He goes, "I can't believe you're playing in the Old Firm. What an opportunity." He passes the phone to Rob Jones, "Best of luck. Wish I was up there watching," and all that. Robbie [Fowler] comes on the phone and says, "All right mate, I hope you get fucking battered." I'm like, "Cheers Rob," and he says, "I'm Rangers aren't I. I swear I hope they fucking do you." I'm like, "Cheers for that." His agent at the time was a Scottish fella and Robbie was his only client.'

The atmosphere was electric and something that Warner had never experienced before. 'Around Parkhead was chocker on the coach to the ground and I knew this was another step now,' he says. 'This was a different level. They had Giovanni van Bronckhorst and they had Jorg Albertz, the German fella that could hit them from 35 yards. A French fella up front [Stephane Guivarc'h], who had won the World Cup the year before. [I thought] they have got some players here. It's November and it's fresh, there was like a crust on the pitch. The game starts and they had a man sent off, so they are down to ten early on. We just pummelled them. It was 5-1. I couldn't have had a better introduction to Parkhead.'

Warner had sat on the bench at Anfield and heard 'You'll Never Walk Alone' sung on the terraces numerous times, but here he was on the pitch hearing it at the start of an Old Firm derby. 'It was brilliant. It was the loudest atmosphere that I had ever heard. The noise was just ringing in my ears. I couldn't hear. I can remember shouting at Stubbs on the edge of the box and I was screaming at him, but he just wasn't acknowledging me. I thought this is great. Goals were flying in, so I was buzzing. Then, they scored one because I hadn't lined up the wall properly and Van Bronckhorst just whipped it around, in off the post. I can remember the manager [Josef Venglos] having a go at me at full time saying, "What were you doing? Your wall wasn't right," and I was like, "I know!" I thought that's right, we have won 5-1, but I have to hold my hands up for that.

'When we were scoring goals, I was doing airplanes and that. The Rangers fans were on the left-hand side and they were fucking fuming. A few weeks later I went into a bar and there was this fella standing there. "All right, I was at the game the other week and I'm a Rangers fan." I'm like, "Okay, you weren't happy then, were you?" He was like, "You and your fucking airplanes and that." I'm like, "Yeah, I know!" You could tell you had to take him seriously, as he wasn't a kid. He said, "I wanted to fucking slash your face, when you were running around like that." I said, "You know what, if I had have been there [in the Rangers crowd], I would have wanted to do the same thing." He was like, "Cheers!"'

Warner had some more enjoyable moments when out on the town though. 'I can remember dining out on it loads of times. If I was out in Glasgow, people would just say, "I'll pay for that!" People would just buy you drinks. The year after, I went to Millwall and I was out with the lads on a Tuesday night in Leicester Square. We were in this place that had a little door and it was dead smoky. This big fella came bowling over with a big bottle of champagne and put it down. He said, "Tony Warner?" I was like, "Yeah!" He said, "5-1!" Then walked off into the mist. The lads were like, "What's all that about?" I only played three games and dibbed in and out, but I did it at the right time. I was involved in a legendary game. I think it was the biggest score in 36 years. A couple of seasons after they won 6-2.'

Warner also got to play with Henrik Larsson, who he describes as the best player he ever appeared alongside. 'He was just a god up there. He was a quiet fella, reserved. He was an athlete. He was lightning quick and made all the right decisions all the time. He was a goal-scoring machine. He is like the king of Celtic. He went to Barcelona and changed round a Champions League final. Went to United and they recognised his quality. He was a top player. There was Lubo Moravcik, a Slovakian fella. He played for Saint-Etienne. He wasn't quite as good as Larsson, but he was a superstar up there. He was only a little fella, but he was just unreal.'

Gérard Houllier arrived at Liverpool in the summer of 1998 and was named joint manager alongside Roy Evans. But while Warner was in Scotland, Evans had been let go. 'We just became a bit more professional. The fitness aspect became more apparent. The diet changed and the stretching. He wanted athletes to compete and over-run teams. To have base fitness and endure hard games. We had the Carlsberg lounge and I remember when it happened, they just stopped alcohol in the players' lounge. We were like, "What! What are you doing! It's the players' lounge, you've got to have a drink!" It was the right thing to do, as football was changing. It was getting quicker and you needed more endurance. He recognised that. Tactically he was pretty sharp, but the one thing that I do remember was that he raised the fitness levels. I wasn't there for that long with him.'

I met Warner in Hope Street Hotel, which is opposite the Liverpool Philharmonic Hall. It's now the base for the squad before every home game and another former Reds keeper, Daniele Padelli, stayed there for the six months he was on Merseyside, with his Ferrari parked outside. We spent a couple of hours chatting and drinking coffee, which flew by due to Warner's natural charisma. He now works as the goalkeeping coach at Accrington Stanley. He laughs about how he came to leave Liverpool but it clearly hurt him at the time.

Warner was in his last season at the club and he had signed up for a loan move to Aberdeen. He had an ankle injury which prevented him from making the switch, but the Scottish side requested that he joined up with them once he was fully fit. Meanwhile, at Liverpool the squad were preparing for one of the social events of the calendar year. 'There was a players' pool and we could go to Aintree in a box on the ale, it was great,' Warner says excitedly. Just five miles separate Liverpool's home ground and the racecourse which hosts the Grand National.

'There were 20 lads going and four injured players as well. Phil Thompson come in one day and went to Incey who was captain at the time, "What's going on with Aintree?" Incey was like, "I haven't even booked the staff in!" There were four staff and Joe Corrigan, but what they realised was that there wasn't enough space for them. So, what the staff done is they said the injured lads aren't allowed to go which frees up space for them. The injured lads aren't best pleased, we are like, "It's our players' pool!"

'The next day, Fowler had to go and answer a charge at the FA for the "sniffing the line" celebration. Houllier said to him, "You have got to go down at a certain time, you have got to come in at eight o'clock to train for shooting and stuff." He said, "You have got to come in early with Fowler to do shooting tomorrow." I was like, "Fuck off! I'm injured one day, and I can't go the races, but I'm fit the next day to be cannon fodder." I said to Joe Corrigan, "I'm not doing it," and he was like, "Well it's up to you, do what you want!"

'So next day I came in at normal time thinking I'm great and that. As I'm driving in, Fowler's just finishing off shooting against one of the young lads. I went in, sat down and had a cup of tea. Someone said, "Phil Thompson wants to see you." He was in Gérard Houllier's office. This was early April with about six weeks left of the season. He lined me up a treat, he said, "You know that you're supposed to be going to Aberdeen when you're fit." I was about ten days away from being fully fit. "I've just spoke to Mark Leather the physio and he said you're fit, so get your boots and fuck off! Get out the ground now!" I'm like, "Hang on, I'm not fit." He said, "You are fit now fuck off, you're gone." I said, "If I leave now that's it, I'm gone because my contract finishes." He said, "I don't fucking care, who do you think you are, get out!" He said, "Listen, you have let Joe down and the manager had okayed it, you are getting launched."

'I remember almost being in tears. I said, "Get Joe in and I will apologise to him." I thought Joe will have my back because me and him were fairly close. So, Joe came in and he took their side. He said, "You have let yourself down and I stand by what the manager says." It was just a hard way to go. I knew that I was going but I thought I would be able to come back at the end of the season and say goodbye. I did really well not to start crying. Joe came out the office and I said, "Joe, what were you doing?" He said, "Look it's come from the manager, there's nothing I can do." I said, "You have thrown me under a bus a little there." He said, "No, you have thrown yourself under a bus!"

'I wasn't happy with Joe for a long time after that and I definitely wasn't happy with Phil Thompson for years. I hated on him really. But now with me doing coaching, I can see the point of it. Looking back retrospectively, you have got Phil Thompson who is dealing with a lad who doesn't want to turn in, when he is fit is going on loan and has only six weeks until the end of his Anfield career. I lined myself up there. I speak to him now and we are fine. I know people have issues with him because he can be a bit abrasive. I wasn't getting away with that with Phil Thompson. He probably thought, "I've won loads of fucking leagues, won European Cups and FA Cups, played for England and all that, and you yer little fucking prick, you don't want to turn into work when you are told to because you have got issues with the races."

'He gave it to me big style with both barrels, so that weren't nice. Looking back as a coach, if someone was doing that to me, then they would have to get told. If it had been earlier on in the season, then I might have got a fine and a kick up the arse. The timing wasn't good. I couldn't have timed it any worse. Then, funnily enough, I went straight home, and my mate was at the races at Aintree for the National weekend. I said, "Right, I've been kicked out, so I'm coming the races." Then, I remember that McManaman and Roy Evans were there. I was like, "They have fucking kicked me out," and Roy – who had been sacked by then – was like, "Come in our box, we will have you!" So, I got to the races in the end!'

Warner's agent also represented Middlesbrough's Ben Roberts and he had been at Millwall in 1998/99. They were in the old Second Division, England's third tier. 'He said to me, "Millwall would be a good fit for you!"' remembers Warner. 'I was coming out of Liverpool and you do have these high opinions of yourself. I was like, "I don't want to drop down that far, I want to play in the Championship." He said, "It would be a good fit, so I will arrange a trial." I said, "Okay! Fine!" I went on holiday and I kept myself fit. It was the first time I had been out of work since I started footy, so it was a little bit daunting for me. I thought that I might end up in a media centre or something, I didn't know how it would work. I went to Sardinia and was running every morning and night for 40 minutes in the scorching sun. I thought I've got to get myself right.'

He went down to London and he was immediately impressed with what he saw. 'Steven Reid was whipping balls in and I thought he is all right for 17. Paul Ifill was doing the same. Tim Cahill was in there, and I thought these are just good lads and a good-quality team. There were little talks of people saying that we could get promoted this year.' Warner was faced with joint managers yet again, as Keith Stevens and Alan McLeary were in charge of the Lions. He quickly realised that they were keen to sign him and even though chairman Theo Paphitis was haggling over the contract a little bit, he became a Millwall player.

'It was great,' admits Warner. 'It was probably the best move that I have ever made! I started at Liverpool, but for me personally it's where I enjoyed my football the most because it's where I played the most. Millwall is my club really to be honest. I felt like a football player. Saturday, Saturday, Saturday, Tuesday … You have to prepare yourself and make sure you're right. I was 25 then and had [only] played 11 games before that. The lads were superb and the atmosphere.

'I liked what Millwall was about. I enjoyed the atmosphere and the aggression. Teams would come to us and they would be tough and dirty as well, but in a fair manner. We would just take everything to the line. I was aware of teams coming down and they just didn't like it and I thought, "Great!" There would be fellas hanging over the walls. That's been lost in football these days, everything is kind of sterile. I don't mind a bit of intimidation. Leicester went there in the cup and there was a lad that didn't want to take the throw-ins, well that's great. If you don't want to take throw-ins, then there is something wrong with you. My first game for Millwall was Cardiff away. There were people screaming at me and I just turned around and gave it them back.'

The Millwall fanzine *A Lion's Roar* has been running for 30 years and back in Warner's time, copies would be given to the players. 'The lads would read it at the training ground. It would say, "Warner was shit this week" or "Warner threw one in this week". They would give you scores, and all the lads would like to have a look to see what they thought about you. I remember Sean Dyche– ahead of his time the fella – would come in and say, "What you reading that for? If some fucking dickhead in the crowd, who has probably never kicked a football in his life, he doesn't know what you go through, why has he got an opinion on you that you value?" Then, some of lads would be reading it and they would say, "You were shit!" And he would be melting before the game. He would go mad. "You shouldn't allow it in our place of work." He was pretty astute, and he had his head screwed on with certain things. I still speak to him now and he is spot on.'

Millwall finished in the play-offs in Warner's first season and then were promoted as champions the next term under Mark McGhee. Their success continued in 2001/02 as they finished fourth in the First Division, as it was at the time. Warner made 51 appearances the following season and he was voted Player of the Year by the supporters. He was loving life as number one at The New Den and Dennis Wise was now the boss.

He was also attracting praise due to his penalty-saving exploits. Warner said, 'There was a secret. Steve Gritt, who used to be joint manager of Charlton with Alan Curbishley. Gritty would sit down every Sunday to watch the football and anyone who took a penalty in England or Scotland, he would mark it down. He had like a bible of penalty takers. He would have them in team order and then personnel order. He was like an anorak. I'm talking around 2003. He would mark them down and look at the sequence. So, he would say, "This lad takes two to the left and 12 to the right, so I'm going right." You could also make them go that way by going half one way and then go back. I never let anyone know about it because once people are on it, then they change it. It was just our secret. In two seasons, I saved more than I conceded. I think in one season I saved about six out of ten and in another seven out of 12. I can remember people saying, "He's a penalty-saving genius!" It was just Gritty's book.'

Warner entered into his fifth season at the club. 'I was yet to sign a new deal and Wisey was saying to me, "You might get injured." I was like, "Hang on mate! I've been here for four years; I haven't been injured yet. I hand injuries out; I just don't get injured." He kept on at me to sign, but I didn't think they gave me enough time. I felt it wasn't at the level that they were putting other people on, as a goalkeeper.' He had a move lined up for Wolverhampton Wanderers and was due to go to the Molineux ten days later. A cruel twist of fate saw him pick up a neck injury in January 2004 and he was out for six weeks. 'I came back, and I was fit for about two weeks and then I came flying out in training and a stupid challenge from John Sutton fractured my kneecap. That put me out for 12 weeks. This was about early April.'

Millwall would go on to reach the FA Cup Final, which was to be held at the Millennium Stadium in Cardiff, but it didn't affect him introspectively. 'I had played against Walsall and there were a few rounds still to go, so it wasn't as if I was injured the day before the final,' confesses Warner. 'I knew that I was injured a long time before. I had accepted it. There was me and Kevin Muscat that had injuries and operations. Danny Dichio played against Nottingham Forest away and him and someone had some handbags thing for pushing and he got a second booking and got sent off. It put him out for the final. That put him in trouble mentally. I remember that we went to Cardiff the day before to look at the stadium and I was fine, but he said, "I can't handle this!" He had to go sit on his own for a little bit. When people say you missed the final, I didn't miss it, I was out months before.'

When Millwall beat Sunderland at Old Trafford in the semi-final, Wise spoke to Warner and Muscat. 'He said, "Now we are in the final, I want you two to lead out the team because you have missed out and we want you to feel involved in the team." We were like, "Fucking brilliant! Thanks for that!" We went to Cardiff and Theo comes walking in. He says, "Listen, the FA are trying to quash you two walking the team out because every time the FA Cup Final has been contested, the manager has always walked the team out. They are trying to say no! I'm going back in a minute and I'm going to try and get it our way." At Cardiff, you would walk up the steps and then to a bit of a canopy that pulled out. The FA said, "If Wise walks them out under the canopy, then officially he has walked them out, so a box has been ticked. These two can then stand there and walk out." So, we were like that's fair enough and a good compromise.

'We were by the tunnel and Alex Ferguson was at the front with me and Muzzy. I had my operation in the April, so my knee was all right but Muzzy had his not long before the final. He was proper in a brace and hobbling a bit. The referee was like, "I have been told to get Wisey to the front," and he was like "No!" We walked out and I'm trying to keep up with Ferguson, but Muzzy was proper struggling, so it was just me and Ferguson. I was hurrying up. I was like, "When I come up them stairs mate, it's me and him. The world's watching, if you're not keeping up, then see you later."'

Warner's contract expired and he was picked up by Cardiff City. 'Cardiff were a little bit like Millwall, as they were a little rough and tough, but they weren't the same. It was an all right club. I went to Cardiff at a bad time; we had good players but as a team we weren't very good. For one reason or another, I can't put my finger on it. As a team we weren't cohesive, there was something not quite right about it. I was injured and I didn't really enjoy my time there, but it happened. I'm not saying it was a bad move, it just didn't suit both parties.'

He did manage to get one over an old friend though, when Cardiff played Blackburn Rovers in the FA Cup, even though the Bluebirds failed to progress. 'Tony denied me my first ever hat-trick,' says his former Liverpool team-mate David Thompson. 'When I was playing for Blackburn, I had scored two goals and in the last minute, we get a free kick right on the edge of the box.' It was the closing moments of a 3-2 defeat for Cardiff in the replay at Ewood Park, but the goalkeeper still had work to do. 'I'm looking at it thinking, "Come on Tone, you've got to let this in, my first ever hat-trick and the game's dead anyway." I absolutely nailed one and it's going right in the top corner, it must have been going 100mph. I'm thinking to myself, "That's in, all day, that is in!" And he's only sprung from nowhere and tipped it over the bar. I thought, "You have absolutely killed me there mate!"'

In Warner's second season with Cardiff, Dave Jones arrived, and he preferred Neil Alexander. 'It's always disappointing especially as a goalkeeper if you're overlooked, as you know it's going to be a hard season for you. It was the second game of the season, I got a phone call off my agent to say that Fulham wanted me, and I would be playing on the Saturday for the opening game of the Premier League season. I'm 31 at this point. I had been to Liverpool and it didn't really work out for me there. I had been on loan and had been to Millwall which was great. I had an injury and then I nearly got there with Wolves, but my injury ended that. Then, I went to Cardiff and I'm on the bench and I'm not happy. I thought Premier League football was beyond me and past me. If you had said to me, "You're going to play Premier League footy," I would have laughed at you. I got this opportunity and I thought, "Right! Now is the time that you are going to get to where you want to be!" I jumped at it. I can remember playing Birmingham on the opening day of the season and standing in the tunnel just looking at my arm. You know the Premier League triangle, I can remember just looking at it and thinking, "You have finally got it!" It was brilliant and no one can take it away from me. We drew 0-0 and it was a really proud moment.'

Warner lived in Wimbledon village next door to team-mate Carlos Bocanegra, while he also met his wife while he was staying in one of the most beautiful parts of London. Fulham had a decent squad that would finish 12th in the 2005/06 campaign. Steed Malbranque, Zat Knight and Brian McBride were just some of those who Warner shared a dressing room with. 'A harder fella you will never find,' says Warner about American striker McBridge, who became captain and a firm fan favourite at Craven Cottage. 'To look at him he is just a nice fella, he is not nasty or anything, but I tell you what he will put his head in anywhere. I've seen him get scars and just get up and put a bandage on it. He was brilliant. He was one of those that had that hang time to get the perfect header over you. It was a really good group. I didn't play as often as I would have liked, I started about 20 games there. We beat Everton, we beat Liverpool, we beat [Manchester] City.'

He will never forget when he played Liverpool for the first time since leaving the club. It was October 2005 and a trip out in the morning proved to be the moment when he clocked where the future Mrs Warner was working for a later date. The match kicked off and an hour into the game, first-choice goalkeeper Mark Crossley picked up a hamstring injury. 'We were winning 1-0 and I thought, "Do not come on and fuck this up!" It would just justify everything; why they let me go and people would be like, "He's doing it because it's against his old team" or "He's just shit".

'Liverpool had just won the European Cup as well. I played out of my skin and pulled off a number of decent saves. We were hanging on to a 1-0 lead. We were just wasting loads of time. I can remember one [Liverpool] fan going absolutely mad at me. I was like, "What do you want me to fucking do mate?" We got a second goal late on and then we could relax a little bit. We were 2-0 and we had beaten them. You are in it for yourself, wherever you are at. The week after we beat Everton 1-0 and that was good because my mate Timmy [Cahill] was playing and Ferguson. That was nice. After that game, Dave Beasant phoned me and said, "I know you are only on loan, but we are going to try and tie you down permanently." My uncle was an Everton fan and even he was like, "Get in there!"'

Warner joined Fulham on a permanent basis in the summer of 2006. 'It was a superb club, really well run. [Chris] Coleman was superb, brilliant fella – one of the lads. A really good character, everybody liked him. I thought he was superb. He pulled me and told me, he was laughing, "You were fourth on the list you know, you weren't our first choice!" I was like, "Oh! Okay, cheers!" He said, "But you're here now, so I can tell you!" There was an Italian that was meant to be coming but couldn't agree the money. Someone else came in but failed his medical. Then, the other one was Stefan Postma, he was on the list.'

Postma's ex-girlfriend posted a pornographic video on YouTube which showed her penetrating him with a strap-on. 'He was going,

"We are going to end up with Postma here, he takes dildos up his arse off his bird on video for the last six months, we can't have that at the club, who's next? Warner! Well get him in then!" That's how far down the list they were! I will have to buy her a drink, if I ever meet her because she made me a few quid!'

Warner increased his playing time with loan moves to Leeds United, Norwich City and Barnsley. Roy Hodgson arrived in December 2007 and imparted his own style on Fulham. 'He is quite methodical and meticulous with his training. I must admit, it was a bit boring his training, but he got the job done. He only really asked for an hour of your time a day really among everything else and to concentrate on his plan. He made it work for Fulham. He really did.'

Fulham had won only two games previous to the season that Hodgson took the reins. He kept them in the top flight and then in the next term helped them to seventh in the league. In 2009/10, they miraculously reached the Europa League Final, where they lost 2-1 to Atletico Madrid after extra time. This was clearly an overachievement for the side, but when Hodgson moved to Liverpool in 2010 he found that his philosophy wasn't quite so easily transferable. 'The difference with Liverpool was that maybe the bigger players weren't prepared to listen to what he would talk about because they maybe didn't like it, whereas at Fulham they didn't really have an option. He came in as an international manager and no one was that big at Fulham, where they could shout the odds. The lads listened to exactly what he had to say and did it to the letter. We got to the Europa League Final and done really well in the league – upset some teams.'

Warner didn't play that much under Hodgson, although he did have a solid relationship with the manager. 'Personally, I got on really well with him. I didn't have any problems with him at all. I think that just goes to show.' Warner spent the next two years at Hull City, Leicester City, Charlton Athletic and Leeds United, but his time on the pitch was limited. He found himself without a club, and a phone call from Hodgson, who had now started at Liverpool, helped him prolong his career. Hodgson told Warner that he was free to train with the Reds. 'I was there for a couple days with the first team and it was just after the World Cup in South Africa. [Alberto] Aquilani was there and Albert someone, big fella with black hair and a left pegger?' 'Riera!' I suggest after a pause. 'Yes, him. It was like a skeleton squad. I was there for a couple days and then they all packed up and went on pre-season tour. Then, Roy said to me, "Melwood is getting shut down, but the academy is still open. You are more than welcome to go there. If it's for you then great and if it's not, then that's also great. It's up to you. I won't think anything of it. You just use it as you have to."

'I went to the academy and played with Suso, Tom Ince and Nathan Eccleston. They were just top-level young players. I was about 35 and it was just what I needed. They had a full-time goalkeeper coach, so that was great. I was there for about six weeks to two months. I remember some of the players coming to me and saying things like, "Hasn't your agent found you anything yet?" I was like, "Mate! You are here and I'm here now, this is the real world." I was on a downward spiral. The goalkeeper coach kept me mentally straight so I will always be thankful for that. There were a few lads that left Hull the same time as me and never played another game, but I just kept on training. If you don't keep yourself fit, then you are finished. Earning a grand in the real world is very hard. Whereas you can go in and do a job for someone and earn a grand just like that. I wasn't working, so I thought if I just keep training then something will come.'

Warner had arrived in July 2010 and it was now November. 'I can remember pulling the academy manager and saying, "Listen, if I'm overstaying my welcome, then let me know?" It sometimes happens, I've been at clubs before and people have been saying, "What's this cunt still doing here?" That's what happens. I had it at Bolton, and we were like, "This bloke has been here for ages, what's he doing?" But because it has come from the manager, no one wants to go, "Hey Roy! Are we going to launch him or what?" But he said, "If you come in and you're doing sit-ups and press-ups in the gym and not drinking tea and having toast, then you're actually a good influence." He said, "As long as you need to keep coming, then you keep coming.'"

Then, after months of just training, Warner's hard work paid off with a move to Scunthorpe United. 'Joe Murphy got injured at Scunthorpe and I had to go straight in against Watford away. I could go in just like that because I was fit and ready, and we beat Watford 2-0. That was one of my proudest moments because I hadn't played professional footy for a year. Watford were a good team. We got caned by Leeds 4-0 the next game and then Murphy got fit then. I can remember losing my head a little bit after that and I didn't go to Liverpool for about a month.'

It was almost Christmas and with the January transfer window approaching, Warner phoned the academy staff to see if he could train with them again. That enabled him to get a move to Tranmere Rovers. 'Without that training it has a knock-on effect,' says Warner. 'Playing for Tranmere was great, and I was back on track again. Then, I nearly got a move to Blackburn off the back of that, they wanted me to sign and I had agreed the money. My missus was concerned that we would have to move, and I can remember telling her [that we wouldn't need to] and she started crying because she was well happy.

'I spoke to Bobby Mimms and I said, "Am I coming in or what?" He said, "What it is, we have got two keepers and we are trying to get this lad out on loan. We don't want to upset anyone, just hang fire." Paul Robinson had been injured during the season, so Blackburn were forced to recall Mark Bunn from Sheffield United. Young Jake Kean was getting sent out to Rochdale on loan, while they also allowed Frank Fielding and Jason Brown to leave the club. 'I said, "Bobby, I can't hang on all the way through July for you to pull the plug and I can't go anywhere." He was like, "We won't!" But they fucking did. My agent phoned me and said,

"They have pulled it!" I told my bird and she was fucking crying her eyes out. She was like, "What are we going to do?" I was like, "I don't know!" It was a week before the season started. I tried to ring Bobby, but he wouldn't pick up the phone. I rung Steve Kean as well, as he was my assistant manager at Fulham, but he wasn't answering either. I was like, "I'm back to square one now!"'

Warner's career then took an unexpected turn and for the first time he ventured outside the British Isles. 'The season started, and I remember just lying in bed, and my mate Paul Ifill rung me. He said, "What you up to?" I said, "Nothing!" He said, "We need a keeper, I put your name forward and they said yes, they will have you!"' Wellington Phoenix of New Zealand was to be Warner's destination, for a stint in Australia's A-League. The Rugby World Cup in New Zealand meant that the season had been delayed by four weeks. 'He said, "You have got a month to get fit. We have just started pre-season." I was like, "Cracking! We have got out of jail here." My missus was well happy to go.

'It was really nice. You think New Zealand is close to Australia, but it's four hours. It was like from here to Italy for a game and that was the close ones. It was like a nine-hour flight to Perth and different time zones. They never really did that well when we went to them and they never did that well when they came to us. I had never been to Australia, but it was great. Bouncing round Melbourne, Perth and Sydney. It was a nice opportunity.'

Warner came home and then went to Maltese club Floriana. 'Some divvy, who lives round here, a bit of a local villain, had a club in Malta. He said he would get his mate to meet me and he would just give me the wages. That happened for a few months. Then, he decided to not pay me. It went to a tribunal and he pulled out blag payment slips. It had to go to lawyers. He tried to put the frighteners on me and sent people round to my doorstep and all that. That's the shit end of football. You are in slight desperation really and you run into these crackpots and dodgy characters. It was hard times towards the end.'

As always, he can see the funny side to events as he recalls his manager, who was also a part-time accountant. 'He was fucking shit,' jokes Warner. 'We would get beat and he would be just standing there eating a piece of cake. He would be like, "Go get in the shower lads!" I can remember going berserk, screaming and kicking stuff. He was like, "We can't win the game now, can we?" I was like, "Fuck off!" He would say to the other Scouse lad, "What's wrong with him?" The other Scouse lad was like, "Generally in England, Gaffer, if we get caned like we did then, the gaffer normally says something." He was like, "Well, we can't win the game now!" I always remember him going straight to the cake. Me and Franny Jeffers were over there, but this madcap chairman put Franny on a fortune and they just couldn't sustain it.

'We played Valletta at the national stadium and we lost. The kit man was like Manuel from *Fawlty Towers*. He would have a chopped-up Mars Bar on a plate and a plastic cup with Coke in [to give to the players]. I was like, "Fuck off!" and I smashed it all out his hands. The plate went flying over his head. There was all this match fixing. You would think, "Are you doing this because you have been paid off or are you not very good?"'

Warner was the goalkeeping coach at Chennaiyin when they won the Indian Super League Final in 2017, with former Aston Villa manager John Gregory in charge. He is now enjoying his time at Accrington Stanley, having previously held a playing contract there in 2015 while coaching at Bolton Wanderers at the same time. It was then that he almost went to India for the first time with North East United. 'I signed a contract and they wanted me for 12 weeks. The first-team goalkeeper coach left at Bolton and went to Charlton. I had already handed my notice in at Bolton, but they said, "Step up!"' confesses Warner.

'I went in and they had Ben Amos. Neil Lennon kept hanging on and hanging on, whilst India got wind of it. He said, "The first-choice goalkeeper wants a more experienced coach." I was like, "Hang on a minute! He hasn't played anywhere, no games.

How come he makes the decision on who coaches him?" He said, "Goalkeepers are different." I was like, "You're fucking talking to me! We aren't unicorns or unusual creatures; we are just goalkeepers!" He said, "Well! I have made my decision." I said, "I handed my notice in 10 days ago, the India thing has gone and now this was gone. I can't just go back to coaching the 18s." He was like, "I will try and get you in the 21s!" He was just hanging on and I was phoning him all the time. Then, the money started to go out the club and he got sacked. Have a guess who came in? Bobby Mimms! I was fuming.'

Chapter 7

Michael Stensgaard, *It's Not the End of the World*

'A TYPICAL Danish upbringing in a typical Danish town,' says Michael Stensgaard when asked about his childhood. The goalkeeper grew up in the south of Copenhagen, close to the centre. His parents were very supportive of him from an early age along with his brother Thomas and sister Annette. His father's company DER sponsored KBU in the 1980s, who were one of the biggest clubs in Denmark at that time.

When you walk through the centre of the city, it's impossible not to notice the vast number of bikes that are used for transport. Stensgaard would take his to school, as his own kids do now and it's a mode used by a large proportion of the population in Denmark when travelling to work. 'I wouldn't take my bike in the UK,' he laughs. 'Copenhagen has changed a lot. It's a nice place to grow up. Denmark is a relatively safe country to live in. Copenhagen has developed into a good food and culture place, but it has always been quite a safe place compared to over big-cities.'

He was just five years old when he went to his first club, Greve Fodbold, situated in the eastern side of the Zealand island, but only 13 miles away from Copenhagen. They had the biggest youth system, with six teams for every year group. Stensgaard stayed at the club until he was 17 and after he made his senior debut, he moved on to Hvidovre. 'They saw me play for Greve and they approached me,' he explains. 'At that time, bigger clubs were looking [at me], but for me it was important to get playing time especially as a goalkeeper. That seemed to be the right move. I moved to Hvidovre and I was quite lucky to get into the under-21s because at that time no one really played for their first team so young, as I was 18.'

Stensgaard had just finished college and didn't have a contract. His parents told him that he could live and train like a professional for a year without getting paid and they would support him financially. 'I took one year and then I got a contract with Liverpool,' he says proudly. The youngster made his debut for the Danish under-21s and he was instantly likened to Peter Schmeichel. He certainly didn't let it go to his head and dismisses the idea. 'Basically, every time someone could catch a ball they said, "He is the new Schmeichel." To be honest, I didn't pay too much attention to it because I primarily just focussed on playing. I just took one game at a time, but of course there was a big fuss around things because I had made my under-21 debut. That was in Germany and I played probably my best game ever. Then, I played Spain and England and did well. After that it seemed like many clubs were interested.'

Several Scottish sides were keen on bringing him to the United Kingdom. West Ham United were also interested and Stensgaard had a trial at Bolton Wanderers, who were in the Premier League at that time. Everyone in Denmark knew of his emerging talent and that was beginning to stretch further afield. 'At that time there was no data access, so you could only go and watch them [players]. So, if you played against the big teams and did well there, then that was a good mark on a career. Today, you can follow every step of someone's career. That could make it more difficult, but sometimes also easier if you had a few good games.'

Liverpool watched Stensgaard for the national side and had little trouble convincing him they were the right club, even though he was talking with several teams. 'They saw the under-21 games and then they went to see me in Denmark and approached me. I have been a Liverpool supporter since I was six or seven, when I got my first shirt from my dad because he travelled to England. From then on, I always supported Liverpool. So, when they came in for me – I had other offers – but it was never really in doubt.'

Roy Evans was manager in May 1994. 'He was a really nice guy, not your typical English manager of that time. He had a really good human side. He didn't say too much. There were many things that I had to learn of course, but he just said, "Go in and do your best." I didn't feel too much pressure from anyone. It's such a huge club to come into especially when you come from a small club in Denmark, then it's another world. I didn't find the pressure from the gaffer too big. He was really good at just making sure you just focussed on football.'

Stensgaard remembers that from a philosophy and tactical point of view the players were on board, but there were a few issues with attitude and application. 'That was a big thing because I almost lived more professionally than the professionals,' he says. 'We didn't have that much of a drinking culture here [in Denmark]. It did give us some good relationships and the team bonded, so it wasn't only bad. But if you saw how people lived compared to today, then it's crazy. There was a big difference. [As a player] you can't live the way they lived at that time. I could catch a ball, but I also think I was recruited for my professionalism. They wanted to change a few things. The culture in football can be a bit difficult. Me and Stig Inge Bjornebye lived a bit of a different life to some of the other players,' he chuckles when assessing the situation.

Just six months after signing for Liverpool, Stensgaard dislocated his shoulder in training. It was common practice at the time not to operate at first and after working on it for a while, he played in a reserve game. However, it was away from the pitch that saw a recurrence of the injury. At home, he simply moved an ironing board and his shoulder popped out as it was not strong enough. 'Ironing Board Ruined my Life!' was the headline of the *Sunday People.*

'I got so much stick for it,' he admits. 'How I did it I don't know? I called the club doctor and said, "I have just moved my ironing board and my shoulder popped out, but it's back in." He said, "Okay! Come in tomorrow and if it's back in, then no problem!" I came in and the manager told the press. The players were just laughing. It was fine. I could handle it.' The dressing room was full of characters that certainly liked a joke, so which one of Neil Ruddock, Steve Harkness and Jamie Redknapp gave him the most grief? 'Everyone!' he laughs. 'They couldn't stop. I think I should have just said that I did it moving a box. I wouldn't say ironing board [again].'

In Denmark, schools teach English from the age of seven. The language may not have been a problem, but the culture and social norms are certainly different. Stensgaard could utilise the experience of Jan Molby, who had made the same move ten years prior. 'It was good for me to have him when I came. I was 19 years old and it was good to have him around. It was good to be able to speak Danish to someone. It was before the internet, so it was much more difficult to move abroad. You couldn't just see what was in the Danish news.' Molby also helped him grasp the practical information. 'When you start any new job in a new country, there are so many new things. It makes it a lot easier just to have someone to say, "What time we meet?" or "What's the normal practice?"' The deep-lying playmaker had similarities in his footballing style to Xabi Alonso, although he was now 31. 'He was fantastic. He was at the end of his career when I came, but his team quite often won the five-a-side. He was a great player.'

Stensgaard came into a talented squad, but it didn't take long for him to get accustomed to life wearing the Liver Bird upon his chest. 'It's like with everything, when you have done it for some weeks, then it [becomes normal],' he recalls. 'No doubt, the first couple of days you are starstruck and then everything goes into a routine. Then, you find out they are normal and have the same problems as you. For me it was a great experience, but it's not something that I sit back and remember every day.'

The goalkeeper continued to have complications with his shoulder. 'It was difficult. I kept having problems. I went through two operations and I was trying to get back, but it was quite painful all the time.' The shoulder consists of four muscles and one of those muscles still doesn't work properly for Stensgaard to this day. 'I kept trying and, in the end, I felt it wasn't that important to me to be honest. I decided to stop and go back to university in Copenhagen and get another life, you would say.'

Club doctor Mark Waller felt they shouldn't risk a third operation, even though there were some doctors that were advising to do so. Stensgaard trusted the advice that it was too high risk and it could cause further complexities with his health. 'The decision was made a little bit easier because I went to college, so I had an education,' he admits. 'I could then go straight into a university. I was only 21. To begin with I was gutted, I was so gutted because it was my big dream, but I have always been quite optimistic. I thought that it was a shame, but I said to myself, "This isn't good!"'

He realised that he had been fortunate to have gone to the club in the first place and that at least he had 'felt it from the inside'. His contract was cancelled my mutual consent. 'The club were absolutely amazing. They didn't try to save any money or anything. They were really good. I have always respected them, and I have nothing bad to say about them.'

Stensgaard is a positive character and he doesn't waste time worrying about eventualities outside of his control. 'Even in those times and it is even more crazy today, but you get a good start to life financially. That gave me a head start when going to university. If you look at it that way! When you can look around the world, at how many people are suffering, I couldn't really feel sorry for myself. I quite quickly got into my new life at university.'

Taking the positives out of negative situations certainly helps with the mental challenge. 'I could go straight into law school. I lived in a nice big flat in Copenhagen, while I was studying. I had a better time studying than most. When I first stopped, of course, it takes a little time to get into it. But you just have to tell your brain that this is the situation you are now in. I think that's a really interesting point, when you see how many players go bankrupt. I think it's because they live in the past. If you are a footballer and your identity is football, then I think you have a problem. Because life is not being a footballer. First of all, you are a human being. What I saw in football and also at Liverpool were players that had been through bad times financially and everything. I think that's because of identity.'

Mental health problems are on the rise in football, despite the large wages that many get paid. 'I tried to see myself, not only as a football player, but as someone who also wanted other things in life,' says Stensgaard. 'That helped me because I could go straight into something [else]. When I meet old team-mates, then you see the difficulties that they have. They are only living in the past. They don't get up in the morning and say, "I'm going to make a difference." You should have a relationship with other people. It's hopefully a third of your life. I think we will see even more difficulties, even though people have enough money. The goal isn't to get rich; the goal is to have a nice life. Those two things aren't always the same.'

While Stensgaard was at university studying law, he was able to goalkeeper coach back at his old side Hvidovre. 'I wanted to give something back,' he says. 'It was a good way of still getting out there and getting a feel from it. I wasn't bitter, which is why I could do it. I could still be part of a club.' He worked with a young goalkeeper called Jorgen Nielsen, who also made the switch to Liverpool. 'It was me that set up the move,' confesses Stensgaard. 'I got him over, trained with him and then they took him. He was a really nice guy. He is still similar today and he has got an education also.'

Nielsen spent five years on Merseyside, but never played a competitive game. His shirt was used against Everton though, as Steve Staunton had to borrow it for the final 13 minutes of a match after Sander Westerveld was sent off and the Reds had used all their substitutions.

Stensgaard started to feel his shoulder getting better and the prospect of a full-time return to football grew larger. 'When I stopped playing the doctor said that it might over time recover, but they couldn't say [for definite],' he says. 'They thought that other muscles might take over, so that it could be stable again. In training, it felt okay. It didn't feel like it did when I was at Liverpool. Then, March 1998, I thought to myself it feels okay.'

He enlisted the support of former Olympic canoeing champion Arne Nielsson. 'I was the first to get help from a mental coach. I went in and said, "What do I do?" We set some targets for the next few months. At that stage, I hadn't played a game for three-and-a-half years. It was a long time. We made a plan that I would go into FC Copenhagen and I would play the first game in August. That was the goal.'

It's fair to say that football in this period viewed outside influences in a negative fashion, with England manager Glenn Hoddle's use of his faith healer Eileen Drewery the most notable example. However, Nielsson wasn't a spiritualist, but someone who improved people's mental capabilities. 'It was tough to do that because everyone said, "Are you sick?" "Do you need a psychologist?" I just said, "No!" I just saw what they had done in golf! I just saw what they had done in individual sports and I thought we can take that. Nowadays, everyone is using them. Every club has one attached. It's happening across Europe. Many players have them on their own as well. It's not a big thing anymore, but in 1998 it was not normal. It got me back into playing. At least I got some more experience.'

Stensgaard hadn't even trained since his Liverpool days when he and Nielsson had their initial consultation. 'My first training session with Copenhagen was a disaster, even my mom could have done better. Because I hadn't trained in a proper way [for some time]. My first reserve game, I let in four goals and I cost three of them, I think. It was a disaster.' But then he improved. 'In the first game for Copenhagen, I was lucky that the other goalkeeper got injured and I played, and I was man of the match. That whole experience was in four or five months. They normally say that you need to spend the same amount of time [coming back], if you have been out with an injury. I did it so fast compared to the rest.'

Stensgaard had a run of games for the club and even featured in the Champions League. 'That was good,' he says. 'It was probably my best six months because at that time Copenhagen played Chelsea. I only got a six-month contract because they didn't know if I could last, but that was a good thing for me because I could just play.' A 90th-minute goal from Marcel Desailly denied Copenhagen a famous victory at Stamford Bridge, while they lost the return fixture due to a strike from their fellow countryman Brian Laudrup.

'Then, I went to Southampton,' continues Stensgaard. 'Wrong move, wrong manager. It's a great club, but it was the wrong move. It was bad advice from my agent. It was not good with the manager.' Dave Jones preferred to use his namesake Paul Jones between the posts and Stensgaard felt that it wasn't a fair competition. 'The goalkeeper at that time, they were quite close, so there was no chance that I was going to play, no matter how well I did. So that was a bad choice. He was not a nice man to be honest.'

Stensgaard did get the opportunity to train with Saints legend Matt Le Tissier and couldn't fail to notice his ability. 'I think he was one of the best players that I ever trained with,' he admits. 'He was so good, but also, he didn't live up to his potential. He could have been one of the best in the world, if he had really wanted to. He was amazing in training. The things that he could do. If you played a game on a smaller pitch, his team always won. He was a really good footballer.'

The Dane returned to his home nation after a frustrating six months. 'I started having other problems. I went back to Copenhagen, where I had two years.' Roy Hodgson became manager at the club in his second season. 'Roy was a really important manager for Copenhagen at that time because he moved the bar a bit. He came in with a more professional way of thinking and demanded more of the players. Prior to that we always thought that training should be fun, but he said, "No! Training should be important so that you can win games." He came in with a winning attitude and I think that was the first building stone for Copenhagen.'

I refer to Hodgson's brief tenure at Liverpool, where many of the players felt that the training was boring. 'It was,' agrees Stensgaard. 'It was not fun training, but at that time it was exactly what Copenhagen needed. They needed structure. They needed to get results and he won the title when he was there. Copenhagen was a bit unorganised. They were a big club, but there was a little chaos around it. He came in and put everything into a structure. He wouldn't allow anyone not to go in the same direction and that's what Copenhagen needed at that time.'

Nowadays, Copenhagen are dominant in the league, with former Wolverhampton Wanderers boss Stale Solbakken in charge. They have won eight league titles across two different periods under the manager. 'He didn't really have a successful time in England, but he has done well for Copenhagen. He has done a great job. He has built on what Roy Hodgson did, when he was here. He has been really important for Copenhagen.' Hodgson's title was the club's first in eight years, but Stensgaard could only feature in five games, as he realised, he would have to give up on his football dream for a second time. 'I had a disc go in my back. It had come over time. I started to be a bit negative. Because when you set yourself goals and you can't achieve them due to things outside your control it's frustrating. At that time, I was almost done with my law degree. I thought I can do other things in life.'

The next chapter of Stensgaard's life began. 'I was studying next to football and then I started working for one of the biggest Danish consultancy companies, while I was finishing my law degree,' he says. 'We built up a sports management department. I knew I was never going to be doing law within the state because that would be boring. I wanted to find something that really interested me. Because I had done that [mental] coaching thing and was the first in that area, then I developed into helping others. When I got into negotiation and conflict management, then I found this really interesting because it was not too far from me. What questions can be asked to open up a human being or what questions could be asked to start negotiations?'

Stensgaard attained new skills which developed his ideas further. 'I took a course for negotiation group resolution and I did my final exam when I was at university. That went really well. They have a big competition across all the universities in the world called INC [International Negotiation Competition]. The Copenhagen university asked me if I and one more wanted to go and represent Denmark. We did and we won. I think we are the only non-English speaking country in the world to have won. We won it in Paris. I have also judged a few of them afterwards. It was a great experience. In England they have regional championships and then the best ones get sent to the nationals. That was probably the hardest thing that I have ever done, but it was fun, a good experience.'

He started People in Sport, which is an agency with a difference. 'We have 60 football players around the world. We have around 300 handball players; we have ice hockey players and now e-sport players. It is now the fastest growing sport in the world. With my law background, football background, coaching, and mental coaching side, then we have a pretty good platform for making a difference. I'm not your typical football agent, who is just doing it for the money. I like to build things. We have built up a company and we want to make a difference. We are trying to improve football by being transparent. We want to bring everything out to the players, so that all the players know what they are getting.'

The company has players from around the world including England, Italy and Germany, while Belgium, France and the Netherlands are also key areas. Borussia Dortmund's Thomas Delaney is one of their most high-profile clients and is joined by former Manchester United goalkeeper Anders Lindegaard.

I met Stensgaard in his office, which was just a two-minute drive from his house that he shares with his wife Lavina and two children, Noah who is Lavina's son from a previous relationship, and Rosa. His job involves lots of travel and watching plenty of matches. It's clear that he has a fondness for people, which has been refined by his own experiences. The subject of mental health is clearly close to his heart. 'I think it's important,' he says. 'I think there's something wrong, but that's a whole new book. The whole culture in football is wrong. We don't do anyone any favours. It's all around the world. Three out of five [footballers] in the UK go bankrupt. That's not because they don't have the money, it's because of mental health. There was a study in Denmark that said 20 per cent had the start of depression and anxiety. From the outside, you would look in and think what's going on? Everyone wants to be a footballer! So, when you are there, you don't want to be there? The pressure is getting so high. The whole image of going into an English club or German club where you make a lot of money, the first thing you have to do is buy a big car to fit in. The whole atmosphere is to buy the most expensive stuff. Do you pick your wife because she looks good? Or do you pick your wife because you want to have a good life?

'I am quite critical around the football business because I don't think that the values that people have are the right ones. When people get older, they look back and think that wasn't important. Why did I do that? That's what we want to do. We want to try to make a difference. We have not had any players with problems in areas such as gambling or whatever. We try to set up the right values, so that they can be successful. You cannot be successful if you have problems in many areas. That's something for me that's very important. What you find out, is that the more people you know in the business, you will find out that everyone is being really macho and acting as if they have everything under control. When really, they aren't secure, the pressure is too high. Everyone says it is fun to play in the big games, but in fact most people don't like it because of the pressure. If you don't play well in those games, then you don't get to the next level. The whole thing is to learn how to live in that area.

'I can understand it when people say it's just spoilt kids that get paid too much money and that they would give their right arm [to be in their position]? But you come from different ways. The perfect way would be to go out and get a proper job first like a director or coach at a football club and then be a player. Then, you are seeing it from the outside, but the problem is players only see it from their side. They build up a bubble and they see the world [that way]. Life isn't like it is when you live as a football player. It's all about money, money, money! It's not about giving anything to anyone! When clubs say that they have to visit handicap kids or whatever. Then, you see players saying, "That's fantastic!" and "I want to give something back!"

'But in fact, many of them don't want to give anything back. They are just there because they have been told to by the clubs. In the dressing room before they are saying, "I don't want to!" and "It's a waste of time!" The football business is just one big show. You just see what you want to see, with Instagram and everything. Now it's even worse. It looks like the perfect life and they are all balanced, but in fact many players are not balanced. That's exactly what we are working with. We want to create results, but we also want to create human beings.'

Chapter 8

Sander Westerveld,
Houllier, The Treble and Spain

'THE EAST is known as the "Farmers" part of Holland,' explains Sander Westerveld. The goalkeeper grew up in Enschede, which is in the province of Overijssel and in the region of Twente. There are 160,000 inhabitants of the city, which borders Germany, while almost a fifth of those living there are students. 'Everybody in Holland says it's far away from the real world. It was quite relaxed.' The people from the area are known for their down-to-earth personalities. They view the flashier west as 'big-time Charlies' and they don't like vast shows of wealth. The philosophy of treating everyone the same regardless of their financial situation can certainly help those stay grounded. 'That mentality helped me I think as well,' he adds. 'There was a lot of space for a child and a lot of freedom to grow up. Also football wise, there wasn't a lot of pressure like they have at Ajax and the other western sides. I grew up playing football for fun and then getting better along the way. Just making steps higher up the ladder.'

There weren't many football teams in the area, with FC Twente the biggest. 'That was my club,' admits Westerveld. His earliest memory is from around eight years old. A friend would go into the game with a ticket, then get another ticket from someone else inside the stadium. He would then come back to the young

Westerveld and they would use that ticket to get into the match. 'We would sit on the fence behind the goal watching the games. They were fairly successful. Not winning the league, but always in the top five. They were a great club to be involved with. I played in the amateurs and my dream was to play for Twente.'

Sitting behind the goalkeeper was perhaps a sign of Westerveld's future aim. 'They had a goalkeeper that is probably known in Britain as well, his name was Theo Snelders. He played for a long time at Aberdeen and then ended up at Glasgow Rangers as well. He was a fantastic goalkeeper. I was always into goalkeepers. He was my childhood hero. I really looked up to him and watched him train.' Snelders made over 200 appearances in his 11-year span at Aberdeen, while his save in a penalty shoot-out won them the 1990 Scottish Cup Final against Celtic. 'I remember when I was younger, after training he gave me a pair of his gloves. He became the goalkeeping coach at Twente and I still see him now.'

Westerveld was training for an amateur club when he was selected for the district team at 12. The best players from the east would play against the west in a tournament and then the youth national sides were chosen. This meant that he had the opportunity to play at Wembley at just 15, when they lost 1-0 to England schoolboys. 'When I was 16, they picked me for the under-19 team,' he says. 'So, then I moved to Twente. They had three teams at the time – a 16–19 team, a reserve team and the first team.' Westerveld played for three years in the under-19 side and when he was 18, he signed his first professional contract.

'When you start playing, everybody has a dream club. Being from the city, it was the biggest I could achieve. It was my dream to play professional football for Twente. I must say, I had a strange beginning to my career. It all went by itself.' Westerveld improved year after year. There was a natural progression to his career in those early years. At 19, he was promoted to back-up goalkeeper by manager Issy ten Donkelaar. When first choice Sander Boschker was injured, he made his debut and got to play three successive games. The year afterwards he played the final 11 games of the season with German boss Hans Meyer at the helm. Westerveld's contract finished and although they talked about renewing his deal, he was unsure how much game time he would get, with Boschker just four years his senior.

'There was a lot of interest from other clubs,' confirms Westerveld. 'When Vitesse came and gave me the chance to play the first ten games, I said, "Okay! Let's leave! I have got ten games to show what I am capable of." They were an ambitious club and they had a president that thought they were going to be champions in the next ten years. They were building a new stadium, so the project was perfect for me.' Westerveld was happy at FC Twente but knew that it would be better for his advancement to join Vitesse Arnhem. 'It was sad because I didn't want to leave in the end. Sometimes you have to think about yourself. I thought this was a chance, I would be at least playing Premier League 100 per cent and not fighting for my place at Twente, where I wasn't sure they would pick me.'

Westerveld's choice proved to be correct. 'From day one, I had a fantastic time at Vitesse. Played well in the first year, in the second year we were playing in a new stadium, which was amazing because there was a full house every week. In my last year, I was Player of the Season. We finished third in the league, which is still the best in the history of Vitesse.' Karel Aalbers took the presidency at Vitesse when they were bottom of the second tier in 1984 and completely transformed their fortunes.

'It was very difficult especially for Vitesse because they had just come up. They hadn't been playing in the Premier League for a long time, just a couple of years. We had a great team. We had a good balance – some experience, some younger players, hungry players. We had a top striker in Nikos Machlas. A Greek guy, who became European top scorer.' Machlas scored 34 goals in 32 league games in the 1997/98 campaign to win the Golden Boot. He joined Ajax a year later for a then-club record in Amsterdam.

'In Holland it's the top three, now you have AZ Alkmaar, but normally it's basically Ajax, PSV and Feyenoord and then the rest,' admits Westerveld. 'So, it was difficult to get between them.' Vitesse have finished in Europa League positions in five of the last nine seasons, which illustrates how well they did in this period. They played very attacking football with a high press, which was enabled further by playing in front of their own supporters. The GelreDome was revolutionary in Europe when it was completed in March 1998. Like the Johan Cruyff Arena, which had opened two years before, it has a retractable roof, while it has a convertible pitch which can be removed for music concerts. 'We were a year and a half unbeaten and not only unbeaten but winning all our games at home,' says Westerveld. 'The other thing was that we never won away, only once or twice. We could have made it maybe even higher.'

Roy Makaay was another striker who helped Vitesse to improve before they sold him for a profit. 'When Roy Makaay was young, he was the same as when he finished his career – he was a lazy striker. He became a good friend of mine, I played alongside him for the national team as well. I think I played three years with him at Vitesse, then he moved to Spain. It was unfortunate that he never played in England because he was one of them strikers that could put a defender to sleep. One ball and he is out of there. Inside the box and outside the box. If you didn't make a save, then he would score. He would never miss. He would always put the ball on target, kicking from every angle.'

Westerveld recalls a game from later in his career, when his Real Sociedad team travelled to Makaay's Deportivo de La Coruna. Makaay struck a ball from an acute angle in the fashion of Marco van Basten's volley in the final of Euro 88 against the Soviet Union. Westerveld managed to just about tip it over the bar because he was expecting the outrageous. Had it been someone else taking the shot, then it would likely have taken him by surprise and beat him. Westerveld regards Makaay in the same category as Robbie Fowler and Michael Owen, when it comes to natural finishers. 'In the box he was just lethal,' he adds.

Vitesse had several managers during Westerveld's tenure, but Leo Beenhakker made the biggest impression. 'He took me to the club,' says Westerveld. 'I have said it in other interviews as well, I was young, and the press rated me as the new number one for the national team. They put a lot of pressure on me right from the start.'

Beenhakker had shown faith in Westerveld by allowing Raimond van der Gouw to leave for Manchester United. In Westerveld's first couple of games he didn't make the saves that he would normally make, and the media started to doubt his ability. 'I was well known for having a lot of confidence and showing it as well. Beenhakker came to me one day and said, "You look like a goalkeeper that is 6ft, but you are 6ft 3in. Normally, when you play you are 6ft 5in. I just need a goalkeeper that shows that. Be yourself, you are allowed to make mistakes.'

The next game was the derby against NEC Nijmegen, which Vitesse won 1-0 and Westerveld was man of the match. 'He was exactly what I needed. He gave a player confidence instead of warning him.' Many managers in his position would likely have applied more pressure on a young goalkeeper and probably have taken him out of the side. 'He is a lovely man. He is one of those people that is a man-manager. He takes everything away from the player in a positive way. You can't play bad with him.' The relative success at Vitesse meant that it wasn't just the players that left for better sides, as the coaches often got approached. 'We had great managers like Hen tenk Cate, who put a style of football into the team. It was very attacking. It put a lot of pressure on me because,4 with attacking football, the defence struggles, but we dealt with it. It went fine. It was great to watch those games.'

Westerveld was enjoying life at Vitesse and had just signed a new five-year deal. He once did an interview at the tender age of 18, where he mapped out his career plan. To play in the

Netherlands was the first objective, then at 25 he wanted to move to England and then on to Spain. It was naturally met with a little laughter in his home country. 'We played a game against Ajax and afterwards I heard that Liverpool were there watching Edwin van der Sar,' confesses Westerveld. 'We won at Ajax 1-0 from an assist through me, with a long kick. From me to Machlas, then he rounded the goalkeeper.'

Van der Sar said no to Liverpool because he didn't think they were big enough for him. 'I was on that list of goalkeepers that they had, and they remembered me from the game with Ajax. They saw me in three games; after the first game they came to my apartment. Joe Corrigan, Phil Thompson and Gérard Houllier. Corrigan said that he knew after the warm-up and they asked me then if I wanted to play for Liverpool next season. Obviously, I said, "Yes! Next question?"'

Westerveld dreamt of playing for Vitesse, but when those dreams became a reality his ambitions grew, and Liverpool had long become the ultimate aim. The success of the club as he grew up in the 1980s gave him fond memories, as he was able to watch *The Road to Wembley* on FA Cup Final day. 'With all due respect of other clubs and I won't mention names, but if other clubs in England had have come with interest [for me], I wouldn't have signed for them. I left only because it was Liverpool. It was just a dream come true.'

Houllier overhauled his squad in the summer of 1999 with Westerveld presented to the media alongside Erik Meijer, Vladimir Smicer, Titi Camara, Stephane Henchoz and Sami Hyypia. 'To be honest, the first time I saw Anfield, I thought I have seen it on telly, but it looks small to me,' he laughs. 'I looked around and said, "I thought it was bigger." That was until the first time I could see a full Anfield. It was an amazing feeling to be stepping on the pitch and holding the scarf when I signed. It was all a dream. It went so quickly; I didn't get a chance for it all to sink in. It was only when people came over to watch games and talk about it, I was like, "Oh yeah!" For me it was all just normal.'

Westerveld had worked hard to be in the position that he found himself in, but he was unsure what to expect. His career had continued on an ascent. He spent a lot of time with Hyypia and Meijer, who both spoke Dutch and that was a big help when it came to adapt to a new way of life. 'I was really impressed when I met all the players for the first time at Melwood. Michael Owen was there and Robbie Fowler. People I had watched on BBC. Owen was in his prime, it was just after the 1998 World Cup. I was living the dream and it sounded like a dream. I was on, how do you say? Cloud nine!'

Houllier handed all but Henchoz their debuts along with Didi Hamann on the opening day of the season in a 2-1 win over Sheffield Wednesday. The French boss then used three different defensive units in the next four games. They kept just one clean sheet in a win over Arsenal, but the influence of Hyypia was already beginning to tell. 'Looking back at it I think it was harder for me because I was well known in Holland for being an English goalkeeper,' admits Westerveld. 'They said that my strengths were my kicking ability and playing like a centre-back. They used to call me [Franz] Beckenbauer. But also coming for crosses and commanding my area. Not only corners, but everywhere in the box. Coming and collecting the ball. I think that's why Houllier took me as well. My style was perfect for the Premier League.

'But when I came, it was more Sami than Henchoz, he was taking a lot of the work away from me. In one way, it made it easier for me because he was so good in the air, I didn't have to come for crosses. Because it was my first year and people didn't know me, I couldn't really show what I was capable of. After a couple of games, the newspaper journalists wrote he might be a good goalkeeper, but we still haven't seen anything from him. I think it was after game five. I couldn't show myself to the world because Sami was too good for me. So, in one way it was great.

It's great when people know you, you're playing there and we're keeping clean sheets. I think we were the best defence in my first year. But for me personally, maybe I could have done better with a less good central defender, who gave me a little bit more work, so that I showed myself more to the people. He was just amazing for the club and from day one he just played like [Virgil] van Dijk. He played like he had been there for ten years. He just makes it easier for goalkeepers, it was a similar situation at Vitesse.'

Westerveld had joined Liverpool for a Premier League record for a goalkeeper at £4m. 'I had a lot of pressure being the most expensive goalkeeper. I wanted to show myself to the world. I remember the first time they started criticising me for not coming for crosses. I was like, "Who wrote this? This is my biggest strength! I'm famous for that in Holland and now they are criticising me for not doing this!" So, it was a really strange start for me. It was not easy to really fit in and make a name for myself. I never felt any pressure during games, I am really relaxed. I remember Houllier told me when I first arrived, "Don't believe the press and don't read the press!" I was trying not to.

'But when you are the most expensive goalkeeper and they had just kicked out David James after ten years, then they expect a lot from the new goalkeeper. They say, "Okay! If they have paid a lot of money for him, then he must be good!" I couldn't really show myself in the first couple of games. It's always difficult to start as a goalkeeper, if you use the examples of [Loris] Karius and Alisson. Karius is a great goalkeeper, but the first couple of games he played, the mistakes he made cost them games.

'Whenever you make mistakes you have to be lucky. Alisson made his first mistake, when he was dribbling the ball by the by-line. They still won 2-1. So, it didn't cost them the game and so everybody forgets. He started well and made some good saves. Suddenly, you get that name, "He's a good one!" With me they started doubting. They said, "We haven't seen anything" and "He doesn't come for crosses a lot". Which I thought I didn't have to because sometimes it's too much risk to go out there when it's busy and you have a centre-back that is good in the air. You don't need to come for crosses! But people expected that from me, then suddenly I was like, "Okay! Maybe people are expecting," so I wanted to do things that I shouldn't have done. I came for crosses that I shouldn't have come [for]. I just wanted to go out and show everybody, "This is me!" Maybe I was too eager to show myself. I wanted to quickly establish myself as a good goalkeeper. It was strange. It was a slightly difficult start for me.'

That start got even more difficult as Liverpool entertained Manchester United. A Ryan Giggs cross was headed past the helpless Westerveld by Jamie Carragher after just four minutes. Just 15 minutes later United were 2-0 ahead following Andy Cole's header from a trademark David Beckham free kick. Debutant United goalkeeper Massimo Taibi failed to claim a cross and Hyypia pulled one back for Liverpool. Then referee Graham Barber missed the pretty obvious deliberate handball from Nicky Butt, which would have given the home side the chance to level the game. Another Beckham swinger caused a succession of rebounds which resulted in Carragher getting the final touch past Westerveld once again. Patrik Berger made it 3-2, but United held on in the closing stages to claim the victory.

'Afterwards, I was walking off the pitch thinking it was one of those games,' said Westerveld at first before he reassessed the situation. 'Then I watched them back after I started doubting myself! It's the most difficult thing for a goalkeeper – a cross coming into the box, especially low ones.' A journalist from the Netherlands was one of Westerveld's harshest critics, although the goalkeeper appreciated his honesty. 'I remember him saying after the game, "If you had come for one of those crosses!" They were David Beckham crosses. Those I think are still the most dangerous and difficult balls for goalkeepers. If you come for a cross and there are so many people in front of you, then you end up beaten because you are in no man's land.' I think the balls were so low and had so much curve, I don't think I could come for those balls. If I would have gone for one of them, then maybe they would have headed the ball before me. Those are the most dangerous ones. It was just unfortunate that it happened twice in a game like that.'

Westerveld knows that it can go wrong if he attempts to take a cross and someone heads it before it reaches the intended target. He recalls the Alaves goal by Jordi Cruyff in the 2001 UEFA Cup Final. 'I will just say they are great crosses,' he laughs.

A fortnight after the United game, Westerveld was under the spotlight once again in his first Merseyside derby. 'A lot of people remind me of [it],' he admits. 'The biggest thing was that we lost that one. I was playing with a lot of aggression and I wanted to win every game, always giving 100 per cent on the pitch. It was a mixture of emotions and we were losing at the time. I don't think we had a lot of chances either, so it was a very difficult game for us. I really wanted to win; it was the derby. I knew the expectations of the fans and I really wanted to win the game for the fans. I really understood what it meant to play the derby.'

An early Kevin Campbell goal had given Everton the lead at Anfield and with only 15 minutes remaining, Westerveld was involved in an altercation with Toffees striker Francis Jeffers. The goalkeeper said, 'When we had a bust-up. I still don't understand why I got a red card and I didn't expect it in that moment. He tried to get the ball. If you see the pictures, then he tried to hit me, and I tried to defend. I never expected to be sent off. When I was, I was really pissed off and disappointed. I really had a feeling that I had let my team down. We lost and as a goalkeeper being sent off! It was obviously already 1-0, but still! I felt really bad!'

The following day, Westerveld was summoned to the gaffer's office. 'I thought, "Oh! Fuck! He is going to give me a bollocking!" The first thing he said to me was, "I really liked this! I thought you showed a lot of commitment and you wanted to fight. I want a goalkeeper with that aggression. I want a player that leaves everything on the pitch! I like this! Obviously, I don't want you to have red cards, but at least you showed fighting spirit!"' That moment gave Westerveld the courage and belief that stylistically he was doing the right thing, even though he was disappointed with the experience.

'I was playing with a lot of confidence, but I was also taking a lot of risks. With my kicking as well, I was always trying to kick it further than everybody else. Sometimes from ten kicks, I would have two miskicks. I could kick the ball easily over the halfway line, but I didn't want to do it easy, I wanted to put them straight through one-on-one with the goalkeeper or perfectly for [Emile] Heskey to control the ball. I took a lot of risk in my game as well coming out for one-on-ones, flying in. Thinking before the shot, anticipating, and once or twice it cost me. I remember a game against Southampton, where the ball came to the second post. I was like, "The only option for him now is to head it back," and there was someone free there. So, I had already taken a step and he headed the ball in the near post. That was a mistake because I was taking risks. If you do that, then you are always going to get beaten and criticised.'

Westerveld improved as the season progressed and so did Liverpool's defence as a unit. He kept six clean sheets in the final 11 league games and conceded just seven goals. 'I was very happy after the season. I don't think I had too much criticism, it was more like the people didn't know what to expect and didn't know me still as a goalkeeper. So, they weren't convinced. It wasn't like they were criticising me all the time. It was more that they weren't sure. I had the most clean sheets and the best defence. Which for me went perfectly. It was my first year, so it was always going to be difficult. If you tick all the boxes that they wanted at the beginning of the season – they wanted a settled defence, a goalkeeper that keeps clean sheets. That's what I did. I think I delivered! I'm always looking at the bigger picture. I thought, "We have the best defence now, with the most clean sheets. It's my first year, it's ok, it didn't go too bad." I was always trying to improve, and I think I improved.'

Patrik Berger scored nine league goals that season, with Owen the only Red to net more. 'He [Berger] was one of those players that had a lot of energy and a lot of technique,' says Westerveld. 'He was just amazing to watch especially his long-range shots, which were just unbelievable. He was a good friend as well. With Vladimir on the other side, a very technical dribbler. Paddy was just a quick and strong player. He was a great player to watch. All the goals that he scored – most of them were outside of the box. Long-range shots. It was just amazing. I knew how difficult it was to stop them shots in training. It was amazing to watch him play.'

Houllier's squad contained a lot of important players and Westerveld noticed that the level changed throughout his time at the club. 'I felt when I came from Holland and I played for Liverpool that these players were just different class. If you see the passing of [Jamie] Redknapp, if you see the shots of Paddy Berger, if you see the technique of Michael Owen, the finishing of Robbie Fowler and the defending of Hyypia. I had a lot of admiration.'

In the summer of 2000, Liverpool bolstered their squad with a number of free transfers who added greater depth. Gary McAllister, Jari Litmanen and Markus Babbel all joined, which not only complemented the established stars but assisted the youngsters who were progressing quickly. 'In my first year, I think we were limited on the bench, we didn't have too many options and I think we had a lot of injuries as well. Jamie was injured a lot, so we couldn't rotate too much. In the second year, we had more options especially up front but also in midfield, when Gary McAllister came, and Stevie G. [Gerrard] was really stepping up his game. Carragher came into the team as well together with Markus. In every position, we had another player, not like a reserve player. I think we had 22 starting players that year, which was really great because every week we could play with a different set-up especially up front where we had different styles that we could play.'

Houllier now had four strikers at his disposal who all offered different characteristics, which made his side more flexible tactically. 'We could play with Robbie and Michael, and then you know we had to play the passing game to get to the box. Then, in the box, you just had to give the ball to Robbie. If he had the ball in the box, then it would be a goal because I still think I haven't seen a finisher as good as him. Michael could obviously play on the counter-attack and he was amazing in the box as well. Even headers, he would score with headers as well,' said Westerveld.

Emile Heskey joined Liverpool in March 2000 for a club record of £11m and instantly offered something different than their other strikers. The large fee received negativity in the press as Heskey wasn't a prolific scorer at Leicester City. However, his strength and power gave them style alternatives and he was also extremely mobile at the time. 'Then, you had Heskey, which was good for me because I could put all my long balls and long throws into him, and he would flick it on for Robbie or Michael and we could play from there. That was a different style, we could play long ball. If your opponent put a lot of pressure on you and we couldn't play our passing game, then we could just change it and put the ball long to Heskey.'

Fowler, Owen and Heskey scored a combined 63 goals in all competitions that season. Individually they had various attributes, while they also gave defenders differing problems when working in a pair. However, Liverpool's attacking prowess wasn't just about the sheer amount of goals, they could also break down stubborn defences with a player that would find space between the lines. 'Litmanen was like a number ten that would make all those little passes in between the defence,' Westerveld adds. 'He was a very talented player, who gave the assists. He could read a game, so he was so important for us. We had a lot of options there, we had Smicer, Nicky Barmby, all those options. We could change the team without it getting weaker. That was the biggest strength we had.'

Steven Gerrard was just 20 and Jamie Carragher was 22 in Westerveld's second season on Merseyside. Carragher was critical of the goalkeeper in his autobiography, saying he 'didn't rate' him. 'He wasn't my type of fella and we didn't see eye-to-eye,' wrote Carragher. 'I thought he was an average goalkeeper who seemed to think he was Gordon Banks.' Westerveld insists he never had any issues. 'I never had a problem with anyone in my time at Liverpool, when we see each other for legends games there's still a great vibe,' he admits. 'When people ask me what the difference is between Dutch and English football, I'm always using Carragher and Stevie G [as examples] because those are players that in the dressing room after the game, after every game, would just be lying on the floor or in the bath tub totally drenched in sweat.

'I have always said that in Spain and sometimes in Holland, you would come into the dressing room and you have players that you felt could play another game. So, the mentality is different. In England, you have Carragher and Stevie G. that give everything on the pitch and they can't really walk because they just give everything. That's what I really liked about them. Being from Liverpool they had the fans behind them which gave them a lot of confidence and it was great to see them develop and become the players that they went on to be.'

Carragher was a regular in Houllier's team, although he didn't have a settled position, as he was used across the defence. 'I remember that Carragher didn't understand in the beginning the way that I played. I was outside of my box one day with the ball at my feet, he was free, and I passed the ball to him, he kicked it straight back to me and started shouting, "What the fuck are you doing?" He was expecting goalkeepers just to get it away, but I wanted to pass out from the back. I quickly noticed that it was better to play the ball to Stevie G. than Carragher. It was just great to have players like them and also good for the fans to have homegrown players in the team.'

The 2000/01 campaign proved to be one of the most dramatic and memorable in the club's history, even though their wait for another league title and their fifth European Cup would take a little longer. In the league, results were initially mixed before a strong run ensured they qualified for the Champions League for the first time since the Heysel era. Westerveld also had his mixture of high and low moments. A goal conceded at Middlesbrough from a Christian Karembeu strike on Boxing Day saw Westerveld ridiculed by pundits and supporters. 'The pitch at the Riverside had a lot of ice on it,' said the goalkeeper at the time. 'My feet and gloves were soaking, and it was unbelievably cold. It doesn't seem that Middlesbrough have undersoil heating, which is a pity because, on occasions, you'd see the ball with ice stuck to it.' Some of the observers that day agreed with the assessment, as the away end was absolutely freezing. On BBC's *Match of the Day*, former Liverpool defenders Mark Lawrenson and Alan Hansen would regularly analyse Westerveld's all-round game and offer negative opinions throughout the season. 'I never really felt the criticism,' says Westerveld now. 'I didn't really understand or hear the criticism. I was just playing my game and I thought I was doing okay and getting better and better. It doesn't matter if someone has a different opinion of me.'

Liverpool reached the League Cup Final and were favourites to win it against Birmingham City. Fowler opened the scoring after half an hour of the first final at the Millennium Stadium in Cardiff, but they failed to add another goal despite creating a number of clear opportunities. Trevor Francis's men were resilient and refused to give in and that was rewarded when they scored a late penalty through Darren Purse to take the game to extra time. The Reds won 5-4 in the shoot-out when Westerveld saved spot kicks from Martin Grainger and future Everton striker

Andy Johnson. 'I remember after the game that I was so happy because I was like, "Whatever happens now, at least I have shown everybody that they have a goalkeeper now that they can win things with," especially in the way I won that game, not only for the two penalties but I made a save in extra time as well. I knew I was important in that game.'

Westerveld thinks that an ideal way to win a match is by a 1-0 scoreline with the goalkeeper making numerous saves to prove his worth, although he knows that the scorer would still grab the headlines. 'This was just for a goalkeeper,' he confesses. 'This was the best way to win a game, on penalties and saving the deciding penalty. It was the first trophy after ten years for Liverpool and looking back I think it was the most important one because it was the first one that set off a whole vibe in the team that we were able to win things. It gave us a lot of confidence to go on and win the treble. For me as a goalkeeper that was one of the most important – not best games or memorable – but most important game for me in my time at Liverpool. I could show to the world, "This is me and also with me you can win things." For me personally it was important.'

Houllier's side finished the campaign extremely strong in all competitions, as they lost just two of the final 20 matches. They beat Tranmere Rovers and Wycombe Wanderers in the FA Cup to set up another final date in Cardiff, this time against Arsenal. 'I remember that was a game that we were battered,' admits Westerveld. 'I think we had one chance that [David] Seaman saved on the line, a header.' Heskey's point-blank effort was palmed away by the England international with relative ease. 'It wasn't a difficult save. I think it was the only time he touched the ball in the game. They had so many chances. We were just having – not only luck – but we were just trying to keep everything out with Henchoz with his hand and Hyypia with three goal-line clearances. I remember I had a one-on-one with [Thierry] Henry, so I made a couple of saves.'

The Liverpool goal led a charmed life, which meant the manner in which they conceded was even more frustrating. Westerveld holds his hands up and confesses to his own part in Arsenal's solitary goal through Freddie Ljungberg. 'We conceded a shit goal as well,' he says. 'It was a back pass and I remember I tried to kick the ball away, then in the last second I saw Stephane Henchoz. So, I thought I would kick the ball to him, and I kicked it fairly hard, but still. He controlled it, turned around then lost the ball. Again, I took too much risk. When it's 0-0 sometimes you just have to kick the ball out of the stadium, and I could have done that easily. If we had lost 1-0, then I would have kicked myself and not forgave myself for taking too much risk. Fortunately, Michael saved me.'

Westerveld was staring at the clock with just ten minutes of the game remaining. 'I was thinking, "Please! Blow your whistle!" If we lose 1-0 it's okay because we should have lost 3-0, 4-0. I remember thinking 1-0 is not too bad. I should have known better. We had a team that doesn't need a lot of chances. We had strikers that don't need a lot of chances to score. I didn't really have that confidence in that game.' McAllister's free kick was headed down by Babbel and Owen acrobatically finished to the delight of the travelling Scousers behind the goal. 'When Michael scored the first one it was just an unbelievable feeling because then I thought maybe it's going to be penalties. I felt confident that we would win on penalties.'

Then a long ball from Berger caught Arsenal out on the break in the 88th minute as Owen outpaced a 37-year-old Lee Dixon and the then 34-year-old Tony Adams. His finish in the far corner was unstoppable for Seaman and the somersault celebration moments later has been shown numerous times through the years. 'Then, Michael went through on goal and scored the second one. I don't think I have ever been happier in my life,' says Westerveld forgetting his wedding and the birth of his four children for a split second. 'If you win games like this, first Birmingham and

151

then the FA Cup, then it's just amazing. It's just an amazing feeling.'

The drama wasn't finished for Liverpool as they still had to travel to Dortmund for the UEFA Cup Final just four days later. Alaves were the opponents and although the Reds were the heavy favourites, they did things the hard way once again. 'I think you could see that Alaves were really nervous and that we were really up for it. We had so much confidence and we had so much experience from the previous finals we had played especially the FA Cup Final just a couple of days before. From the first minute, we were all over them. It was the opposite way around from the Arsenal game. We just didn't give them a chance, 1-0 up, 2-0 up quickly, easy. It almost went too easy.'

Goals from Babbel and Gerrard gave the Reds a comfortable lead before Ivan Alonso's header pulled one back for the Spaniards. Westerveld then closed down a Javi Moreno effort when it appeared the striker would score and made a save from a long-distance shot by Ivan Tomic. 'I don't think anybody knows that, when they think about me, they think about the mistake that I made against Jordi Cruyff in the last minute. It was one of the most frustrating games that I have ever played in. I never felt that they were in the game. I didn't get a lot of back passes and I didn't have too many saves to make. Like you said, there was the double save when it was 2-1, but they weren't important saves. I never had a feeling that I was really into the game.'

McAllister extended Liverpool's lead from the penalty spot after Owen was pulled down by Alaves goalkeeper Martin Herrera. Moreno scored two goals in quick succession after the break. 'Of course, the second half starts and within five minutes it's 3-3. Suddenly the whole game has turned around and we are suddenly under a lot of pressure. It was a difficult game from then on. We were 4-3 up, when Robbie scored that goal.' Fowler cut in from the left-hand side, beating two Alaves defenders before nonchalantly passing the ball into the net.

With just a few minutes remaining, Cruyff headed past Westerveld at the near post off a corner. Westerveld explains how keepers will always be beaten if they choose to go for the same ball in that situation. They have to make a decision whether to potentially allow the cross to go into the centre, while staying on their line trying to make a save. Westerveld was given stick for his decision, but Cruyff was left completely unmarked by the Liverpool defenders. 'There must have been a conspiracy against me,' wrote Fowler in his autobiography. 'I couldn't believe my eyes, and I wanted to go over to Sander and shake him by the throat.'

Fowler didn't have an issue with Westerveld, but that comment did hit a raw nerve with the keeper. 'I remember in Robbie's book, he said I destroyed his dream. Because he scored the goal in normal time and if I hadn't conceded the goal, then he would have been the hero. I never did it on purpose of course. I was trying to save the ball! I was trying to help the team! It was just one of those shitty goals for a goalkeeper to concede and of course a shit moment as well in the last minute. Fortunately, we scored the winning goal.'

Delfi Geli saved Liverpool's blushes when his misdirected header from McAllister's set piece gave the club a 5-4 victory with three minutes left of extra time. 'I was so happy with the free kick,' Westerveld says. 'I had forgotten about the golden goal rule. I was always celebrating with our fans in every game we had and always tried to have contact with them. I remember that the own goal went in and I turned around to celebrate with our fans, then a couple of seconds later, I turned back around and saw everybody on the pitch. I was like, "Oh shit! We won!"'

For Westerveld, winning a European trophy was the highlight of his career, but also a bittersweet moment. 'In my eyes it was the biggest cup because for a foreigner one of the European cups is more important than any cup. I was still walking off the pitch having conceded four goals, so it was a difficult game for me. I wasn't 100 per cent happy. Of course, when I had the cup, I was happy. For a goalkeeper, it was a difficult final. It was also easy to forget because at the end we got our hands on the trophy and that's what I kept telling myself afterwards as well.' He now feels content with his role within the treble. 'I can easily talk about that mistake in the final. It would have been so different if we had lost. Sometimes as a goalkeeper you have to be lucky. If I made that mistake in the FA Cup Final and we lost 1-0 and then I made another for the Jordi Cruyff goal, and we would have lost. I would have killed myself, almost. Now because of the result, you can forget about those goals.'

However, Westerveld can never really forget about the goals. In the age of social media, he will often hear audio footage that castigates him in some of the biggest matches of his career. 'If you are being criticised so much, then it's difficult to get interviews. I had the feeling that I had to talk it right all the time and I had to fight the criticism all the time. Sometimes it was unfair. If I made a mistake, then I made a mistake.'

Carragher and Fowler weren't the only former team-mates to draw attention to his misdemeanours in their books, with Danny Murphy's thoughts particularly standing out in his mind. 'They talk about me and say that, "He was a good goalkeeper, but he was always finding excuses for goals," explains Westerveld. 'Which was the opposite of what I did, because every goal I conceded, I always thought that it was a mistake. I always should have done better. I was my biggest critic! But when you're being criticised so much, obviously you try to defend yourself. That's probably what happened. I felt I had to defend myself all the time. That felt a bit unfair. I think it was always my mistake.'

Journalists and some supporters were also quick to offer negative judgements. 'I had a lot of critics. I still have a lot of positive vibes about the club. Every time I come back to Liverpool, then nine out of ten people are positive to me. Of course, they talk about 2001. I know I done okay! It was a bit harsh that I had to leave, but there was a lot of criticism from day one until the very last day, I think. Is it fair? If you pay so much money, then people expect you to be the best goalkeeper in the world. It wasn't my mistake that they paid so much money. It wasn't my fault. I couldn't do anything about it! The only thing I can tell you now, is that if I played those two and a half years again, then I would do everything exactly the same because I left everything on the pitch. On the training pitch, I did everything I could. I was a professional and I tried to improve every day. I gave 100 per cent in training and all the games. I never of course tried to make those mistakes, they just happened. Afterwards, I would think about it, "Oh shit! What did I just do?" You can't help it.'

Houllier would say to him after he made a mistake in a game that at least he knew that he would play well for the next three games because he always responded. The Frenchman was a really important manager for Westerveld, despite the way his time at Anfield ended. 'I think it was all positive. He was positive for two and a half years. He helped me in everything from day one. He gave me confidence and put me in the team. If there was criticism in the press, he would say, "Don't listen to them!" He was great with me. I felt really confident with him. He always gave me the feeling I was number one. Until he signed [Jerzy] Dudek, he never gave me the feeling that he would sign another one. He always made me feel and he said it a couple of times that he thought I would be one of the best three goalkeepers in the world. That's what he told me and that's what I believed as well.'

Westerveld had held talks with the management about renewing his contract in the winter of 2001. 'We have talked about that first year, it was a difficult year, but they told me when I came that they had a problem with the defence, and they wanted to fix it. I was 24, I was a young goalkeeper with a lot of pressure on my back from being the most expensive one coming into the Premier League, then in the first year ending up with the best defence. I think I played well that season. I had a lot of games where I won points for the team. I think in my first year, I had a decent year. The second year was obviously the year we were winning all the prizes and of course I was making mistakes. In no way did I think it was possible that they were going to change me.

'One of the things he [Houllier] told me was that he wanted to get a new goalkeeper, the only thing that he didn't know was if he was going to take an experienced goalkeeper and we would both fight for a place or a young goalkeeper for the future. That was it. I remember pre-season in Austria, a month before. They were talking in the press about Van der Sar. I came into training one day and he said, "Don't believe the press! I still think you can be one of the three best goalkeepers in the world and you're still my number one!" I was really confident. I played and we won the Charity Shield and European Super Cup. The Charity Shield was two weeks before the transfer deadline and I had my best game for Liverpool. It was one of the best games I have had. Even Mark Lawrenson on the BBC said, "Okay, I think we finally have our goalkeeper for the next couple of years."'

Markus Babbel is a close friend of Westerveld and he felt that it was difficult for the goalkeeper due to the success of the team among his own indifferent form. 'I came from Bayern Munich and it was normal to win trophies,' says Babbel. 'The next season you start on zero and you start again. Sander had never had this experience. He was playing for smaller clubs and they never had this expectation to win trophies. But if you play for a club like Liverpool, even at this time it was clear, if I go on the pitch, I want to win something. I'm not playing to finish fourth or fifth in the league and then drop out in the cups. It was clear that is the past and it's a new season. You have to show your performance again. I think it was very difficult for Sander to manage this because he had never had this experience before. It is a normal reaction. You can see it with young players when they have an outstanding season before, then the next season the expectation is higher, and you can't bring the same performance again. You put so much pressure on yourself, but the expectation from the people around you is higher than before. You start to make mistakes.'

The stress on Westerveld's position did continue to mount as the rumours regarding a new goalkeeper arriving persisted to grow. Liverpool had beaten Bayern Munich in Monaco to claim the European Super Cup and then they travelled to the then-titled Reebok Stadium just three days after. Westerveld was pleased with his overall performance that day, but then disaster struck in the closing seconds of the match. Dean Holdsworth's long-range effort squirmed under his body and Bolton snatched a surprising 2-1 victory. His wife was in the stands watching the spectacle unfold and they both at that moment felt that it was probably his last game for the club. 'Houllier said afterwards in the dressing room, "Okay. I don't want anybody blaming Sander. He won us a lot of points and he will win us a lot of points in the future as well." So, I was actually quite confident after the game. I thought, "Okay, maybe it's not the last game I will play."'

At the end of August 2001, Westerveld was sitting reading Ceefax (a news system on televisions), as there were no phone updates in those days or Sky Sports News. He was looking to see which goalkeeper was coming to join him at Liverpool. He was in the Netherlands with the national team and a number of their journalists had told him it was likely to be Jerzy Dudek. Westerveld told them that Houllier had said he was his number one. Marc Overmars and Dennis Bergkamp knew of Westerveld's situation. 'I remember Overmars came to me and said, "Hey! Look, all that worrying. They have bought a young goalkeeper, so you will be No.1 and they have him for the future, so you were worrying for nothing!" A 20-year-old Chris Kirkland had made the move from Coventry City to Liverpool. 'I was obviously happy for a couple of hours, until they bought Dudek. That was a big shock for me. Then, I knew it would be difficult for me.'

Westerveld instantly understood that he would no longer be first choice, perhaps even now only the third option. He couldn't leave for another club because it was the last day of the transfer window. He met Dudek in the airport the following day on his way back to John Lennon International. 'He wasn't the problem. I couldn't blame him. So, I started speaking to him and congratulating him on his move. I was talking about how good Liverpool was and what a great club it was. How lucky he was to sign for Liverpool!'

Houllier had told Westerveld on several occasions that the press was wrong and that they hadn't made any approach to Dudek. The Dutchman asked Dudek's agent if that was true. 'He was saying that they had already spoken a couple of months before about the move and that they had already been negotiating. Then, I knew this was something I don't like. I like honesty and I know the football world is not always honest. I am an honest guy and sometimes I got myself in trouble with the press for talking honestly about my opinions. I expect people to be honest with me, which is a bit naive because in the football world sometimes you have people like that. He should have been honest with me. If he had told me that he wasn't happy with me, then I would have been able to find another club before the transfer deadline. He could have given me the opportunity to leave. I know everybody knows of the story now that they fucked up with the signing of Dudek and ended up with two goalkeepers instead of one. It was a mistake from Liverpool, they never wanted it, but I was the one to blame.'

It wasn't so much that Liverpool no longer wanted him, it was the manner in which it happened. 'I was heartbroken,' Westerveld admits. 'It was so difficult for me. I would have accepted anything, except for this.' Westerveld had played an important role in helping Liverpool qualify for the Champions League, but now he wasn't even allowed to travel with the squad to away games. The option of appearing in the reserves was also taken away, he was effectively fifth choice. 'From number one winning five cups to being number five on the list was for me ... And playing for my dream club that I wanted to play for ten years! That was very difficult to take. I said some things in the press afterwards also about Houllier, which maybe wasn't right, but at that moment I felt like this. It took a long time to get over that feeling.'

Westerveld looks back at his time at Anfield with fondness, but it's impossible for him not to still feel sadness with the way his dream ended. 'I think still looking back on those two seasons, I was getting better and better. I remember of course I made mistakes; I remember also I was playing better. You can't win five prizes with a bad goalkeeper. I must have done something right. I think it was unfair that he bought two goalkeepers instead of one. So, I never had a chance to fight back. I would have been happier if he had bought Dudek and put me on the bench. According to him, I was making too many mistakes, when I asked him, "Which ones?" He could only come up with three mistakes! I told him, "I have played 103 games, so three mistakes are not bad." He said, "I want a goalkeeper that never makes mistakes!" Which for me was just end of story.'

Westerveld understands the nature of football, but still feels it could have been handled better. 'I think it was harsh. I think everybody knows that if a goalkeeper is not performing or you have higher standards than the goalkeeper, then you buy another one, but at least let them fight for their place. I was still young; I was still getting better and better. I'm 100 per cent sure that if I had still been there, I would have fought my way back into the team as well. I'm 100 per cent convinced.'

Westerveld signed his contract for Liverpool at the airport just before he flew out to make his international debut in Brazil. In the same interview that the young Westerveld conducted all those years ago, he also stated that he wanted to be one of the three goalkeepers for his country at Euro 2000. That ambition was fulfilled. 'The national team is the highest you can achieve as a football player,' he says. 'To be able to do that – I felt so proud. I was really over the moon, when I knew I was in the team.' Westerveld was in the squad for the World Cup in France in 1998 and enjoyed the experience of visiting new countries. He liked the special atmosphere and travelling to different hotels.

Two years later the European Championship came 'home' for Westerveld. 'It was really strange that we were in Holland. Playing all the games in Holland, in our own stadium. It didn't really feel like a Euro in that way, but on the other hand it probably gave us a lot of confidence which is why we played so well.'

Manager Frank Rijkaard didn't have a pecking order of goalkeepers behind Edwin van der Sar for the tournament, so neither Ed de Goey nor Westerveld knew where they stood if there was an injury or suspension. The Netherlands beat Czech Republic 1-0 in the opening game in an unconvincing display, but they improved to score three goals in a 20-minute period against Denmark in the second encounter. Van der Sar gave away a late free kick in Rotterdam but injured himself in the process. 'When Van der Sar got injured, I was like, "Okay!" He [Rijkaard] was looking at the bench and he said, "Sander, warm-up!" I was like, "Wow!"

'When I stepped on that pitch, I knew I was playing in a Euro. It was just the best feeling ever. I ended up making three caps in that Euro, coming on twice and then playing a full game against France. It felt amazing.'

His personal satisfaction was contradicted with the feeling that the team underachieved. They might have reached the final four but they certainly expected to win the tournament. Defenders Jaap Stam and Frank de Boer were in their prime, the midfield had strength and technique in Edgar Davids and Phillip Cocu, the wide players had speed and guile in Overmars and Bolo Zenden, while the combination of Patrick Kluivert and Bergkamp in attack was simply frightening. 'I think we had one of the best teams in [Netherlands] history at that time and we should have done better,' admits Westerveld. 'I think it is still the biggest shock and the most negative thing that all the players involved experienced that we were kicked out in the semi-finals on penalties, after missing two penalties in the game.'

*Michael
Stensgaard
appears much
more content with
life away from the
pitch than on it.*

*Ray Clemence
orchestrates
his Liverpool
defenders.*

David James was often cruelly maligned in his time at Anfield but he had a long and successful career.

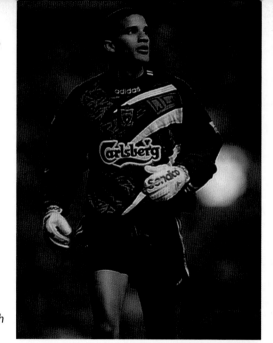

Tony Warner never played for Liverpool's first team in a competitive match, although it did help shape his future.

Sander Westerveld
applauds the
supporters in his two
years at the club.

Pegguy Arphexad and Emile Heskey celebrate the UEFA Cup in 2001.

Wayne Allison beats Bruce Grobbelaar as Bristol City surprisingly hold Liverpool in 1994.

Jerzy Dudek and Chris Kirkland join Liverpool together on deadline day in August 2001.

Scott Carson was just 19 when he signed for Liverpool; three months later he was playing in a Champions League quarter-final.

Martin Hansen never felt valued on Merseyside but he learnt from the experience.

Brad Jones and Peter Gulacsi never made a significant impact at Liverpool, although they both had outstanding careers on the continent.

Loris Karius and Simon Mignolet had a solid relationship in their rivalry to be Liverpool's number one.

Danny Ward felt he didn't get enough opportunities at Liverpool.

Van der Sar made 130 appearances for the Netherlands, while Westerveld made just six. There must have been a sense of disappointment not to have played more and been given a greater opportunity? 'No, because the good thing was that I knew it was Van der Sar. I would have had a problem with it, if it had been any other goalkeeper that I was fighting for the number one spot with.' Following the treble season, the Dutch press were advocating that Westerveld should replace Van der Sar as the national side's first-choice goalkeeper. Van der Sar had just encountered a difficult year in Italy with Juventus. Westerveld felt that he was getting closer to his compatriot's level and he didn't completely rule out the prospect of replacing him in the future. However, he also knew from training camps with him that he was perhaps too good to overtake.

'He was the best goalkeeper in the world at some stage and for me he was one of the best goalkeepers in the world all the time. It's like sitting behind Alisson now! Every reserve goalkeeper behind Alisson isn't happy about the situation because he is back-up, but still he can live with it because he knows, "I'm on the bench behind the best goalkeeper in the world." I had the same feeling! Of course, I wanted to play and of course I was hoping for more opportunities especially if you're with the national team for five years and you're only able to play six games.'

Most other second- and third-choice goalkeepers on the international scene would have a higher number of appearances over that period, even with a top-class goalkeeper ahead of them. 'Van der Sar was never injured, I don't know whether he was afraid, or he just wanted to play all the games and all the friendlies, he never gave me a chance. You have to hold your hands up and say, "He was better than me! Fair play."'

Westerveld's final five months at Liverpool was a frustrating period for the goalkeeper. 'I had to get away,' he confesses. 'I wasn't even involved in matches; I wasn't in the stands and I couldn't travel with the team to away games. I was just training.

You can ask everybody at Liverpool, I tried to be a professional. I never made any problems there. I gave 100 per cent. It's bad for a goalkeeper if you're not involved, so I had to get away.' A couple of English clubs were interested in taking him, but Westerveld didn't want to play against Liverpool. That meant he had to go abroad. Former Liverpool striker and then Real Sociedad manager John Toshack had also been present at the ill-fated Bolton match in the prior August. Toshack preferred not to focus on the late error, but instead was impressed with Westerveld's overall performance in that game. It was a clear example of how different managers think and operate. 'I moved to Real Sociedad, which was another step. I wanted to play in Spain, but not so early in my career. I had an opportunity and I took it. Although they were bottom of the league, I just thought, "I will play for six months and show myself to the world again. Hopefully, I will make the step back up the ladder." Half of that was true! I never left after six months and I stayed there. I ended up almost winning the league with them and had the most amazing three years of my career.'

Real Sociedad survived relegation and finished 13th for the third season running. Toshack was relieved of his managerial duties and Frenchman Raymond Denoueix took the helm. Their first fixture of the 2002/03 season was a Basque derby, which La Real won 4-2. 'That was great,' says Westerveld. 'It was a home game as well. Before, they tried to tell me how important it was, a Basque derby. I remember telling them, "Please don't tell me anything about derbies! I played in Vitesse v NEC in Holland and I played in the Merseyside derby." I told them, "Don't worry, I know what it means for everyone to play derbies!"' The build-up to derby games proved to be a little different though. Everyone wants to beat their local rivals, but Sociedad's fans are happy to lose games in the run-up providing their team shows up on derby day. The matches with Real Madrid are also especially important to the supporters, as it feels as though they are battling with the establishment.

Sociedad's improvement was huge, and they spent the majority of the season on the top of La Liga. Their title challenge went to the final day, when Real Madrid's 3-0 win over Athletic Bilbao denied them the championship by two points. Sociedad also won 3-0 on the day against an Atletico Madrid side that contained Luis Garcia and Fernando Torres, but they ultimately needed their arch rivals to do them a favour. The draw with Valencia and defeat to Celta Vigo in the matches prior had been the real reason they weren't celebrating their first league title in 21 years. 'I still think we should have won the league,' says Westerveld.

The team had a solid Basque core which was complemented by a selection of foreign players. The Russians Valeri Karpin and Dmitri Khokhlov provided goals from midfield, while Norwegian former Liverpool defender Bjorn Tore Kvarme did make some appearances. However, strike pairing Darko Kovacevic and Nihat Kahveci made a telling difference with 43 goals between them in La Liga. A 22-year-old Xabi Alonso was also part of that Sociedad side. Westerveld remembered, 'You could see the talent he had. He read the game and his passing was just unbelievable. He scored against Real Madrid at home, in the 4-2. It was a long-range shot that he curled past [Iker] Casillas, you could see he was special. I never expected him to be this good, you can never know when they are so young, there's so much that can happen still. I remember him talking about Liverpool. He was one of the players that could speak English. I had a good contact with him, and we spoke about Liverpool.'

After the Atletico match, the Sociedad players still commemorated the occasion. They may not have won the league but it was still an outstanding achievement. Their supporters also enjoyed the festivities, and tributes to their heroes were forthcoming. Westerveld had friends over from Liverpool and one of them gave Alonso a beer mat to sign. His signature was for a joke contract to join the Reds for £1. Just a year later, Alonso did make the switch to Liverpool in an arrangement that was more legally binding.

The severe disappointment of the premature end to his time at Liverpool was finally beginning to disperse and Westerveld started to feel content with his footballing life once again.

In his third year at the Anoeta, Westerveld suffered an injury which kept him out for eight weeks. A shot from Juninho in the Champions League game with Lyon broke his little finger. He also injured his ankle later on in the campaign, which ruled him out for another few weeks. This saw his playing time restricted to just over half of the league games but he still did well when he played and finished 2003/04 as La Real's first choice. With just a year remaining on his own deal, Westerveld agreed terms with Atletico Madrid on a five-year contract. It took the two parties just 20 minutes of negotiations to finalise the most lucrative package of his career.

However, for Westerveld this wasn't about money. He knew that a move to a prestigious club like Atletico would give him the progression that he desired. Sociedad wanted €3m for the stopper, which was quite a bit considering he had only 12 months left on his present agreement. Atletico offered €2m and Westerveld thought that would be sufficient for him to get his desire to switch to the Spanish capital. 'The only thing was the president kept saying he wanted more money,' he says. 'At the end of the day, the deal didn't go through because they still wanted their €3m. That was very disappointing.' Atletico signed Argentine goalkeeper Leo Franco from Real Mallorca instead.

Looking back on his playing career, Westerveld now realises that it was another pivotal moment in his overall journey. 'It wasn't as disappointing at that time because I thought, "You know what! I'm happy here! I have had a good year; I will just finish my year on my contract, and I will be able to leave for free." It wasn't a big deal at the time.' It was the end of May and Westerveld was on holiday in Italy. Real Sociedad president Jose Luis Astiazaran phoned him to say that he was going to sell him to Manchester City. 'First of all, I didn't want to go back to England, I wanted to play for

Liverpool and not some other club. Secondly, it was Manchester City where David James was, and he was number one for England at that time. I knew it wouldn't be for a number one position. I was like, "No way am I going there!" He said, "No, we already have an agreement and they are willing to pay the fee!" I was like, "No! I'm not going! I wanted to go to Atletico Madrid, and you asked for too much money. That's fair enough but I'm going to stay now. I'm not going to any other club unless they are better than Real Sociedad. Don't think I am just signing to just go and sit on the bench somewhere." Things went downhill from there.'

Sociedad threatened not to give Westerveld a squad number for the coming year, which meant he would only be able to train. He spent every day of the remainder of his holiday talking with Astiazaran about potential moves. 'They wanted to push me to Mallorca. I told them, "I'm not going to a club like Espanyol or Mallorca, I'm at Real Sociedad, we almost won the league. I'm not going to go to a relegation [threatened] team again. It doesn't make sense!" That was the politics of football.' He came back for pre-season and he made it known that he was happy to fight for his place. Sociedad remained undeterred and they told him he would have to train with the reserves if he didn't leave.

Westerveld spoke with Real Mallorca and decided in early August 2004 that he would have to go there on loan for a year. Having allowed Franco to leave to join Atletico, the islanders now needed a replacement. The issue was still far from straight forward, as once again Sociedad's demands were unreasonable. It took until the final day of the transfer window to be resolved, when Westerveld, who felt he had no other option due to the exertion of pressure, left at the last possible moment. It was a cruel twist of fate having to replace the man that had effectively taken your proposed position, even if that wasn't Franco's fault. 'For the second time in my career, I was pushed out of a club. It was a bit harsh. It was the second time in my career that I thought about retiring. My whole world had collapsed again.'

The blow of not making the transfer to Atletico was just about tolerable, but the negative experience of exiting Sociedad in this manner was too much. 'It destroyed my career,' says Westerveld. Mallorca boss Benito Floro told the Dutchman that he needed an experienced first choice for the season, so that their newly promoted youngster could learn from him. However, as the campaign had just started, the young goalkeeper had made his debut in a 1-0 defeat to Real Madrid and was the man of the match. That youngster was Miguel Angel Moya, who went on to play for Valencia, Atletico Madrid and Real Sociedad.

'I arrived on the island on the Thursday and we had a game against Getafe away [at the weekend],' says Westerveld. 'I trained with the team for two days and then the coach said, "I can't put you in the team because of this guy. He had a good game and you have only trained with the team twice." So, he plays against Getafe. We won 2-1 and he is man of the match again. The whole of the island press is like, "Here we go, a kid from the island, just 17, the new Casillas!" The coach comes to me and says, "He will probably be inconsistent, so we will just give him a couple of games. I can't take him out of the team. You will be in the team as soon as possible." A year of this life. I was on the bench the whole year, I played six games. That was it. That was probably the end of my career then.'

The succession of obstacles thrown into Westerveld's path had taken their toll. His motivation for the game was at its lowest as he knew this season without regular football would deny him the chance to find a decent club at the highest level. At least he could take some solace in his environment. 'I had a great life in Mallorca. Every day after training was like I was on holiday. For my family and me it was great, but from a football perspective it was a disaster.' Mallorca did offer to sign Westerveld at the end of his contract which illustrates his professionalism, although if he did accept it, he would only receive half his current wages. He naturally decided that the weather wasn't going to be the deciding factor. 'I thought, "Wow!" I'm not sitting on the bench again behind a young kid. I can wait for my chance, but I know how good he is. He has shown it in the years after.'

Moya was Atletico's first choice for the 2014/15 campaign when he replaced Thibaut Courtois and it was only once Jan Oblak settled that he lost his place. He has played over 300 top-flight games in his career, although he featured in just 30 matches in all competitions for Mallorca in the next two seasons after Westerveld departed as another former youth product, Antonio 'Toni' Prats, took his position. Westerveld wasn't to know that. 'Like I said, I enjoyed my life in Mallorca, but I wasn't there to enjoy my life. I was still a football player and I wanted to perform at the highest level [possible]. I had lost my place in the national team because I wasn't playing for a year. I thought it would be over because there wasn't a lot of interest. It was also a time when not many clubs changed their goalkeepers – not in Spain and not in England, so there wasn't a lot of options.'

Portsmouth had been promoted to the Premier League two years previously with Harry Redknapp as manager and Milan Mandaric as chairman. Redknapp left in November 2004, when Velimir Zajec arrived to become director of football and the Croatian became the manager for the next five months until they found their replacement, Alain Perrin. 'He [Perrin] wanted to sign me. I was like, "This is the best option for me, at least it's Premier League." It was a chance again to show myself on the big stage.' Even though Westerveld was a free signing, the move to Fratton Park came quite late in the summer. It made it a difficult transition. 'I missed the whole pre-season. I joined them in France, which was about a week before the new season started. I wasn't 100 per cent fit of course.'

The combination of missing so much game time in the previous 12 months and the lack of meaningful training sessions meant that Westerveld didn't have the foundations to make an immediate impact. To arrive into the world's hardest league in such a manner is far from ideal for a goalkeeper who felt he still had much to prove. 'I had a lot of energy and fighting spirit, but I wasn't fit enough,' he says. Perrin still played him in the season opener against Tottenham Hotspur. 'The coach put me in the team and said, "I know you're not fit, but just play your games and you will get fitter every week and we will take it from there."' Westerveld featured in the next three games, but a match against Manchester City changed everything. With Pompey ahead for the first time that season, he misjudged a cross from Joey Barton and the resulting error fell to Claudio Reyna to level the score. Andy Cole ensured that City won 2-1 and Perrin's team had just one point from their opening four fixtures.

'He came to me and said, "Make sure you get fit and I will put Jamie [Ashdown] in for now, a young goalkeeper. Whenever you are fit, I will put you back in. I don't think you are 100 per cent fit at the moment." So, he took me out and I was on the bench.' Portsmouth won their next fixture 1-0 at Everton and recorded three draws from the following four matches. However, Westerveld still felt confident he would get his opportunity. 'I had a personal trainer come over from Holland to work on my fitness. I was getting fitter and fitter, but unfortunately for me they didn't have the confidence anymore in Perrin and they kicked him out.'

The Frenchman was sacked after back-to-back defeats in November 2005, the last of which was Westerveld's first return to Anfield, when he watched his side lose 3-0 following goals from Zenden, Djibril Cisse and Fernando Morientes. Perrin had his lowest win percentage of his career at Portsmouth and quickly regained his credibility by winning the Coupe de France with Sochaux in 2007 and then Ligue 1 with Lyon a year later.

Having left over control on transfer issues, Redknapp returned to Portsmouth. 'Harry Redknapp came and bought 11 new players and a goalkeeper,' says Westerveld. 'He took all the signings of Perrin out of the team and put all his own players in. That was the end of it for me.' It didn't initially appear to be the end though, as when Redknapp arrived there was still a month until the January transfer window opened. 'He told everybody when he came, "Everyone is going to have a real chance of showing themselves."'

Westerveld had met Redknapp a couple of times when he was at Liverpool, as he was team-mate Jamie's father. He regards him as a 'great guy, a lovely fella' and says his man-management skills were very good. It didn't do him any favours when it came to team selection though. Redknapp's first two games saw Ashdown play in defeats to Manchester United and Tottenham Hotspur, conceding six goals in total before Westerveld was given his bow. They beat West Brom 1-0, but despite a good game from the Dutchman, Ashdown was selected on Boxing Day against West Ham United and then two days later for the 4-0 loss at Arsenal. Redknapp collected his second win when Westerveld kept another clean sheet on New Year's Eve in a home game with Fulham. 'Then, one game we lost at Blackburn Rovers away and it was 2-1, but I was happy with my performance,' admits Westerveld. 'I was fit and playing well.' It seemed that Redknapp wasn't convinced with Westerveld or Ashdown. 'He still bought a new goalkeeper. Then, that was me [done]. I don't know if it was because I was a signing of Perrin – like I said he kicked all the signings out – or if he wasn't happy with me. Obviously, he knew me from Liverpool, but I don't know!'

Dean Kiely joined from Charlton, making his debut in a 2-1 defeat to Liverpool, and Westerveld spent the remainder of the season on the bench, apart from a brief moment in the February. On the drive to the Champions League encounter between Chelsea and Barcelona in the snow, he had a phone call from Spanish football journalist and pundit Guillem Balague. The two are friends and were meant to be watching the game together at Stamford Bridge. 'I've got David Moyes that wants to talk to you,' said Balague to Westerveld. 'Are you willing to speak to him?' 'Of course!' came the reply.

Nigel Martyn and Stephen Wright were both injured at Everton, while the young Iain Turner had just been sent off nine minutes into his Premier League debut. Moyes desperately needed a keeper and after a brief conversation, Westerveld agreed to help him out for a month. 'I put down the phone and was like, "Oh crap! This is Everton. What did I just do and say!" The funny thing is during my time at Liverpool, nine out of ten friends I had were Evertonians for some reason. I quickly phoned a couple of friends on my way home.'

Westerveld was no longer on the way to London to watch Ronaldinho and co. as Moyes needed him on Merseyside the following morning. His mates were quick to reassure him that both sets of supporters in Liverpool would understand the context. 'Straight away they were like, "No, look at the situation, you are not a player that came from Liverpool straight to Everton. You are not a player, who was just sold like Michael Owen or just left. You have been kicked out! Everyone knows about your story at Liverpool! We know the story of why you are at Everton, so you won't have any problems there."'

The circumstances justified a reprisal for someone who had felt so much professional heartache in the previous four years. 'It was one of my most memorable periods of my whole career. I played football for 20 years, but it was something special. Maybe because I was afraid beforehand. "What will be the reaction of the fans? I'm still a Liverpool fan. I played in controversial derbies." But then the warmth and welcoming from the fans from the very first day until the day I left was just heart-warming and just amazing.'

Francis Jeffers, who Westerveld infamously got sent off with in his first Merseyside derby, recently explained to him, 'They knew your situation and I wasn't surprised. It doesn't matter who you are, when you put on the Blue jersey and Everton crest, then you're an Evertonian. They will support you all the way.' Jeffers had the same issue when he rejoined the Toffees from Arsenal. He was booed during the warm-up, but the second he played, the supporters were behind him. 'That was the same for me,' says Westerveld. 'I only played two games and stayed the full month, but it was just amazing. Everyday again. The way they treated me, the players and the fans were just amazing. Looking back, it was one of the best moments of my career. I'm really happy that I did it.'

Moyes thanked Westerveld for his services in front of the dressing room before the 3-1 win over Fulham, with Wright now recovered from his ankle injury and back in the side. The Scotsman gave him the opportunity to stay for another month, but Westerveld felt it was too difficult as his wife was pregnant with their second child at this time. He was training with Portsmouth on a Monday and Tuesday and then flying to Liverpool on his day off on the Wednesday, where he would train at Finch Farm for two days before games at the weekend. 'I would have loved to have stayed a little bit longer, another month. In the ideal situation, I would have done it.'

Westerveld also needed an operation on his knee, so he took this chance to get it sorted as he wasn't going to play. He returned to his home in Holland and then in July, he had a telephone call from the relatively unknown Almeria boss Unai Emery, who went on to manage Arsenal. The prospect of playing in the Segunda Division didn't particularly appeal to Westerveld. He then had a second phone call, which this time was from their sporting director Roberto Olabe, who had previously been at Sociedad when Westerveld was there. 'He explained to me the project. He explained the situation and what had happened at Sociedad. It was a good sign that he wanted me back.'

Westerveld was struck by the club's philosophy and his love for the country was enough to persuade him to give it a go. 'Unai Emery was the same Unai Emery that was at Arsenal. He was full of energy and ambition; he drew me a picture of what he wanted. Looking back, it was one of the best years of my career on a family and personal level. We made the most friends in all the 20 years of my career at Almeria.' The city is located in the south-east of Spain on the Mediterranean coast. 'Football-wise it was great. It was just an amazing year. We played amazing football, very attractive football. We got promotion.' Almeria finished second in 2006/07 after several seasons in Spain's second tier. Westerveld loved the community that the place created, with families socialising after training and the wives watching away games together.

His one-year deal expired in the summer of 2007 and the now 32-year-old knew that he hadn't played consistently at the top level for a number of seasons. He saw a switch to either Japan or the USA as realistic expectations. 'They start their leagues in March, so I just needed a club for half a year,' he said. Westerveld's father passed away in the June, and he knew that he needed to be closer to his mother for the foreseeable future. Former Ajax and Netherlands midfielder Danny Blind, who was the technical director at Sparta Rotterdam, was next to pick up the phone to Westerveld. Their goalkeeper Harald Wapenaar had undergone an operation on his back and wasn't due to play again until the winter. 'It was perfect for me,' says Westerveld. 'I could play there until December, then make the move to the USA or to Japan. I could help the team, then when their goalkeeper was back, they had their goalkeeper. So, it was a win-win for both me and the club.'

Another twist meant that his well-thought-out plan never came to fruition. 'I don't know if this is the story of my life that sometimes you have to be lucky and then other times unlucky. In the October, the Japanese federation changed the rules so they would only take one foreigner instead of three. They all wanted the Brazilian strikers and the number tens. They didn't buy foreign goalkeepers anymore. So, Japan was out.'

Salt Lake City were the only team in Major League Soccer (MLS) that needed a goalkeeper. 'Salt Lake City didn't look interesting enough to me. I wanted to go to MLS, but I was hoping to go to a team in New York or San Francisco or Chicago for the family. At that stage, I wasn't playing at the top anymore.

I wanted to move somewhere for the family, so we could enjoy life. It's a big life experience for me and the kids. Salt Lake City didn't look like it could help me and wasn't appetising enough.'

The circumstances at Rotterdam also changed, as Wapenaar needed more time to recover. Westerveld decided to stay for the remainder of the season and continued to play every week. He was offered another contract, but his desire to see more of the world meant he would soon be on his travels once again. 'I still had a couple of years left in me, but not in Holland. I just wanted another adventure for me and my family. After my knee operation my knee wasn't 100 per cent, so I couldn't play at the top anymore, even if I wanted to.'

A conversation with another Netherlands midfield legend ensured that Italy was his next destination. 'Clarence Seedorf phoned me. He said, "I've just bought a club in Italy, do you want to come over to be the sporting director and help me set up the club. You can play for as long as you can."' The idea appealed to Westerveld, but his family had to come first. 'The first thing my wife said was, "Italy, we have never been in Italy before!" It was just unbelievable. Sometimes you need luck with your family as well.'

Westerveld spent two seasons at AC Monza in Serie C. The global financial crisis at that time made it very difficult for Seedorf to develop the club the way he wanted. It cost him millions and he struggled to get sponsorship deals. He was still playing for AC Milan and he wanted an arrangement to use their young loan players as a stepping stone for their careers, but that never materialised. 'After two years, he said, "I'm going to have to let you go because I'm going to sell the club! This is not what I was thinking before,"' said Westerveld.

The goalkeeper wasn't too disheartened. He spoke to someone about the prospect of playing in South Africa. 'I said, "No way! I don't want to play there; I have heard a lot of bad things about South Africa!"' He had enjoyed his time in Lombardy, but he was happy to go back to the Netherlands to retire. On the drive back home from Italy with the family, he spoke with Maarten Stekelenburg (the now Netherlands assistant manager, not the Everton goalkeeper). He was coach at Ajax Cape Town. Westerveld knew that Cape Town was very different from the rest of the country and that the team have the same mentality and playing style as the Ajax in his home country. They offered him a one-year contract, but they agreed upon a two-year deal. 'We ended up living there for four years; as a player for two years,' he says. 'Everyone from the whole world is visiting Cape Town now because it is one of the best cities.'

Westerveld expected more from the football though, given that the World Cup had been there just a year before. Rugby and cricket are the major sports in the country. 'The stadiums were empty. The level of football was no better than amateurs. It was very difficult to make a difference there.' When his playing career was finished, Westerveld decided to stay in Cape Town because his son was another year away from progressing to senior school. 'They said, "Okay! You can be our goalkeeping coach if you want?" I ended up for two years as goalkeeping coach and assistant coach at Ajax.'

Westerveld and his family decided that Mallorca would be the perfect place to settle as they enjoyed the Spanish lifestyle the most and he still has a property on the island. However, he allowed his wife, three boys and daughter Evi to take a holiday back in the Netherlands in the interim period. 'She said, "We have to go to Holland. We have four kids, everywhere we go we are taxi drivers. They have to go to horse riding, football, swimming, to and from school." That week in Holland, they could walk into the city centre and they could take their bikes. They had so much freedom.'

The family are enjoying their life in the Netherlands and have done so for the last four years. They decided against going back to the east and instead moved to Hilversum, which is located more centrally. It's 15 miles from Amsterdam and only a short journey to the beach, while he takes just an hour to drive to visit friends and family back in Enschede. The kids use the cycle lanes to get about and they attend an international school, with friends from Sweden, Wales and Scotland. When they are older, then the option to spend more time in Spain is there.

All of Westerveld's children play football, but it's not something that he ever bestowed upon them. 'I let them do whatever they want. If they don't want to play football and go to ballet or whatever, then that's fine by me. But obviously, I know what it is, and I know how it feels.'

His oldest son Finn is also a goalkeeper and there's a video on Twitter of him making an excellent reflex save. 'To see one of your sons making the steps that you did when you were younger. Obviously, I'm a little bit afraid. I know the negative things as well.'

Westerveld knows that talent alone isn't enough, and that luck will also play a huge part. As a parent he is concerned how it will affect him. 'I was never ever nervous for any game I played in my life. It was a thing that I was well known for. Which is sometimes good and sometimes bad! It's bad for your concentration. Sometimes it's good to be nervous. Now, every game I watch of his, I'm sweating. I know now how my parents felt. I never understood why my wife didn't want to go to games because she was too nervous! Now, every ball that comes close to the goal, I'm like, "I hope he saves it!" or "I hope he doesn't drop it!" I know what stick he will get and the pressure they put on a goalkeeper.' His other kids all play as strikers, which doesn't raise his own anxiety in the same manner. 'I really hope he can make it or at least be happy. He is really determined; he has the right attitude and he is working really hard for it. It makes me really proud!'

For Westerveld personally, he prefers to have a number of simultaneous projects, as it gives him the flexibility that football never did. His full-time job as a father is supplemented by goalkeeper coaching for the Netherlands under 18-side, legends tournaments for Liverpool and Holland, working for a federation called World Coaches and video analysis tool Metrica Sports, while providing occasional commentary for Astro TV either on the pitch at matches or in the studio in Kuala Lumpur, Malaysia.

'Everything is football related, but none of it is one job. I like to do all this stuff together. I can do so many different things. For Liverpool, I went to Ghana for a week to organise a corporate tournament for Standard Chartered.' He has found the balance between domestic bliss and maintaining a work life that still enables him to see the world.

Westerveld still misses the day-to-day routine of professional football, with the end goal of playing at the weekend. The Liverpool legends games have an added importance for former players, as they aim to be in their best possible condition for a match that can take place up to six months later. 'If you are able to play legends games, again have banter in the dressing room, playing games but a little bit more relaxed as well. At Anfield, in front of 55,000 people, it's always sold out wherever we go. We played at the Bernabeu against Real Madrid three years ago and there were 90,000. You play against [Zinedine] Zidane and [Emilio] Butragueno, last year we played against Milan with [Paulo] Maldini, Pippo Inzaghi and [Alessandro] Costacurta. It's the closest you can get now to playing for Liverpool in the Premier League. As long as I am fit enough to do that.'

The matches generate so much money for the LFC Foundation and recently the Sean Cox Rehabilitation Trust. It's a rewardable partnership for all involved. Some of the more senior players only make fleeting appearances in their former shirts nowadays. 'Aldo [John Aldridge] only plays for a couple of minutes at the end,' says Westerveld. 'If I am fit, I'm in the team until Pepe Reina retires!'

Chapter 9

Pegguy Arphexad,
Lucky Omen

'ALL THE time I was talking to him,' says Pegguy Arphexad on his relationship with Gérard Houllier. 'It started okay, but me and Sander didn't understand that after the first year we won three trophies and then we signed two keepers. We didn't understand. When we asked him why he signed two keepers, he said, "We were supposed to sign just [Jerzy] Dudek, but he couldn't pass his medical. Sander also made too many [mistakes].' I said, "Sander had a good year! In 2001, we won all the trophies we could have won apart from winning the league. You signed me for one year and then you signed two keepers. When you signed me from Leicester you said you were going to give me a chance to be a competitor for Sander. When that chance came you signed two keepers." He said, "Well, I needed international players." I said, "Why? If I played for Liverpool, then it would be easier to be an international player. If I had been Georgian or Armenian, then I might have been an international, but I'm French!" We had [Fabian] Barthez, I said, "Before you can be an international you have to play!" After that my head went down.'

Arphexad was brought up in Guadeloupe, which consists of six inhabited islands and many uninhabited islands in the Caribbean. It's situated south of Antigua and Barbuda. The Grand-Terre island is positioned in the eastern half and Arphexad grew up in Les Abymes, which has a population of around 60,000 people. It has still produced a number of footballers including ex-Marseille defenders Ronald Zubar and David Sommeil, along with Pascal Chimbonda, who spent several seasons in the Premier League. 'It was very nice, and I was surrounded by my family,' he explains. 'I was there until I was 15.'

The keeper then moved to France to join the Brest academy. 'I came from a sunny island and when I went to Brest it was very cold,' laughs Arphexad. 'I couldn't believe it. It was raining every day, but the people were really nice. It was lucky because there were four of us coming to the academy, so we were with each other all the time. We could speak to each other and take it from there.' Teams in France would regularly try to recruit players from this region of the Caribbean mainly due to the fact that they share a language. 'It doesn't work like this now,' he says. 'There's now an academy in Guadeloupe, where players from all over Guadeloupe will go to because it's the best one. I got picked up for Brest because I was in a tournament in the south of France. After this tournament, I was asked to go to Brest.'

Arphexad was playing for the national team of Guadeloupe in the competition aged just 15. There were sides from different regions across France including Brittany and Provence-Alpes-Cote d'Azur. The goalkeeper also enjoyed the sport of handball, but he had been between the posts from a very young age. 'When I was six, I used to be playing in goal against kids that were nine years old,' he continues. 'All the time I played with older children than me and I was in goal because I was the smallest. I liked it and took it from there.' It's a cliché among English supporters that many foreign players don't like the weather in the United Kingdom, but it could also apply to many other places within Europe. North-west France has a similar climate and if you're conditioned as a child to a particular atmosphere then naturally it will take time to adjust. 'At the start it was difficult because

I was coming from Guadeloupe where it was sunny, and it was raining all the time. The first year was really difficult because I was doing normal school and I was at the academy. I had to get the balance.'

Arphexad would start school at seven in the morning, then break off for training for two hours at midday. He would then return to his academic studies until five, when he would have another two hours of training. Finally, he would go back to school for a third time to do his homework. 'It was very hard,' he admits. 'I was very tired. It was very physical. The four of us would stick together and when the others felt low, we would pick each other up.'

He made his first professional start for Stade Brest at just 17 against Red Star FC, who are now a third-tier team in the suburbs of northern Paris. 'We had a very good team like [David] Ginola,' he recalls. The former Tottenham Hotspur and Newcastle United winger was a late developer and he never left the Stade Francis-Le Ble until he was 22. Claude Makelele, Bernard Lama and Stephane Guivarc'h were also in the squad. 'The club went bump and then all of us were free to move on!' says Arphexad. He then moved to the other side of north France to Lens, which was 442 miles away. 'It was really nice because it was like a family team. We all stuck together.' It was here that he obtained his baccalaureate, a diploma that French children receive on completion of secondary school. 'Before you go to university you have an exam,' explains the stopper. 'I went to university and did football. My family wouldn't let me give up school. You never know what could happen. If I completed school and wanted to concentrate on football, then I could do that after.'

Le Racing Club de Lens were regulars in the French top flight at this time and even won the Coupe de la Ligue (which was abolished in April 2020). Arphexad has strong memories of the events as he trained more frequently with the first-team squad. 'When I went to Lens, I finished with the academy and signed as a professional. I was very happy and grateful to be in Lens. The fans were great. They were very good with me.'

Patrice Bergues was his manager and he would later play a defining role in Arphexad's move to Liverpool. Bergues spent four years at Lens before becoming Houllier's assistant at Lyon and then at Anfield. 'He was very good. He was a very nice person and a very good coach also,' says Arphexad about the man who had such an influence over his career. Bergues had been the coach of the Lens academy and his success with the youth players allowed him the opportunity to manage in Ligue 1. 'When he won the French Cup with the youth team, he was promoted to the first team and he took many of us with him,' says Arphexad, as he bursts into laughter. It's not that he thinks he wouldn't have made it as far without his mentor, but he's certainly happy to give him credit for his tutelage. 'We are still in touch now,' he adds. 'He is a very nice guy. A really nice human. He would speak to you if you were having a bad time. He was one of the main reasons that I came to Liverpool.'

Arphexad made his debut for Lens against Montpellier in the 1995/96 season. It was the end of April and Lens needed the win in the fight for a European position. Guillaume Warmuz started for Lens, which he did over 300 times for the club. He picked up an injury after an hour with the score level at 1-1. 'We had to win this game to qualify for Europe,' recalls Arphexad. 'We had a lot of pressure from the fans. It was very nice and after we won it was a great day for me.' He was 22 at this time and the injury to Warmuz meant that he would make another two appearances. That Lens side also contained another future Liverpool player Titi Camara and Marc-Vivien Foe, who appeared for West Ham United and Manchester City before tragically dying on the football pitch for his country at just 28 years old. 'He [Foe] was good, he was a tremendous player,' Arphexad states. 'He liked playing with me. He was a good player and good man. He was younger than me. When he died it was really sad!'

Vladimir Smicer also played at Lens in the latter stages of Arphexad's period at the club. 'We had a good team. I enjoyed my time at Lens. I would have preferred to have played more games, but sometimes in football it's like this.' Despite playing his part in the club's qualification for European competition, Arphexad went to Lille on a one-year loan. 'I did all the pre-season games and just before the season started, they said, "You have done well, but you are too young," and that they needed a more experienced goalkeeper, as they were also playing in Europe.' The switch was made easier by the close proximity to one another. 'I said, "Okay, I will move to Lille." It wasn't too far, I didn't need to change where I lived,' he confirms. 'Lille to Lens is only 20 minutes. They rung me and asked me, if I wanted to come and I said, "Yes!" The atmosphere was good, and the goalkeeping coach was very good. I improved a lot.'

Arphexad then made the move to the United Kingdom. 'I was supposed to go to Motherwell in Scotland. Alex McLeish was the coach. I had done a trial and I had done okay. I played a few games and they wanted to sign me. They wanted to sign me for a month!' He can certainly see the funny side of the situation now, but at the time it was clearly not enough to make such a switch. 'Their goalkeeper was injured, and my English was very poor. Willie McKay was my agent. I was one of the first players that he signed in England. I went with Willie, then afterwards I called him and said, "No! No! Willie! I don't want to go there because I have two years left on my contract in Lens!" He said, "No! Stay!" I said, "I don't want to stay, I want to go back to France! I don't want to cancel my contract for a month. If it doesn't go well, then after a month I will be out of contract!"'

Arphexad decided to travel to the airport with McKay with the intention of returning to France, when his agent spotted in the newspaper Leicester City required a goalkeeper. McKay knew Leicester's assistant manager John Robertson, or John Roberto, as Arphexad affectionally calls him. He rang him straight away to tell him he had solved his dilemma. Robertson was also concerned about Arphexad's tender age with Europe on their agenda and Kasey Keller having a number of qualification games for his country during the season. McKay was persistent though and told him that he should at least take a look at the keeper in a training session. Robertson still wasn't interested, but McKay wouldn't take no for an answer! 'Willie said, "I will bring him tomorrow for training," and John said, "I will have to ask Martin O'Neill. Come with him and I will ask Martin. I don't know if he will be able to train." I went to Leicester and Martin came into the dressing room, he said, "Okay! He can train with the goalkeeping coach Seamus McDonagh!" I had a really good session and Seamus told Martin O'Neill to come and have a look.' Arphexad was given a week-long trial and after he impressed in two practice matches, he joined the club from the East Midlands.

O'Neill left a lasting impression on his new signing. 'He was a very good man-manager. I couldn't understand his accent at the start. He used to talk to me, and I couldn't understand nothing!' Arphexad had signed as the second goalkeeper in August 1997, but he wasn't in any of the first few matchday squads. 'I was training well and after five games I hadn't been named in the squad, not even as a substitute, nothing! I went to see him and said, "Coach, what's going on with you? You ask me to sign and then I'm never in the team?" He said, "Yeah because you don't speak English!" He told me that if you don't speak English, how are you supposed to talk with the players? I said, "Okay!" Then, the week after I learnt English. I learnt the basics like wide left, keeper, man on ... The most important things very quickly, then a week later I was talking all the time in the training session. The week after he put me in the squad, and I played my first game for Leicester against Chelsea.'

At that time, you could sign a player before one o'clock on the Friday and he would be eligible to play on a Saturday afternoon. Keller picked up an injury in training at ten past one. 'He had to play me,' jokes Arphexad. 'He couldn't sign anyone for a month, so he had to play me, and I had a wonderful game at Chelsea. They had [Gianluca] Vialli, Tore Andre Flo, [Dan] Petrescu, [Gianfranco] Zola, [Roberto] Di Matteo and Mark Hughes. It was a big squad. I said to myself, "Fucking hell! What a gift, you get to play your first game at Stamford Bridge!" I had a very good game and even Ken Bates came to the dressing room to give me man of the match.' It was normally a Chelsea player, but the then chairman had been impressed by his display, even though a late Frank Leboeuf goal had given Ruud Gullit's side the three points. 'Martin O'Neill wasn't happy, he was like, "Fuck off!" We had lost 1-0 with two minutes to go. It was right in the top corner and I couldn't do anything about it! I had a good game though and Seamus was very happy. He used to like me a lot. He was very happy because he had said to sign me.'

There were some interesting personalities in the dressing room at Filbert Street such as Robbie Savage, Steve Claridge and Matt Elliott. 'Yeah, it was very good,' adds Arphexad. 'There were some strong characters. Robbie wasn't a strong character. There was Steve Walsh, Claridge, Ian Marshall and Elliott. After that Robbie became a strong character, but before that he was just following everyone. Now he has got a big mouth.'

A young Emile Heskey was Arphexad's room-mate. That season he scored ten league goals for the second consecutive year. 'It was nice. We are still in touch now. Emile is a top man. He was good as well. He was a very good player. He was so fast. I think he was under 11 seconds for the 100 metres. He was fast and strong.'

Arphexad made some important penalty saves in shoot-outs during cup competitions. 'I have very good memories because at Leicester they used to like me for saving penalties. I was lucky. After training, I used to practise a lot with Seamus for penalty shoot-outs. I was trying to make the player strike the ball where I wanted him too. Make him think I was going to dive the other side and try to make him put it the other way. Sometimes they would score and sometimes I would save it.' He managed to get the psychological advantage over many of his opponents. In January 2000, he saved penalties from Lee Dixon and Gilles Grimandi in the FA Cup fourth round against Arsenal. He arrived from the bench at full time to replace Tim Flowers and made important interventions to deny Patrick Vieira before they won 6-5 from 12 yards. It was the second time in a month that he had been their hero in a shoot-out. The League Cup quarter-final against Fulham had proved more decisive though, as the club went on to win the trophy at the end of the campaign, with Arphexad an unused substitute in the 2-1 win over Tranmere in the final.

'It was tremendous,' he continues. 'In my three seasons at Leicester – we finished tenth, tenth and eighth. We won the League Cup and lost once in the final. It was very nice for Leicester because financially compared to the other teams we done very well. We had a smaller budget, but we were finishing in the top ten all the time and winning the League Cup. It was very good. The fans were very nice.' Leicester had won the League Cup in the March before Arphexad had arrived at the club, so it was certainly a significant period in their history. They may have bettered those achievements by winning the Premier League in 2016, but the importance of those years at the end of the 90s shouldn't be underestimated.

In April 2000, Liverpool were in a commanding position to qualify for the Champions League and finish third in Houllier's first full season in solitary charge of the team. They had won five consecutive matches, but an unlikely collapse cost them a place in Europe's premier competition. They failed to win any of their final five league games which included defeats at Chelsea and Bradford City along with a 0-0 draw at Everton. Sandwiched in between those matches were a home game against Arphexad's Leicester. The soon-to-be 27-year-old had held talks with Liverpool about a possible switch to Anfield. 'The year before I was supposed to sign for Liverpool, but things didn't go through,' he admits. 'When you haven't signed a contract, then you never know. I had to prove that I was good enough to go to Liverpool. I had a good game.' His clean sheet gave the away team a 2-0 victory and as Leeds United beat the Reds to third by two points it certainly made a difference. 'Martin O'Neill knew that I was in talks with Liverpool. He was supposed to play Tim Flowers, as a few weeks before there had been talk about me signing for Liverpool. O'Neill just decided to play me. I don't know why. He said, "Pegguy, you're going to play for Liverpool? Okay, then play against them!" It was a midweek game on a Wednesday night, and I had to have a good game.'

The week after he had a conversation with Bergues which confirmed his dream would be coming true. 'I went to Liverpool as a free player because my contract was running out. I talked with Martin O'Neill a lot of times about extending my contract, but the thing was I wanted to play. Tim Flowers was there, and he was old. They said when he retired that I would play then, but I didn't know what was going to happen. If in two years I got injured and I had the chance to sign for Liverpool! They say, "Maybe the train will go past another time?" But I had to catch it! I said to O'Neill, "I have to be honest with you that I think I will go to Liverpool because next year I don't know if it will happen again." He couldn't give me an answer to say, "Okay, you will be first choice next year!" Because if he had said that, then I would have stayed at Leicester. I preferred to be second choice at Liverpool than second choice at Leicester, as I felt at this point, I was good enough to challenge Sander.'

Arphexad had belief in his own ability and he wasn't fazed by a move to one of England's greatest clubs. He was one of three French players to sign that summer, while there were already many players in the squad fluent in the language such as Titi Camara, Rigobert Song and Stephane Henchoz. Chelsea were the opponents again when he made his debut, but this time it was at Anfield. 'Even when you're on the bench you can feel the atmosphere, but on the pitch it's different,' he beams enthusiastically. 'I was trying to concentrate on my game because it was my first and I had to show I was good enough to play for this team. Everything went well and we won 2-0. Everything was perfect.'

Houllier's men won the FA Cup, League Cup and UEFA Cup in that 2000/01 campaign. 'The only thing that I wasn't happy with was that I didn't play enough games,' says Arphexad. 'I was supposed to play all the cup games, but I got injured. I got injured before the League Cup quarter-final against Fulham.' He had played in the 2-1 win over Chelsea and the 8-0 thrashing of Stoke City in the earlier rounds. 'I was supposed to come back for the final. I wanted to play in the final. Gérard Houllier told me that, "We haven't won anything yet and you have only been back in training a week."'

Arphexad had to make do with a place on the bench as his side contested the League Cup Final at the Millennium Stadium in Cardiff. Houllier had told Arphexad that he would be brought on should the match go to a penalty shoot-out due to his past record. Liverpool were the overwhelming favourites, but despite this they only drew 1-1 with Birmingham City after 120 minutes. However, the substitute goalkeeper's pre-arranged agreement with the manager stood for nothing because they had used all three of their replacements during the game. Arphexad had to continue watching from the sidelines as his team won 5-4 on spot kicks, but he wasn't bitter. 'It started from there. When you win a trophy, it gives you more confidence to go on and win more. We wanted to do well in the league also. Manchester United were so far ahead of us and then we had to concentrate on trying to win all the cups and to finish in the top three. We won the FA Cup, but we were lucky, very lucky! We were losing that game with ten minutes to go and then Michael Owen scored two. Arsenal were better than us.'

Liverpool didn't play particularly well in either of the domestic cup finals, but that didn't stop them winning both. 'We were very strong mentally,' says Arphexad. 'We also had a very good squad [with players] like [Sami] Hyypia and [Didi] Hamman. I think we had a good team. We could have won the league.' That illustrious league title never arrived, although they completed an incredible treble with the astonishing 5-4 win over Deportivo Alaves in the UEFA Cup Final. 'The atmosphere was tremendous, but we couldn't celebrate as we had a game against Charlton that we needed to win to qualify for the Champions League. It was strange because we had won the UEFA Cup and we were happy, but we couldn't celebrate because we had to focus on the next game straight away.'

Arphexad got on with everyone within the squad, but his time with Heskey at Leicester meant that he was closest to the forward. Houllier's relationship with Arphexad was initially good, but he was bemused by the decision to sign Dudek and Chris Kirkland on transfer deadline day of August 2001. He immediately asked to leave because he knew his game time would be limited. However, Houllier insisted that he needed three good goalkeepers to compete in all competitions and that Westerveld no longer featured in his plans. Arphexad still wanted to move, as he didn't want to sit on the bench.

'I was going on loan to Portsmouth with Harry Redknapp because Shaka Hislop was injured. Harry called me and I said, "Okay, I am coming!" I was meant to go on the Friday, but on the Thursday, Kirkland got injured with his knee and Houllier said, "No! You aren't going nowhere!" I had to stay.' The situation was far from ideal, but Arphexad never held it against Dudek or Kirkland. 'It wasn't their fault. Our friendship was very good. We were very close to each other. Jerzy was a very nice person and Chris also; he was much younger, but he was a very nice person. We worked hard together. With Sander as well, even when we were competitors. The manager makes the choice and we have to deal with it.'

There was certainly no shortage of high-quality strikers to test them in practice with Heskey, Michael Owen, Robbie Fowler, Jari

Litmanen and Nicolas Anelka all at the club in this three-year period. 'Robbie was naturally a tremendous player. He was a top goalscorer. He could score from anywhere. He was instinctive. He was different to Michael; he would stay more in the box. He was a very good player.' Those two weren't the only local-born players that left an impact on Arphexad's time in L4. 'Stevie G. was coming from the academy and already he was like a playmaker and boss of the team, when he was young. Jamie Carragher was different, he was like a hard worker. He used to give 200 per cent every time he was on the pitch.'

Arphexad did manage to get one loan deal to Stockport County, but injury meant that he had to return to Merseyside after just three appearances. 'The thing with Liverpool was that I was happy. There aren't many people that can say that they played for Liverpool. I enjoyed my time there, most of the first year because we had a good run. I would have appreciated playing more, much more! But sometimes it's like this.'

Gary McAllister asked Arphexad if he would like to join him at Coventry City in 2003. 'I had a bad injury at the end of my time in Liverpool with my knee. I had an operation and the surgeon told me that if I wanted to stop, then I could do now because my knee was in such a bad state. Gary Mac called me and asked me if I fancied giving Coventry a go. I said, "Gary, I am injured!" He said, "When you get yourself fit, then I will welcome you!" We were very close.' Arphexad made the switch to Highfield Road, but McAllister left the club at Christmas because his wife was unwell. Arphexad picked up another injury and he was rehabilitated in France. When he returned, Peter Reid was at the helm. McAllister's assistant, Gary Mills, was now at Notts County and he asked Arphexad to follow him there. However, after a couple of games injury struck once again. 'The surgeon was right,' he jokes. 'I couldn't play because at night it was swelling. I wasn't training. I was always sitting on my own, then after that I decided it was time to go back to France.'

His first knee injury had come at the age of 16 in Brittany, while he had surgery in Leicester in 1997. The surgeon wasn't a specialist and from then on in his career he had to rest his knee and get treatment immediately after matches and often after training. It's testament to Arphexad's positive attitude that he doesn't even mention this until the end of the interview. He wanted to return to France, when an unexpected opportunity arose. 'At the end of 2004, I had surgery on my knee again. I went for rehabilitation and Marseille called me and said they wanted a keeper. I said, "I'm coming!" I thought why not!'

Arphexad never played a game for Les Olympiens as back-up to Barthez, but he still lives in the area with his wife, son and daughter. 'I needed the sun,' he confesses. 'From Brittany, Brest, to Lens to England. I need the sun now, so I stayed in the south of France.'

Chapter 10

Scott Carson,
Leeds, Turkey and Lampard

IT'S AUGUST 2018 and new Derby County manager Frank Lampard is speaking to fewer than ten journalists in the press room at Pride Park. The man who would later become the next Chelsea boss is personable to those asking questions and relaxed in his new role, having just witnessed his team beating Ipswich. Outside, Derby goalkeeper Scott Carson is signing autographs and posing for selfies with supporters. He immediately agrees to a future interview, although arranging a fixed date and time proves difficult in the coming months.

I arrange to speak with Carson in March 2019, but then less than ten minutes before the interview is due to take place, I receive a phone call to say he must go for immediate treatment. He misses the next game against Stoke City and his replacement Kelle Roos keeps a clean sheet. Carson doesn't start again that season for Derby as they make their way to the play-off final only to be beaten by Aston Villa. I finally got the opportunity to talk with the goalkeeper when he made the shock move to Manchester City, a year after we initially spoke.

Carson grew up in Cleator Moor, which is about ten minutes away from Whitehaven on the west coast of Cumbria. His mother Gwen raised him and his brother Grant after his parents split when he was just four years old. It's a remote part of the country and there wasn't much to do, so they played sport. 'Any opportunity that we got, we would have a kick about, starting building goals and anything to keep us occupied,' says Carson.

He would play football on a Saturday and rugby league on a Sunday. 'I only think I was any good because I was 6ft when I was 14 and it gave me a big advantage. I used to love it and I still love it now, watching games.' Carson supports Wigan and his uncle would go to the Challenge Cup finals in 1990s. He played for a couple of seasons from the age of 12, but he knew he had to move his focus to solely on football.

Cleator Moors Celtic was his team as a youngster after he turned up with his mates and his goalkeeper gloves. A relationship between a coach at Cleator and the manager of Workington Town ensured he had some extra goalkeeper training, in the time before specific coaches were in place. 'They had a youth cup game and they asked me if I wanted to play,' he says. 'I played this under-18 game, and we got beat 4-1, but I must have done okay because the manager got in touch with Cleator and took me and another lad.'

Peter Hampton spotted him for the Leeds United academy, then following a few games in Dublin, he spent the school holidays at Leeds for training. 'I started coming out of school on a Friday at dinner time and going down, staying at Leeds and then playing a game on a Saturday,' adds Carson. 'I hadn't signed then for Leeds, so I was playing under-16 and under-18 for Cleator and then I used to play for a pub team on a Sunday.' That pub was called The Globe and the team was made up mostly of lads from Cleator Moors Celtic.

When Carson moved to Leeds on a full-time basis, he found the adaption hard. 'It was difficult at first because I had never been away from home much before. It was difficult. I found it tough, but it was obviously something that I wanted to do my whole life – to be a professional footballer. So, I just had to dig in and get through it. At the time that I went to Leeds, it was unbelievable.'

Carson was a ball boy for a Champions League game with Barcelona at a time when Leeds were flying high under David O'Leary. He lived with James Milner, and Aaron Lennon was also in his age group. 'There were a couple that went on to play a little bit lower,' he says. 'When we first went and lived in the training ground, it was like being back at school. It was just a laugh. We worked hard, but we all got on great.'

On his promotion to the first-team squad, Carson began to mix and train with players that had reached the Champions League semi-finals just two years prior. The likes of Robbie Fowler, Robbie Keane, Harry Kewell, Jonathan Woodgate and Rio Ferdinand may have left, but they still had Alan Smith, Mark Viduka, Nick Barmby and Lucas Radebe.

But who stood out the most for their talent and professionalism? 'That's a difficult one,' contemplates Carson after a long pause. 'When I started getting into the first team that's when the trouble started financially, and players were leaving. It was probably because of that reason that I went there.'

Were the players aware that the club was facing economic ruin? 'Not really. It was just what people were saying. We were just concentrating on the under-17 and under-18 football and everything we had to do around the training ground. It wasn't as if we knew exactly what was going on, but you obviously hear all the whispers.

'I was always really impressed by David Batty,' admits Carson, as he returns to the initial question. 'I'm not sure why! He just always looked class on the training ground. He never gave the ball away and never shirked from a tackle.'

The revolving door policy at the club naturally destabilised the team and led to their relegation in Carson's only season with the senior players. O'Leary had spent four years as manager at Elland Road, then Terry Venables arrived to steady the ship before Peter Reid joined in March 2003. Reid was the boss who promoted Carson to the first-team squad. 'I really liked him. I got on great with him. He was really straight up. He came to me and said, "Nigel Martyn's gone, and you have a chance with the first team now." He was brilliant for me. There were a few of the senior pros who weren't too struck with him, but for me I will be ever grateful to him because he put me in the first team.'

Reid had been sacked before Carson made his first-team bow, which was instead given to him by Eddie Gray in strange circumstances. His debut appearance for the Yorkshire side wasn't exactly to script, but Carson enjoyed his brief moment in the spotlight. 'I can just remember sitting there and taking all the tape off my socks,' he recalls. 'I had a sore finger at the time, so I took it off that. Then, the next thing there was a red card and I didn't know what was going on.'

There were just two minutes left of the home game with Middlesbrough in January 2004 when Paul Robinson was sent off. Bolo Zenden had given Boro the lead just after the interval before Joseph-Desire Job added a second. Robinson was dismissed for bringing down Michael Ricketts and Carson's first opportunity in senior football saw him face a spot kick against the man who had just been fouled. 'It was one of them moments that I dreamed of, but it was quite a short and sharp one. I picked the penalty out of the net and I don't think I touched the ball after that.'

Just three weeks later, Carson made his first start in another baptism of fire against Manchester United. Leeds were 19th in the table and their Roses rivals were in second place. 'I can remember not having the best of sleeps on the Friday. I had never been to Old Trafford before and when the bus pulled up, I was thinking, "I'm not sure I want to get off here." The game didn't go too bad. We drew 1-1. It wasn't perfect, but considering I was only 18, I don't think it was too bad.'

Paul Scholes scored off a rebound after Carson had parried a shot from Gary Neville, but the youngster made a string of impressive saves to thwart Nicky Butt and Mikael Silvestre. Ryan Giggs hit the post before Smith equalised. 'To be honest, I can't remember much about the game at all. I kicked one ball out of my hands, and it went straight out of play. David Kelly turned around to me and just ripped me to pieces. I was thinking, "This must be what football's about."'

Carson only played one more game that term, with the club already confined to life in the second tier when they met Chelsea. 'It was a difficult time and once you start losing a couple of games, with everything that was going on, it was difficult. Even though we had a group of players that could compete, it just wasn't happening for one reason or another.'

Robinson left for Tottenham Hotspur that summer, which appeared to give Carson the number one jersey for the campaign in what had been renamed the Championship. He was more than happy with the situation. 'There was basically only me and another couple of young lads. So, I thought, "I'm going to play this season." I was fine with that, it's what I wanted to do. To get more experience and play. We had a friendly the week before the first game and Neil Sullivan came on the bus. It just deflated me. I thought I was going to be playing and no one had said anything to me.' Sullivan had spent 12 years at Wimbledon, then three years with Tottenham before a year as understudy to Carlo Cudicini at Chelsea. He naturally took the goalkeeper spot, although Carson did learn a lot from him and was glad that he joined after the initial disappointment.

Liverpool and Chelsea both agreed a price with Leeds in January 2005, with Carson having just six months remaining on his contract. 'At the time, Chris Kirkland was injured and there was only [Jerzy] Dudek there,' explains Carson. 'I was thinking, "I've got more of a chance of getting a game at Liverpool than I have at Chelsea." There was Petr Cech, Cudicini and however many more goalkeepers there. It just felt more right for football reasons that I should do that. If I did okay, then I had more chance of playing.'

The hopeful Carson could only dream that an opportunity would come in the last eight of the Champions League. He made his debut for the Reds in a 1-0 loss to Newcastle United in the Premier League, but that paled in comparison to the quarter-final against Juventus. Emotions were high at Anfield as the two clubs met for the first time since the Heysel disaster 20 years prior. The home supporters held up a mosaic which read 'Amicizia' (Friendship), while red, black and white wristbands were distributed before the game.

'I didn't go there expecting to play,' admits Carson. 'It was only when we got to the stadium [that Carson found out].' Rafael Benitez was always late naming his side and often left it to just an hour and a half before kick-off. 'I was just thinking, "What a game this is going to be!" I think Jerzy had a slight groin strain. He [Benitez] read the team out. I was surprised when my name was read first.'

Liverpool took an early two-goal lead when Sami Hyypia scored from close range and then Luis Garcia hit a superb half-volley past Gigi Buffon, who was then the world's most expensive goalkeeper. 'Buffon was one of my heroes growing up,' enthuses Carson. 'Any chance I got to watch Italian football on a Sunday, I would watch it. Just to play against him was a great achievement for me and everything I had dreamed of as a kid.' Juve were managed by Fabio Capello and fielded a team that included Lilian Thuram, Alessandro Del Piero, Pavel Nedved and Zlatan Ibrahimovic, while it was Fabio Cannavaro's header that squeezed past the 19-year-old Carson to pull a goal back just after the hour mark. Benitez's team contained Igor Biscan and Anthony Le Tallec. 'It was just some night all round. To be looking at some of the players that we were playing against. I think we had a couple of injuries and a couple of fringe players were playing that wouldn't normally play.'

That result proved to the players that they could compete with anyone and was another part of the building process which culminated in the dramatic comeback in Istanbul. We all know the story of how Liverpool were three goals down to Milan after

45 minutes and Benitez was getting confused with how many players he had on the pitch. However, Carson has a slightly different and unheard perspective of how the side completed one of the most historic sporting moments.

'The main thing I remember was Alec Miller, the coach, was just trying to lift everyone at half-time. He was saying, "If we get one back, then these will start panicking. We just have to keep on going." Rafa made a tactical change when he brought Didi on and it all changed. After that it was just some night.'

Like the 2019 edition, the victory parade on Merseyside was another momentous occasion. 'It was difficult for me because I hadn't played many games in the group stages,' Carson says. 'I obviously played one game. The way I am, if I haven't played in the actual game, then I don't feel like I have deserved it. I was on the bus and I was obviously happy to celebrate with the team, but I just felt that I didn't really deserve the medal or to be jumping around like I have actually won the Champions League.'

The club overachieved in winning that Champions League, but still had some outstanding players in their ranks. 'It was a big shock. I had seen all the first team players at Leeds and trained with them a couple of times, but when I came to Liverpool, they were players that I had seen on TV and in World Cups. I was a little bit starstruck by certain players.'

Steven Gerrard, Xabi Alonso and Garcia were at the Melwood when he arrived, while Fernando Morientes and Javier Mascherano would join in subsequent campaigns. 'It was something that I wanted to do, and I had to basically stick my chest out and try to show everyone that I should be there and that I was good enough to be there.'

Benitez partnered Hyypia and Jamie Carragher at the centre of defence. The Finnish centre-back was experienced and had a quiet authority on the pitch, while Carragher was vocal and playing arguably his best football in his career. It must have made it easier to have such a commanding presence ahead of the young goalkeeper.

'To be honest Sami was a cool guy. I don't know if you have ever seen Carragher in training, he just screams, and he has got this passion that he wants to win everything. The first couple of games I played it wasn't a good experience playing with Carra. He basically coached me through the games and tried to tell me everything to do. Anything that was wrong, he would let me know about it.'

Only James Milner has been capped more times for England's under-21 team than Carson. He was then unexpectedly selected for the senior squad that went to the World Cup in Germany in 2006. An injury to Rob Green gave him the opportunity after he had been out on loan at Sheffield Wednesday just three months before.

'That was something else as well,' he says. 'It was something that I wasn't expecting again. I think I was fourth keeper and Greeny pulled his groin in an England B game. I came on for the second half and played. It was like, "He is going to be out for quite a while, so you're in the squad, get yourself ready."

'It was something that I had not been used to. Even though I was at Liverpool, I was starstruck again and you have to pinch yourself sometimes when you're training with the best players in England. It was just another great experience and one I wasn't expecting.'

Carson joined Charlton Athletic on a temporary basis the next season, after the club ironically failed to sign Green. He was named Player of the Year at The Valley in a squad that contained Jimmy Floyd Hasselbaink, Darren Bent and Dennis Rommedahl. However, he couldn't prevent them from relegation, as they dropped out of the Premier League.

He spent the next year in the Midlands with Aston Villa, keeping 11 clean sheets. 'I think everyone was on a similar level then,' admits Carson. 'Ashley Young and Gabby [Agbonlahor] were obviously getting all the plaudits, but I think everyone knew they were on a similar level, which is why it worked well that season. I don't think anyone thought that they were better than anyone else and everyone seemed to work hard. They all got on really good and it was a good squad.'

In November 2007 his form was rewarded, and he made his England debut in a 0-0 draw with Austria. Steve McClaren kept faith with the now 22-year-old for the crucial match with Croatia just a week later. Niko Kranjcar's long-range shot bounced just in front of Carson and he was unable to prevent it slipping into the net. It was the opening goal in a 3-2 defeat for England and the result meant that they failed to qualify for Euro 2008.

McClaren was sacked the next day and pundits were quick to criticise him for using such an inexperienced goalkeeper in such a key encounter. 'I was obviously disappointed after the game, but I was still inside happy that I had played for England,' confesses Carson. 'Some people will say that I probably wasn't ready and looking back I probably wasn't. But when the manager tells me I'm playing, it's not for me to say, "I think it's a bad decision, I don't think I'm ready." It was a difficult night and it was a difficult couple of years afterwards because it was the only thing that anybody seemed to go on about. It was just one of them things. They do happen and unfortunately it happened then.'

Villa played in the fierce Second City derby and obviously the Bluenoses weren't going to miss an opportunity. 'That was some experience. The Blues fans didn't let me forget the Croatia game,' laughs Carson. 'It was a brilliant atmosphere and we won at St Andrews, so it made it even better as well.'

Carson's error for his country could have had large repercussions on his mental state. 'You just have to forget about it. The more experience you get, then the easier it becomes. When you are young it's difficult, it's all you think about. You probably let it bother you, when you shouldn't do. I think the more games you play and the older you get; you just learn that they do happen, and you have to forget about them as quickly as you can.'

The goalkeeper had spent two years playing regularly and that clearly wasn't going to happen at Liverpool, so in 2008, it was time to make a fresh break and move to West Bromwich Albion. 'I just knew that I wasn't going to get too many opportunities at Liverpool,' he admits. 'West Brom came in and said, "We will take him on a permanent, would you be interested?" I had been in the area while I was at Aston Villa, so it wasn't as much of an unknown. I said, "Yes!" Tony Mowbray was playing good football and it was a move that I was interested in.' Carson has spent eight of the last 13 years of his professional career in the Midlands and this is where he now calls home.

Carson signed for the Baggies at the same time as Borja Valero, although the Spaniard found it tough. Valero spent two of his three seasons at The Hawthorns on loan in his home country with Real Mallorca and Villarreal. He has since proved his quality with five years at Fiorentina in Serie A and now with Internazionale. 'He was a great player,' recalls Carson, who could see his talent. 'I think he found it a little bit difficult, he struggled with the language at first. When he came, you could obviously tell that he was a really good player. Whether the English style suited him, I'm not too sure, but he was a great lad. I think maybe, if he had more time to settle, then he would have done a lot better.'

West Brom were relegated from the Premier League in Carson's first season with Mowbray, but they were immediately promoted back the year after with Roberto Di Matteo at the helm and Carson as captain. 'It was a great achievement. Jonathan Greening went to Fulham and the manager pulled me before the game against Peterborough at the start of the season and said, "I want you to be captain, what do you think?" It was something I had never done or even thought about doing, but I said, "Yes, not a problem, I will give it a go and try and do my best."'

Di Matteo left in February 2011 and new boss Roy Hodgson told Carson that he wasn't going to play and should find a new club. The dramatic change in circumstances saw Carson opt for a transfer to Turkey. 'There wasn't too many options and I just thought, "You know what, I'm going to go and see what it's like.

Just get out of England for a little bit." I went there and I feel that I played some good football. If it had been a little bit easier on the family life and everyday living, then I would have probably stayed longer.'

Carson really enjoyed the football side of his time at Bursaspor, but his private situation was tough. His wife Aimee found it difficult and he had three young boys at this time – Hayden was five, Harley was three and Dane just two months old. 'Everything that we take for granted in England– just nipping to Tesco or whatever it may be,' says Carson. 'The food that we were used to eating wasn't really there, so it was quite difficult and quite boring for us at certain times. It was difficult. You obviously have interpreters and things like that. I knew a couple of words, but it wasn't an easy language to learn. I don't think it was the language that was the problem, it was just boredom really.'

Bursaspor played Fenerbahce in the Turkish Cup Final of 2012. They lost 4-0, but the supporters were something else. 'I can't really remember too much about the final. We went into it thinking we had a good chance and we never really played that well at all. We got thrashed. All the games were unbelievable. It was the thing that I enjoyed the most, the football and atmosphere. They were singing an hour before kick-off. You never really got a bad atmosphere. I think as a young kid it would have been difficult, but if I had been younger, I don't think I would have done it.'

Carson has settled in Yoxall, a small village just north of Lichfield, Staffordshire, and has added a daughter to his family. He and Aimee have opened up a business called BeatBox Studios, which sees high-intensity boxing classes utilising nightclub music. At Derby County, he felt content and his consistency in the East Midlands was all the more remarkable given that he has had seven managers in his four years at the club, while they finished in the play-off positions in three of those seasons.

'I went to Derby and Paul Clement said to me, "It's down to you and Lee Grant to see who will be number one." Thankfully I got the shirt at the start of the season and did okay. I got an injury a couple of months in and missed a few games, but then I think we were on a rocky patch and I came straight back in. I think I played about 140 games consecutively. I loved it there. It was a great place and great people. I think I played my best football there.'

It's not just the dugout that has seen a high turnover of personnel at Derby, with the squad constantly changing. Carson arrived with a further eight players in the summer of 2015 and only Craig Forsyth remains in the first-team group from that time. There has been a high calibre of signing in this period but it's perhaps striking that the loan players have attracted more praise. This instability has cost Derby when it has come to automatic promotion. The various coaches that Carson has worked with at Pride Park have had vastly different philosophies, but which one got the best from him? 'I was starting to get a bit of recognition under Gary Rowett,' says the keeper about the manager who lasted the longest at the club. 'I made a couple of important saves at important times. If a midfielder scores some important goals, then they get all the plaudits. So maybe Rowett.'

Lampard spent 12 months at Derby in 2018/19 and enjoyed living in a local village, Duffield, where his wife Christine would be regularly seen walking with their dog and baby. He enjoyed it so much that he plans to buy a second home in the area in the future.

What qualities did the former Chelsea midfielder possess as a manager? 'Erm,' responds Carson contemplating the question carefully before answering. 'Tactically he was good. He worked us really hard. I don't know, I missed a game and that was it. I never got an explanation, or he never told me why. If he had just spoke to me a little bit more, then things would have been a bit easier. That's maybe his style of management, which is fine. I think I missed the Stoke game because I was ill, then we had Rotherham the next week. I just assumed that I would play because I just missed through illness. I got to the game on the Saturday and the team went up and I wasn't in. There had been no chatter or anything like that. I think as an experienced player or older player, it's the one thing that we all say. If a manager just tells you and pulls you to one side, then you respect his decision, no matter what it is. I think when you don't get told anything, you just see it on the board, then it's pretty difficult to take.'

Carson didn't have an issue with Phillip Cocu, but the opportunity to spend 12 months at the Etihad was too strong an opportunity to miss. He can now add Pep Guardiola to the list of managers he has worked with, which will surely have a major impact on him should he make his own move into management.

Chapter 11

Jerzy Dudek, *Poland,* *Feyenoord and Forlan*

IT'S EARLY December, there's snow on the ground and it's below freezing temperatures in Katowice, which is Poland's 11th-largest city. The area in the southern part of the country is just 70km away from Cracow and the nearest city to Szcyglowice, where Jerzy Dudek lived for 22 years of his life. It's just turning four o'clock and as daylight finishes, the smell of wood burners lingers in the air and there are lanterns with candles inside around religious monuments. Katowice has undergone a major transformation in the last century, as many of the areas and buildings have been modernised. It's a very different place from the one that Dudek and his friends would travel to on the train when they were skipping school and dodging ticket inspectors. It's now a centre for culture, while you can still feel the influences of Germany and Russia which have controlled the region in the past.

Dudek joined Gornik Knurow at the age of 12 and then as he got older, he combined his time with a mining vocational course at college. He would spend four hours of practice in the mine and then in the afternoon he would have football training, at the club now known as Concordia Knurow and in the fifth tier of Polish football. The country still has around 80,000 miners to this day, much to the annoyance of the European Union.

Roman Kensy and Witold Slabkowski were coaches at the side and they assisted Dudek's development in his early years. At 18, he started to train with the first team more regularly and under the guidance of goalkeeping coach Jerzy Ogierman, he made his debut just a month short of his 19th birthday. The team improved with Marcin Bochynek as manager and Dudek's reputation in Upper Silesia continued to grow. Marek Kostrzewa initially tried to sign him for Gornik Zabrze to no avail, but he was eventually able to persuade him to join a new project. A merger between Sokol Pniewy and GKS Tychy had taken place and it meant that they would be playing in the Ekstraklasa (Poland's top league), with Kostrzewa as assistant manager for the newly formed team.

In 1995, after ten years at Knurow, Dudek moved to Sokol Tychy (now known as GKS Tychy) and arch rivals of GKS Katowice, where his brother Darek would later play and manage. It's just a 15-minute train ride between Tychy and Katowice, which makes the meetings between the clubs and hooligan elements particularly fierce. They arrange to fight the day after the game, with GKS Katowice having more numbers and GKS Tychy utilising weapons. The far-right government Law and Justice (PiS) may publicly condemn the violence from the football hooligans within the country as a whole, but there's no doubting their views and policies have encouraged their ideologies even more. The walk down the Generala Andersa road towards the stadium from the train station illustrates the contrast within the place. On the right-hand side, behind a transparent bus shelter is a row of apartments, with 'GKS Tychy Ultras 71' spray painted at the end, then on the left it's the more scenic view of the Park Gorniczy along with detached houses and a small stream in the distance.

Dudek is certainly the most famous player to ever wear the GKS Tychy shirt and given that he went on to win the Champions League, it seems strange that there's little evidence at the stadium of his former presence. With the focus equally on ice hockey and basketball in the region, it's likely that they don't see it as a priority. Inside the club shop, the 22-year-old girl has never heard of Dudek, while it only sells ice hockey merchandise and there are no tours of the arena. The current Tychy City Stadium was only completed in 2015 and it lacks many of the modern amenities found at most European sides given that it still has a capacity of 15,000. Inside the restaurant, there's a view of the pitch which is obstructed by the large plastic fences, and the meal of potato dumplings, red cabbage and pork won't be to everybody's taste, though it's easier to consume with a bottle of Tyskie.

The Polish Army Stadium was the venue for Dudek's debut against Legia Warsaw. They had Juventus goalkeeper Wojciech Szczesny's dad Maciej in the opposite goal and his relaxed demeanour immediately allowed his fellow keeper to feel at ease. His side may have lost 2-0, but Dudek's performance gave him confidence. His maturity was beyond his years and his growing professionalism already saw him stand out from his peers. The senior players in the squad drank after every game, but that didn't stop the team surviving relegation. He made only 15 appearances in total for the club in his solitary season, although it was this experience that illustrated that he was ready for the next level.

In 1996, Sokol took a trip to the Netherlands on a pre-season tour. There they played Excelsior and Feyenoord's reserve team, but after Dudek forgot to pack the team's kit they were forced to wear the Feyenoord's green away kit much to the pleasure of the players. After the game they went for a tour of the De Kuip stadium and Dudek met their goalkeeper Ed de Goey for the first time. 'We were like kids at Disneyland,' wrote Dudek in his autobiography. Six months later they would share a dressing room.

After a nervous trial, where Dudek felt out of his depth, he was given a five-year contract with the vision to becoming de Goey's successor once he moved on. 'At that time Feyenoord weren't winning a lot – they still don't – but at that time it had been long ago,' says former team-mate Jean-Paul van Gastel. The midfielder had signed for Feyenoord just six months earlier and the club had won just one Eredivisie title in the previous 12 years. 'He was very social,' says Van Gastel about Dudek. 'He had come from Poland to Holland and he was trying to learn Dutch. When we went out to play, he always came along. He liked the Dutch music and he really socialised to get the Dutch culture. That was his first steps. Everyone liked him because he was a good guy and he was very pleasant in the way that he was as a human being.'

Ronald Koeman was also at Feyenoord, but the former Everton manager was 33 at the time and by his own admission was no longer the role model he once was. 'For me, playing with Koeman was a dream,' admits Van Gastel. 'He was one of the greatest players in all of that time. He was playing for Barcelona, then he came to Feyenoord. I learnt a lot from him, details like how to move around the midfield. Later, I became his assistant coach. I have known Ronald for many years and for me it was a pleasure to play with him.' Dudek was also fond of Koeman and he even did extra training with him on free kicks and penalties. Henrik Larsson was another on the playing rota for De Trots van Zuid, although he was just starting out, as a 19-year-old. 'Larsson at that time was at the beginning of a great career. That was his first club in a strange country, then he went to Celtic and he got better and better. He is also very professional and a nice guy. I also worked with his son, when I was a young coach at the academy of Feyenoord; Jordan came to practice with us.'

Dudek naturally had to bide his time with De Goey ahead of him in the pecking order, but he was able to use the period to learn off his more senior team-mate. The two would room together on away matches and Dudek was often praised by his goalkeeping coach Pim Doesburg. After an impressive campaign where the team finished runners-up in the league to PSV, De Goey made the switch to Chelsea. Manager Arie Haan immediately promoted Dudek to first choice. However, the Pole was concerned that the club had signed Hungarian international Zsolt Petry especially as the now 24-year-old hadn't yet played for Feyenoord. He needn't have worried.

'He was a great goalkeeper,' Van Gastel recalls. 'When he started in the 11, for the first couple of games he made some mistakes, but then got better and improved. The coaches let him be in the squad, from then he got more confidence and he did really great. I think when he made mistakes, he was a little bit nervous really. I think that affected the team a little bit, maybe the defence? I don't know! The main point is that he always fought back.'

On his debut, he dropped a cross after he collided with an FC Jazz player, although the resulting goal didn't cost them as they won the Champions League qualifier 6-2. Van Gastel scored twice from the penalty spot as he dominated the encounter with Steven Gerrard-esqe quality. The Champions League group-stage match against Juventus saw Dudek commit another error, although he wasn't the only one who played badly as they lost 5-1. Haan stuck with Dudek regardless, but the team's results weren't good enough. 'He made a couple of mistakes. It was a different kind of playing [style] in Holland. The goalkeepers are playing with the other ten players. In the beginning he found it a little bit difficult, but in the end, it was not his strength to play with his feet, like Brad Jones as well. They are very good goalies, but they are more goal goalies rather than playing football goalies.'

Haan was sacked after defeat to Manchester United. The next season Leo Beenhakker took the helm and there was an immediate lift as the team improved by 19 points in the final standings. 'He was like a people manager,' adds Van Gastel. 'He gave the players a good feeling. He made it like a team. When he came Arie Haan had been fired, it was a difficult situation. The next season we became champions. It was very nice. It was very good. We had a team that refused to lose. Leo was very important in that. He let us be professional. He kept us satisfied.'

The Dutch league was wide open during this period, with the previous year's winners Ajax falling down to sixth. PSV were third and Feyenoord finished 15 points ahead of runners-up Willem II. Dudek was instrumental within an attacking style. 'He was very important,' says Van Gastel. 'The one thing I remember is that we had one week of partying after we won the championship. He was going crazy for that week like us. He always liked the Dutch music, so when we went to clubs, he wanted to hear those songs. For the years we were at Feyenoord we always heard those songs.'

Feyenoord finished third the following campaign and Beenhakker left to become Ajax technical director, while Bert van Marwijk replaced him in Rotterdam. 'Van Marwijk was more like playing from the system that he wanted to play,' explains Van Gastel. 'He was more of a trainer. He wanted to play 4-3-3 and he was always making exercises for that system.' The team improved defensively in the 2000/01 season and Dudek conceded only 37 league goals, as the club finished second to PSV. It was expected that he would be leaving and Dudek had been given an incredible reception by both supporters and players, as he was presented with flowers and gifts. He clearly made a positive impression on those at the club and Van Gastel recalls his best attribute: 'His kindness,' he says without hesitation. 'His open character. I think goalkeepers are special. There's something about them that makes them special. I think [Jurek] is a special guy.'

In Dudek's time in the Netherlands there was some interest from Barcelona and Manchester United, but Arsenal made the most concerted effort. Dudek travelled to London and witnessed the training facilities for himself, while Arsene Wenger described the Gunners in great detail. However, the clubs couldn't agree a transfer fee and Feyenoord chairman Jorien van der Herik broke off negotiations. Arsenal signed Richard Wright instead and Dudek had to return for pre-season training with Feyenoord, which was a test of his mentality. He played three games in the Eredivisie against Sparta Rotterdam, Roda Kerkrade and Ajax, but it was when on international duty that Liverpool made their move. Ironically, Dudek saw Sander Westerveld in Amsterdam's Schiphol Airport on the way to John Lennon International. He was polite with his soon to be replacement, but a little taken aback that the rumours in the papers were true.

Dudek joined Liverpool on transfer deadline day in August 2001. 'When he first came in it was a bit of a shock because they brought Chris Kirkland in and I don't think they told Chris that they were signing Jerzy as well,' says former Liverpool full-back Stephen Warnock. 'The pair of them turned up together and I don't know if Jerzy knew that Chris was signing either. They were both top keepers at the time, one up and coming goalkeeper and in truth a goalkeeper in Jerzy that we didn't know that much about.' Another former defender at the club was Stephen Wright. 'At the time, we were going for Chris Kirkland and I think it was getting stalled for a number of reasons,' confirms Wright. 'I know we were after a first-choice goalkeeper. In the meantime, Jerzy Dudek was coming in.' Gérard Houllier broke the British transfer record for a goalkeeper with the signing of Kirkland, but as he was only 20, he wanted to ensure that they had another top-quality alternative.

'As a group we didn't think he was going to be as good as he was,' admits Wright. 'We thought that Kirky was going to be number one and it turned out that Jerzy was in the end.' Warnock was also surprised with how easily Dudek adjusted to his new surroundings. 'When he came in and trained, we knew straight away the level that he was at. The ability that he had. Once he started playing, I think even Kirky turned around and said, "This is going to be difficult for me to dislodge him because he is at such a good level." He was impressive from the get-go.'

Dudek admits that he struggled in the first few days with loneliness, but that eased when his wife Mirella and son Alexander arrived. Houllier's friendliness and the support of player liaison officer Norman Gard were also extremely helpful in the initial adaptation. Former Liverpool defender Markus Babbel feels that Dudek settled quickly because he made an effort to integrate with the other international players. 'He was also a foreigner like us,' says Babbel. 'We knew how difficult it is if you're new to a club and [it takes time] to feel comfortable. That was a great help for him. With Vladimir Smicer, the German guys, Sami Hyypia. We were always together. The English guys stayed together and then the foreign guys were together. For him, I think it was quite easy to settle down quickly.'

The Polish goalkeeper wasn't initially impressed with Melwood, but Liverpool opened a new, modern part of the complex a few months later. He left a greater impression on his new team-mates though. 'At the time, Gérard wanted a high-class goalkeeper and Sander was a good goalkeeper, he had just made some errors of individuality,' says Wright. 'We always had that stigma of goalkeepers that made big mistakes in big games. When they both [Dudek and Kirkland] came in the class in training just went higher. We had the likes of Robbie Fowler, Emile [Heskey] and Michael Owen saying, "We can't score against these two in training," in the small-sided games.'

Dudek was primarily Liverpool's number one, but he maintained a strong relationship with the other three keepers, especially Westerveld with whom he could converse in Dutch. 'He was good,' says fellow stopper Pegguy Arphexad. 'At the start, he had a different way of goalkeeping to us, but then he had confidence. He did very well for Liverpool, and he is a legend.' His English was limited, but it was enough to be courteous. 'He was fine,' recalls Wright. 'He could speak English. When you spoke to him, he was a nice guy. I was only a young lad coming through at the time, I think I was 21. Sitting down with him he spoke really well; he loved the life in Liverpool, and he loved the people in Liverpool as well.'

Babbel could also see an improvement in between the posts, although his viewpoint became more from afar. 'To be fair, I didn't play that many games with him,' he states. 'In my first season I played 60 games in the five-trophy season and that was Sander Westerveld in goal. In the second year, Sander started making silly mistakes and then came Jerzy. From the first minute on he was there, he was unbelievable. He made unbelievable saves. Then, I got my illness. I was more or less in Germany for all the treatment. But I saw all the games. You could see that he was in fantastic form. He kept this form for a really long period, which isn't easy. Sander played a fantastic season in the 2000 year, but in 2001 he was struggling after his big success. Jerzy was always consistently on a high level. For me, he was one of the best goalkeepers in the league at this time. It wasn't a big surprise for me that he was one of the key players in the Champions League Final.'

In October 2001, Houllier became ill during a home game with Leeds United and Phil Thompson took charge in the interim period. 'I think Thommo wanted the local lads in the team and the English boys,' says Wright, although Dudek maintained his place in the side with Kirkland struggling through injury. 'That's the effect I got at the time and looking back at some of the squads it looked like that. I never really spoke to Thommo about it, but he was the one that really gave me a chance and put me in. I don't know what was happening in the background with Gérard, whether he was the sole reason for putting me in or if it was Thommo at the helm.' Kirkland briefly had an opportunity in the Champions League against Galatasaray and in the Merseyside derby, but despite pressure from the media, Dudek returned to the team for the remainder of the season. Liverpool finished second to Arsenal in the league and reached the quarter-finals of the Champions League.

The majority of the players had a World Cup that summer in South Korea and Japan, which left many including Dudek tired and jaded. They also made a number of new signings in the transfer market which created uncertainty, while expectation had been lifted. Liverpool won nine and drew three of their opening

12 Premier League games, despite not playing well. Then Dudek dropped a cross in a defeat at Middlesbrough after colliding with Alen Boksic. It was the start of a poor sequence for the Pole which culminated in the mistake versus Manchester United, which made Diego Forlan a folk hero at Old Trafford. 'I sat in the Anfield dressing room afterwards and I cried,' admitted Dudek in his autobiography. 'I asked myself why it happened to me. I was gutted. The lads were trying to cheer me up, but it had no effect.' Dudek had never been so low following an incident in a football match.

'When you make mistakes as a goalkeeper it's always difficult because it's always highlighted,' says Warnock. 'It's the one position that if you make an error, then it's always leading to a goal. He had a couple of high-profile ones, but you always trusted in his ability. I think it was more a lack of concentration at times and once he learnt from that he was still young enough to bounce back.'

That moment came just three months later in the League Cup Final, against United once again. Kirkland had been given a run of eight Premier League matches following Dudek's error, but Liverpool won just one of them. Dudek was restored to the side at the end of January and the break had done him good. A deflected goal from Steven Gerrard off the back of David Beckham and a strike from Owen gave Liverpool a 2-0 win in Cardiff but the spectacular saves from Dudek made amends for him and ultimately made the difference for his team. 'I told Jerzy three days ago, "I can feel you will be the hero. You were too unlucky when we played them,"' said Houllier to the press after the match. 'Today he was man of the match. But football can be like that. Sometimes you can be at the bottom and then be a hero again. I just had a feeling. I'm a great believer that when you have the right attitude everything else follows. He had a good run after the World Cup but then he made some mistakes and we had to support him.'

Opposition manager Sir Alex Ferguson was equally as complimentary regarding Dudek's contribution to the final. 'Their goalkeeper has won them the game,' admitted the United boss. 'Sometimes you just have to put your hands up on these occasions. Dudek has won them the cup. He deserved to be man of the match. We didn't get a break. Dudek's performance encouraged them to stay near their penalty box.'

Dudek kept 25 clean sheets in his first 50 league games for Liverpool, a statistic that has only been beaten by Pepe Reina and Alisson. 'I think the Liverpool fans and the players especially knew the ability that he had, and they trusted him,' says Warnock. 'That he was the right person to be in goal.' That confidence from his defenders came by the way he dominated his area. 'He was very commanding,' Warnock adds. 'He wouldn't necessarily come and catch things to start with. He would come and punch a lot of things, but once you know what your goalkeeper is going to do, then you work on that and you understand. I worked with Brad Friedel, when he was at Blackburn and Aston Villa as well. Brad was always one of those goalkeepers that you knew, he would make you 15 to 20 points a season. Jerzy was exactly the same, you knew that if they breached your defensive line, then they would have to do well to beat Jerzy because he was such a good goalkeeper. I think that gives you just that bit of extra confidence and that belief. It was always good to play in front of him.'

Wright also felt his presence: 'You knew he was there. You knew that if you had to depend on him that he was there to help you out. Not disrespecting Sander, but late on in his time some of his errors, we were always thinking about what if. With Jerzy in goal, you didn't worry about it. He was so professional. What he does and how he trains. They do train hard goalkeepers; us defenders and outfield players always have a moan about them. When you saw him in the training sessions and in the small-sided games, it's just fantastic, how he works and how he is so good. I think he was the start of goalkeepers changing at this football club. Before that we had a stigma of every goalkeeper that come into our club, really good goalkeepers. With David

James there was the "Calamity James" and things like that, and before that with Brucie. We had some really good goalkeepers, but they struggled to hold down the position sometimes. With Jerzy coming in, he held down the position for a long period, he was our number one.'

Dudek was always well liked and that gave him even more respect among his peers. 'A very nice guy,' says Babbel, who lived close to his fellow Germans Didi Hamman and Christian Ziege, while Jari Litmanen was also a neighbour. The foreign players would regularly meet in the city centre for meals. 'A very nice and handled guy. Definitely not a loud speaker. Very calm. A top professional. I think it was the right time with the right team; we had many foreigners there and we all had this problem that we were away from home and we were alone. Keep us together. Jerzy was a main part and a very nice guy. That's the only thing I can say.'

The English players were also impressed with his overall attitude. 'He was outgoing, he was always up for a laugh with the lads,' remembers Wright. 'But when the hard work come and it was time to knuckle down in training, he was A1, he was quality to be fair.' Warnock agrees, 'He is quite a funny guy to be honest. When he first came in, he was a little bit quiet and shy, which is bound to happen. When you look back now, we didn't have Instagram, we didn't have social media at all really. So, you don't go on YouTube or anything like that, to find out what these guys are like and how good they are. You come into the dressing room and you're a bit of an unknown quantity, when you get brought in like that. So, he was probably very shy when he came in, but once he got to know everyone, he was a bit of a joker of a character and a nice guy. He kept himself to himself, but when he wanted to have a laugh, he would have a laugh as well.'

Houllier's demeanour changed following his operation and he was often more confrontational than he was previously. He undermined individuals in front of their team-mates and gradually the dressing room grew tired of the criticism. Liverpool's results were also poorer, and they finished fifth and fourth in the league in consecutive seasons. Rafael Benitez arrived in the summer of 2004 and he was stylistically very different. 'It might be down to the managers that they are playing under as well,' says Wright about goalkeepers keeping a consistent level. 'You look at David Seaman under Arsene Wenger and Peter Schmeichel under Alex Ferguson, and now you look at [David] de Gea – what a goalkeeper he has been and then the last couple of years he has been nowhere near. Goalkeepers at the time, when you have your best period, should you go to other clubs or should you stay? It's a tough one for goalkeepers! You can't have great seasons every season of your career.'

Liverpool's league form was patchy once again, but in Europe they were a force to be reckoned with. Dudek now had two English goalkeepers pushing him in Kirkland and Scott Carson. 'I think that is always the key ingredient – to be pushed by someone from behind, to have competition for places,' assesses Warnock. 'It always brings out the best in people. Once there's not a great deal of competition, then people drop standards and levels. Scott played in the Champions League quarter-final against Juventus at home and he had an unbelievable game and I think Jerzy was looking at that thinking, "We are progressing here and there's every chance I could lose my position." Once he was back fit, he was desperate to show what he could do. That again builds your levels up and pushes you on to be better. I think Scott was very unfortunate in the fact that he had Jerzy in front of him. The ability that Scott showed when he came into the club, the performances and levels he showed particularly that game with Juventus was incredible.'

Dudek was restored for the second leg in Turin and even faced the media in the pre-match press conference, where he followed Benitez's instructions to try and put the Italian journalists off the manager's tactical plan. An injury-hit Liverpool side drew

0-0 and progressed to the semi-final. Luis Garcia's 'ghost goal' in the second leg against Chelsea set up Dudek's finest moment in a Liverpool shirt. The unforgettable final in Istanbul will be remembered mainly for the comeback, but Dudek was pivotal in ensuring that all that effort wasn't for nothing. His wrist action response to an almost certain goal from Andriy Shevchenko made the supporters believe that the impossible was really about to occur.

When the 120 minutes of football was completed at the Ataturk Stadium, it was Jamie Carragher that gave his goalkeeper a quick history lesson. 'Dudek is one of football's nice guys,' said Carragher in his autobiography. 'That's fine when you want to go for a pint, but when you're looking for that extra edge which is the difference between winning the European Cup and going home devastated, it's time to offer some guidance on the finer arts of craftiness. Prior to the shoot-out I headed straight to Jerzy and told him to do everything possible to unsettle the Milan penalty takers.'

Carragher instructed him to follow the example of Bruce Grobbelaar in 1984. Hamman and Djibril Cisse scored for Liverpool from the spot, while Serginho and Andrea Pirlo missed, as Carragher's plan began to work. Jon Dahl Tomasson and Kaka ensured Milan weren't out of it, with John Arne Riise failing to find the net in between. Vladimir Smicer's strike meant that Shevchenko had to beat Dudek to stop the Reds gaining their fifth European Cup. 'And then, in a moment I'll never forget,' said Gerrard in his book, *My Story*. 'Jerzy psyched-out Shevchenko by staring at him, bouncing on his line and then moving a foot off it – seemingly for the hell of it. Shevchenko, a great player, shot weakly and straight down the middle. Jerzy saved it; and we all started screaming and running.'

Dudek may have been the hero but it didn't stop Benitez replacing him as his number one the next season. Were the squad surprised that Liverpool signed a new keeper after such a success? 'I think so, but then without being disrespectful to Jerzy, if you look at the level that Pepe was at when he came in,' says Warnock, who was now playing more often himself. 'Pepe was an incredible goalkeeper as well. He was arguably one of the best that I have played with and that's saying something when you have played with Jerzy as well because Jerzy was at such an incredible level. I think Pepe was the start of the modern-day goalkeeper. He was comfortable playing out with his feet, he was playing outfield in training and he looked like he could play 90 minutes in midfield. I think it was the start of the modern-era goalkeeper and Pepe was one of them that Rafa knew from his time in Spain and knew he was an up and coming goalkeeper.'

When Reina arrived, Dudek initially wanted to leave, but Benitez didn't want him to go anywhere due to his professionalism. When Carson left for Charlton on loan in 2006, Benitez asked Dudek to stay to provide cover and the Pole agreed. 'I know I will not move somewhere and find a nicer club than Liverpool,' said Dudek to the club's official magazine, as his contract ran out in May 2007. 'I love this city and love this club. If I had gone to the World Cup, then I would have stayed here forever. I told Rafa that too. I would have done everything I wanted to do in my career.' Dudek was offered a new contract at Anfield, but he would have to take a 50 per cent pay cut.

The game may have been changing, but Dudek still displayed some incredible attributes between the posts. 'He made some mistakes in the big games towards the end of his tenure at Liverpool, but he did well for quite a few years, and he won medals,' Wright says. 'His technique was really good. Other than Sander, he could kick a ball a mile. You would look at it and go, "Wow! Look how far he can kick a ball!" It's just nonchalant, it's just with ease. You look at young goalkeepers now, it's just technique and he was really good at that. He was very vocal as well. [We knew] what he wanted from us. With Alisson now, he can play short, but when he needs to go long, the technique's there and he can find them players for the one v ones.' Babbel was also impressed with

Dudek's more traditional goalkeeping traits. 'His reaction on the line,' says the former Bayern Munich defender. 'He was like a cat. It was unbelievable. He was so quick because he wasn't the biggest or strongest, but the reaction he had was unbelievable. He could read the game. For 90 minutes he was fully focused on the game because he knew that maybe that was a weakness he had especially for the English league. It's a tough league with tough guys there. His reaction on the line was just unbelievable.'

Dudek had several offers when his contract expired, but they mainly came from Spain. The influence of the Spanish contingent at Liverpool had introduced him to food like jamon and paella, while they had also educated him about wine. It was goalkeeping coach Jose Ochotorena that informed Dudek about Real Madrid's interest, but after much deliberating on the golf course, he opted to take up Real Betis's offer of first-choice football. However, after he made the trip to Seville and was left waiting for a number of hours, he was let down by the club as they opted to sign Portuguese stopper Ricardo instead. Madrid's sporting director Predrag Mijatovic had previously told him that he could go there as understudy to Iker Casillas should he change his mind and after a conversation between Dudek's agent Jan de Zeeuw and his former boss Beenhakker (who had managed Real Madrid twice), it took just half an hour to agree terms in the Spanish capital.

It didn't take long for Dudek to adjust to his new club, as he spoke English with the staff and Dutch with Ruud van Nistelrooy, Arjen Robben and Wesley Sneijder. The mealtimes were a little different, but he quickly felt like he belonged at the Santiago Bernabeu. 'He is a guy with a lot of confidence,' adds Jean-Paul van Gastel. 'From his coach and fellow players. The first time he came to Holland, he was in a strange country. The second time he went to England, it was a different way of playing the game. I also met him later when I was doing my Pro Licence at Real Madrid.'

Casillas was superb in the 2007/08 season as they won the La Liga title but Dudek's presence had been a positive one, even if his game time was limited. The two keepers became good friends and Casillas used to call him 'Papa Dudek' because he had three kids at this stage. Dudek worked with Bernd Schuster, Juande Ramos, Manuel Pellegrini and Jose Mourinho in his four years at Los Blancos. He especially enjoyed Mourinho's attention to detail and would regularly stay after training to try and stop Cristiano Ronaldo's free kicks. Dudek may have made little impact on the pitch, but he was extremely popular with his team-mates and coaches due to his attitude and professionalism.

Van Gastel spent a week observing Mourinho's methods in Dudek's final year of his playing career and he found a very different person to the one that had arrived in Rotterdam 15 years prior. 'At this time, he was the third goalie,' recalls Van Gastel. 'You saw a person with real confidence, he was walking with his chest pushed out and chin up. He was a very different goalkeeper from the one that started with Feyenoord. His development as a human being and development as a goalkeeper. You could see that he had learnt a lot and he had improved a lot. He had won trophies with Liverpool. It was very nice to see.'

Dudek retired from club football at the end of 2011 and was given a guard of honour by the Madrid players in an 8-1 win over Almeria. 'When my team-mates and friends formed the corridor … I don't have words to describe it,' said Dudek to Madrid's official website. 'Three weeks ago, I already knew I was going to play, but I didn't expect it to be so moving.'

In 2013, he competed as a race car driver and has since been involved in over 30 races. 'He always loved cars, that was clear,' confirms Babbel. 'I think he is a race driver now. If you play as many games as we did – every three days, the national team as well – there's not much time for hobbies. The only thing I know was that he loved cars.'

Chapter 12

Martin Hansen,
The Other Side of the Coin

'HE WOULD give you a bollocking for sure! He would even get the fucking ball out and cross it himself if it wasn't good enough,' explains Martin Hansen about his time with Steve Heighway in the Liverpool youth team. Heighway was a flying winger for the club in the 1970s and then later became academy director, but he never lost that ability to find his target. 'He could cross the ball better than anyone else, so if he was not happy, he would stop the training and do the crossing or the shooting himself.'

Hansen grew up in the suburbs of Roskilde – where they hold the yearly music festival. Denmark's tenth largest city is just 16 miles west of Brondby and 19 miles from Copenhagen. 'There were a lot of kids running about and playing football. It was a quiet place, but a lot of football being played on the small fields around. School was not so far, so I was on my bike every morning to go to school. Nice, quiet area, with lots of kids. It's quite different to England maybe, with lots of open fields and it was a little bit out of the city.'

He was picked up by Brondby as a 15-year-old. 'In Denmark, you play by ages. The best teams have certain age groups who play in the best league. Roskilde, where I played my youth football, was not in the best league. I think we had two or three players, who had the level to go and play in the best league. In the under-13s or under-14s we played against Brondby many times. Then, at under-15s it becomes more of a national level and you travel to all the national clubs around. I had to take the next step and Brondby was interested in taking me to their club and of course it was easy to make that choice. Because that's the next step to get into the national team and all these things. It was quite easy for me to go there.'

Like many hopeful Danish goalkeepers, Hansen was a huge admirer of a certain former Manchester United icon. 'When I was young, I probably looked up to Peter Schmeichel. He was probably the only player. I don't really look up to anyone at the moment, but at that time Peter Schmeichel was a legend. He also played in Brondby. The first-team players; you are just waiting to play with them, but I didn't really have any idols other than Peter Schmeichel.

'He's a big legend, I think in all the clubs that he has been in over the years. He made a big impact on the pitch and off the pitch at any club he has been in. Everywhere he goes really, he does some good work and that was the same at Brondby. Of course, he made his name even bigger when he went to England. I know they are proud of him in Brondby, for sure.'

Schmeichel and his son Kasper are just two of those from the country to have had an influence on Premier League sides. So what is it about Denmark that means it consistently produces top-quality goalkeepers? 'That's a good question,' considers Hansen. 'I think Germany also do. I know we are a smaller country. I don't know! I think Danish teams have had good goalkeepers for a long while, but why? I don't know!'

Hansen pauses for a while to contemplate the question once again before continuing, 'Maybe we see an honour in being in goal and we put a lot of focus on the keepers during training, but I also do think that goalkeeping comes with a strong mentality. That's very important for a player to succeed that he is very strong mentally. That's probably one of the key factors. I do think many Danish people have a really good mentality, when they go into something – they go all in. They want to do everything they can and don't let anyone down. They want to be the kind of person that you can rely on and trust. And this is mostly what I see in Danish players – is that they don't let you down. If you show that you believe in them, then they won't let you down. They will do whatever they can to make you proud in the choice you have made.'

Seven miles separate Brondby and Copenhagen, whereas it's only a mile between Anfield and Goodison, but Hansen can see a comparison in the rivalries. 'It's a little bit similar to Liverpool and Everton. If you take a family of four; two of them would be with Everton and two of them would be Liverpool. It's more or less the same in Denmark with Brondby and Copenhagen. This hate-love relationship you know, many families have two of each and they need to get on with each other. Of course, you have some hooligans, like you have at all other clubs, but it's similar to the derby in Liverpool I think.'

A game between the teams in the Danish Superliga saw a couple of dead rats thrown from the stands on to the pitch by Brondby supporters, although a statement from sporting director Troels Bech suggests it was just a small minority. There have never been rats infiltrating a match at Goodison or Anfield, but there have been a few spotted pitch side across the M62 at Old Trafford. The Merseyside derby goes through stages in terms of friendliness and nastiness, but is that really the same in the battle of the 'New Firm'? 'It's not friendly, but families have to get on with each other,' Hansen admits.

The goalkeeper spent only a season with Brondby before moving to Liverpool. He played in a tournament which consisted of the four regions: Copenhagen, Zealand, Funen and Jutland. The competition naturally attracts scouts from across Europe, while the young national team is also selected from these performances. 'I think that's the first time that Liverpool saw me, at under-15 going into under-16. After the tournament, I got into the under-16 national team and they saw me in Slovakia for my first national game. I played a really good game and after that it really happened. They followed me a couple of times in Brondby after.'

Hansen had trials with Liverpool, Tottenham and Arsenal. He had the option of choosing between the clubs. 'Liverpool just made a bigger effort, they travelled back to see my family,' he admits. 'They had a lot of meetings with me in Denmark and all these things. From the first sight and what I had seen there, made me feel at home. It was an easy decision to make. Steve Heighway was in my house. Billy Stewart, who was a goalkeeping coach at that time, was there. Even the tutor, who had to look after the academy players, was also in my house. They made a big effort to take me to Liverpool and after that it was an easy decision.

'I moved into a family straight away. The first three months were really tough because I had just turned 16. Every time it was Friday, I was getting ready for the game on the Saturday morning and all my friends were already going out or being together having movie nights, whatever. I was sitting in a completely different country having to be a grown-up before I even knew how to wash my own clothes. That was really tough, the first three months were really tough, but every time I was sitting at home thinking, "Ah, is this worth it?" I would just look at the logo and think, "How lucky you are!"

'You are earning money already as a 16-year-old in one of the best clubs in the world. You would sit and be sad, and then you would think about all these good things that you have and all the chances that you can have just there in front of you. It would make you smile before you go to bed. Also, mentally it made me who I am today. This is the only way for me and that's the football way. I want to make it as far as possible and that was the same in England. You have been given a chance, why not go all in, and do whatever you can. When you are old you can look back and say, "You have given everything."'

It's a situation that many supporters don't consider when their club is buying the most talented individuals across the continent and the tone in Hansen's voice illustrates the struggle he had with his own thought process from an early age. That initial adaptation period was assisted by attacking midfielder Astrit Ajdarevic, who now plays for Djurgårdens after spells at Leicester City and Charlton Athletic. 'He was Swedish, so it was quite easy to get on with him. We lived together and we spent a lot of time together. Nathan Eccleston, who was also living in the same house for a while. But really, I got on pretty good with everybody. I don't think I am so difficult to get along with and I enjoyed getting something socially away from football. Anybody I spent time with.'

Many foreign senior players from that era say that Jamie Carragher and Steven Gerrard often explained the history of Liverpool Football Club to them when they first arrived on these shores, so did the young local lads such as Jay Spearing and Stephen Darby feel the need to do the same? 'Not what I remember, or they didn't with me, maybe they did with someone else,' says Hansen. 'You pick it up quickly. Also, the coaches in all these small meetings you have before training. They just said, "Remember who you are playing for!" and, "It's a privilege to be here, maybe you don't see it right now, but you will if you don't use the full potential, you will see it later." Everybody knew about the history of Liverpool. You could talk about it also with a taxi driver, he would also remind you what club you are playing for or what city you are in now. You pick it up very fast. If you are a young player there, you don't miss out on that for sure.'

Hansen confesses that he wasn't that impressed with Liverpool as a city when he joined the club, but that changed in the modernisation just two years later. 'It wasn't so new, it was an old city, but after it was the [European] City of Culture in 2008.

It is unbelievable now. It's a fantastic city and I say to everyone that I meet, even if you want to go for a weekend, it's really nice there. Lots of new restaurants and a lot of things going on there. It's a big part of me still and I do go back when I have the time too.' Music is a big part of Liverpool, so did he also embrace the Fab Four and the Cavern Club? 'Once, but I wasn't really into the Beatles' music. My parents dragged me down to see it.'

Rafael Benitez signed the young Dane just 12 months after they had won the Champions League. 'I was at the academy for the first year, but after that I was a little bit up and down between the first team and the reserves. I got to train a couple of times and see how they did things at Melwood. It's not like I was sitting talking with him, like we are now, but I got to say, "Hello!" and to see how it worked at that level. How they wanted to do things. I started with the first team in the first pre-season that I was there for two weeks, then I went back to the academy again. So, yeah I actually got to see quite early what was going on in the first team and reserves.'

That first season saw tensions simmer between Benitez and Heighway, as both clearly had their own targets and aims. It became obvious to the players that the two coaches had a number of disagreements with one another. 'I think we played in the [FA] Youth Cup. Stephen Darby, Jay Spearing and players like this were in the reserves at that moment. They were not too keen for them to go down one or two days before the important games for the Youth Cup. Steve Heighway was also living and breathing the Youth Cup and that was pissing him off, you could see that. I don't know what else was going on, but you could feel that. Steve Heighway was a big personality also; he did and has done a lot for Liverpool football club and their academy. He was a tough guy and he only demanded quality from everybody and focus. If we didn't give that then we were his.'

Heighway left the club in 2007 after an 18-year stint as head of youth development, but he returned to Kirkby in a consultancy role in 2015, with an emphasis on 15- and 16-year-olds. In that final season, he won the FA Youth Cup for the second consecutive campaign, a competition that Hansen believes should be adopted across Europe to help produce young players.

'That was really a big thing for me because I was only 16 at that time,' says Hansen. 'As far as I know, it was an under-18s tournament. You go into the stadiums and you play in front of thousands. I think they won it the year before also. So, you already heard them [his team-mates] on how great it was to play in this tournament. You are feeling like a full-time professional, when you are playing in the stadiums and people came out to watch you. Because you also played in the under-18 leagues alongside it and there was maybe a couple of hundred watching these games. Then, you move into a stadium and suddenly it was like real football. People are paying to come in and watch the games now. I think that the FA Youth Cup is something different that the leagues in Europe can learn from. It's putting some kind of pressure on the players and giving them a big stage to perform on, a really positive thing.'

The final is played across two legs and Hansen appeared in the 2-1 defeat to Manchester United at Anfield, but he couldn't play in the return fixture. 'Missing the second leg was of course a very big disappointment,' he admits. 'I broke my finger in the warm-up for the first leg but managed to play the game. I also thought that I could play the second game, but it was too complicated, and the pain was getting worse and worse. But again, I felt a really big part of it because I had been a big part all the way through the tournament. I was just happy that David Roberts could go in and win it for us. I think that's a true team if you have players that can go in and make a difference, even though they haven't played for a long time. It was a fantastic feeling to win at Old Trafford.'

In 2007/08, Hansen moved into the reserves under Gary Ablett, the former Liverpool defender who sadly later passed away in 2012 after a 16-month battle with non-Hodgkin's lymphoma.

'Gary Ablett was a really good coach. He was really good to handle all these young players. He could also give you a bollocking, but he could also tell you how he was seeing things in a calm way. He would pull you aside and talk to you like a normal person, not scream in your face. He was kind of the players' man. He was there behind you and he wanted the best of you, but he also expected you to take responsibility for wearing the shirt. That was on the pitch and off the pitch. He was really loved in the club and he was always in a good mood, with a good sense of humour. He also came in smiling and positive every day and it reflected on everyone else. He was a great coach.'

The stars in his team were Argentinean Gerardo Bruna and Spaniard Daniel Pacheco, who Liverpool signed from Real Madrid and Barcelona respectively. They are both now in their late 20s, with Bruna playing at Irish side Derry City and Pacheco now back in Spain with Malaga. 'Pacheco, he was different class,' says Hansen excitedly. 'Bruna also had skills, but he was nowhere near as good as Pacheco. Pacheco could do things that I had never seen before. Bruna was also really good, but Pacheco also had a good attitude and was also working really hard. I think that's the reason he played in the first team more than Gerardo Bruna did. Pacheco was obviously for me, the best player for a long time. He was the one you would think, "Wow, he could go all the way!"'

Pacheco's fellow countryman Suso arrived a few years later and not only did he feature more for Liverpool's first team, but he also went on to become a regular at Milan in Italy. 'Yeah, but I don't think Suso was on the level of Pacheco,' argues Hansen when I suggest that he has developed to a higher level. 'Suso maybe did it a bit later. Pacheco was the player that you think can do something and it doesn't matter who you are playing against, he can turn anyone. A very clever player.'

Hansen also trained with the club's superstars including Steven Gerrard and Fernando Torres. 'It's something that you cannot describe really. I was sitting watching the finals; it was a little bit unrealistic really. Martin Hansen from Denmark is now here, and he is standing in goal whilst these players are now shooting at you or walking past you or sitting next to you. You think, "Should I say something, or should I just focus on tying my boots and go outside." How do you approach players like this? You find out later that they are also just human, but it's a little bit difficult at the start.'

Naturally, Pepe Reina inspired Hansen the most. The Madrid-born keeper had arrived in 2005 and perhaps doesn't get the credit that the likes of Victor Valdes and Manuel Neuer do when it comes to the evolution of the position. 'He was the player who got me to see the goalkeeping playing style [was changing]. He took it to a different level. He kind of invented a new way of playing football as a goalkeeper. It was not just stopping the balls now; it was playing higher and clearing the balls. It was also when you have the ball, you don't spend time on the floor, you see if you can already start a counter-attack. He was showing that you need to be able to play with both legs. He was showing new techniques on the floor; how to get up quicker; how to play the mind games, all these things. He was the guy that was saying, "Goalkeeping is not about stopping the ball, it's so much more." It's reading the game and anticipating, starting a counter-attack. I think the goalkeeping style is going in a different direction than ten years ago or 15 years ago. He was the guy that showed me where the style is going.'

Reina grew up in Barcelona's La Masia academy with Johan Cruyff as manager of the Catalans, while he also played and trained alongside Pep Guardiola when he was promoted to the first team in 2000. 'You adapted and learned from him in training and you saw the games,' explains Hansen. 'Normally, you are proud when you made a good save and caught the ball, maybe you would stay for a couple of minutes. But he didn't even touch the ground, he was already looking for what is the next pass or how he can help the defence when they want to make the next pass when playing possession or whatever. I think the Spanish style that he brought to England; a lot of other goalkeepers learnt from him also. It's not just standing on your goal line. He was showing that you can play 20 or 30 yards out of your goal and you can prevent a chance.'

Liverpool came second in the Premier League in 2009 as they lost only twice and finished just four points behind Manchester United. But that title challenge didn't really stand out for Hansen, who believes that European competition was the main target during his tenure at the club. 'I think at that time, I feel like Europe was the most important thing because they had done so well in Europe. It was such a big thing that we won the Champions League and were in the final shortly after. The focus was a lot on Europe at that time. Of course, if you finish second you are also very disappointed because it was many years ago since they won the title.'

Those infamous European atmospheres left a lasting impression on Hansen and they became normal with Liverpool reaching the final and the semi-final of the Champions League in 2007 and 2008 respectively, along with the semi-final of the Europa League in 2010. 'At the time, I was there, the fans were really there. You could really feel them because sportingly things were really going well. There was Champions League and a lot of good games at Anfield. You could really feel that something was going on for every single game. There was this, how do you say it? This spirit and atmosphere in the stadium, which was something you couldn't really get anywhere else at that time. I remember when we knocked Chelsea out in the semi-finals on penalties [2007]. I had been to Anfield many times, but [on this occasion] my hairs were just raising. I had goosebumps everywhere on my body and I was just like, wow! These nights are something that you never forget,' adds Hansen in a passionate manner.

'Anfield nights are something that you don't get anywhere else for me. Everybody is hugging and everybody is talking to each other even if you don't know them. The taxi driver is waiting outside the stadium and he is going nuts if there has been a good result. Just the city in general, you can smell the football there. You don't get Anfield nights everywhere else, when there is a big important game there, it's just unbelievable.'

In Germany, Hansen played against Borussia Dortmund at the Signal Iduna Park. The Yellow Wall also sing 'You'll Never Walk Alone' before their players take to the turf. 'There's a consistent level in Dortmund for every game, the supporters are really good. Where at Anfield, they can be a little bit after you, but okay, they have high standards and they pay a lot of money to see their team. They just live their football. They really live their football. They don't go to work on Monday after a defeat and leave it, they carry it on to the next game. They live their football and football was invented in England. It's so personal football in England, much more personal than anywhere else in the world.'

Hansen spent a month at Bradford City in August 2011 and made his senior debut ten days after he agreed the move. He played four times for the West Yorkshire side and never won a match, but that didn't dissuade his enthusiasm. 'That was really the first time that I got to play grown-up football, as I would call it. You come out and see how it is at League Two level. You think, "Whoa, there's no bullshit here, you know!" People really playing there for a living. It was really intense. I remember the games. They were really physical. It was everything. "We die out there together" or "There's no chance we are going to lose this game" – that was the feeling all the time. That's also something that I learnt – these guys are really fighting for every single metre, every single spot in the team. "If you break my leg, I will still tell the coach that I can play again at the weekend" – this type of spirit was there all of the time.'

Robbie Threlfall was another young Red on loan at the Bantams and although they finished 18th in 2011 and 2012, there was a real togetherness. 'There was a lot of banter there of course

– it's England. The dressing room was really funny to be in. I was a little bit disappointed it didn't go further than that because finally I got the chance to play real football, not every third week in the reserve team, where you didn't know who wanted to play or whatever. Now it meant something, and it counted,' Hansen announces excitedly.

The moment when Hansen realised that he wasn't going to fulfil his dream and play for Liverpool's first team stands out and was a hard decision to take. 'The first time I realised it wasn't going to work out was when Kenny Dalglish took over [2011]. When Roy Hodgson was there, we were talking with him about a new contract. He believed a lot in my quality and he really lifted your confidence. It's really difficult to be third choice or fourth choice because you don't get any attention. You're just a tool, you're just supposed to do what you are told all the time and you don't open your mouth. These types of things are tough on you. It's something that you can only do for so long.

'But Roy Hodgson came in and he gave me attention. He looked at me like I was a person and talked to me like I was a person. He encouraged me when I did something good, but this was not so much the other coaches. They just focused more on the basic players. The guys who were playing at the weekend. It wasn't so often that you got a tap on the shoulder and say, "Well done, you did great today!" The focus was more pointed at the important players and that's difficult because you really want to get acknowledged for what you do or just feel you are there and that you mean something to them. Otherwise, I might as well just stay inside. That's the feeling that I had. I had it a little bit at the end under Rafa because I think at that time Peter [Gulacsi] was the one who was in front and then Roy Hodgson came in.

'Suddenly, I felt like a football player for Liverpool. I would get spoken to. I would be stopped on the way to lunch to say, "Hey! Great work today!" Then, I thought okay, there is something for me here, I just need to stay patient and work hard as I had done all the time. Then, Kenny Dalglish comes in and suddenly you're just a ghost again. Doesn't speak to you and just focuses on the main players. You go down a couple of times because there are some injuries in the reserves to train and play some games. That was the time that I thought, "Fuck this! I'm not having this one more time. I'm working my balls off every day. I'm not complaining. I'm doing extra work and all these things. The one thing you could do at least is acknowledge that I'm working hard here, not complaining and doing whatever I can." But I was just a ghost again! Nobody looked at me! That was the time I realised; okay this is Liverpool football club but I'm not accepting this again. I want to be someone who is important to a football team. I want to be looking forward to something every weekend. Not just someone who is travelling with the team to sit in the stand in the stadium. Sit there, then fly home and not be part of a win or a loss, or whatever it is.

'You do that every single day, then every third week there would be a reserve game, where it didn't matter whether you lose or win the game. There was nothing at the end. There was no promotion or relegation, there was nothing. It got too easy. I don't want my career to be easy. I want to achieve things. I want to be one who takes responsibility. I want to be a guy who helps others, all these things. But I didn't have that feeling. I was feeling like a tool, a training tool. I might as well just have been a mannequin you put in the ground and have shooting drills around me. That was the feeling I had. I had 18 months left of my contract and I thought, "I need this excitement." I need to get in my car in the morning and feel, "Wow! I look forward to this day. I look forward to the training. I look forward to this important game we have in this week."

'This, I didn't have in England. I had it for a very short period at Bradford and I was so happy every day. I was really looking forward to train and to see the guys who were playing under the same pressure. That broke me a little bit because it was only a month, but there were some circumstances at Liverpool which meant I couldn't stay, and the coach got sacked in Bradford. Finally, I was feeling part of a team and part of a group of guys socially. They are talking to me like I am a player like themselves. When you are sitting there in the dressing room in Melwood, you were not spoken to in the way that they would to Gerrard, Reina or whatever. You are just third or fourth keeper. And you feel it! My ambition has always been that I want to go as far and as long as possible.

'When Dalglish came, I was older then, but I was treated like I was 16. I thought, "That's it, I'm not doing this anymore. I need to go out and restart my career." I believe in myself and I did all the time, but if you cannot show anyone. Because no one is standing on the bench outside Melwood looking over the fence at what you're doing in training. I wasn't able to show anyone. I wasn't able to go out and say, "Hey, this is Martin and I know how to play football." I needed that in my life. I was miserable at home. I was like, "What is the point! I don't care about the money anymore; I just want to play football because that's what makes me happy." It took me three months to convince Damien Comolli that I needed to leave. That I needed some fresh air. That I needed to kickstart my career. At the end, he said, "Okay."'

Hansen sat crying in Comolli's office. 'I was not happy anymore. I needed something else. I needed to feel like I was a football player, not just a nobody. I was a nobody at Liverpool, I know that, but I wanted to go to that level, and I knew that it wasn't going to be at Liverpool at that time because I could see how they were treating me.'

Hansen signed for Viborg in the Danish second division, who were managed by Jan Molby's cousin Johnny between 2015 and 2017. They were promoted in his first season at the club and it must have been a relief to return to his homeland after the disappointing end to his time on Merseyside, but his response came as something of a shock. 'That was unbelievably tough. In

Denmark, you are not allowed to think you are someone. Now, "Martin Hansen from Liverpool was coming back and he was a big failure. He couldn't handle the pressure. He couldn't do this, and he couldn't do that,"' Hansen surprisingly says.

'But nobody knew the real story that I took responsibility of my situation myself. Nobody, no agent, no coach, no one else. I went to Comolli, who I had only spoken to once or twice [beforehand] and said, "Listen, I am done with this. I believe enough in myself that I can go and build myself back up again." That's the truth! Everybody was making a statement about, "What is Martin? Is he a failure?" or whatever. Nobody knew the truth that I could have stayed in Liverpool and probably signed a new contract if I wanted to. But that wasn't me, I want to go out and play football because this is what I like, and this is what I love. I'm not a Monday to Friday keeper, that's not me. It was so tough to try and explain to people the truth. That I took that decision, no one else! Many people probably just shook their head when I looked away and said, "Hey, he's just telling a story." Me and my wife were the only ones who knew the truth. It was a tough period. Then, you need to go out every single day and show your level in training and in the games. You need to show everything now. That you have been at Liverpool and the quality that you have gained from that period.'

It's hard not to feel a sense of compassion for Hansen and empathise with the situation. He spent 18 months at Viborg and not only received the admiration of his own coach and club legend Soren Frederiksen, but also of rival managers. He left in 2013 to join Superliga runners-up FC Nordsjælland, where he played in the Champions League qualification games against FC Zenit Saint Petersburg. It was just one season for Hansen at the Right to Dream Park before he joined ADO Den Haag on a two-year deal in the Netherlands.

'You see straight away that football in Holland is very different to Denmark or England. There's a lot of attacking football and not so much defending,' says Hansen. That adjustment period occasionally led to irritation, as he was left exposed by his defenders. ADO played SC Cambuur in January 2015, with the fans singing a powerful rendition of 'You'll Never Walk Alone' before kick-off. It was a tribute to 21-year-old supporter Kaja who died suddenly the week before and the club organised the pre-match eulogy which included flags and fireworks. Fellow supporters wore the club jersey with the name Kaja on the back and a huge banner was unfurled which contained the slogan, 'Only The Good Ones Die Young'.

ADO let the lead slip in the 2-2 draw and the dissatisfaction of the occasion saw Hansen leave the stadium straight away in his own car without showering. He took to Twitter that evening to defend his decision. 'If people wish to make a drama of the fact that I have to leave the stadium immediately: go ahead,' was his first message, followed by, 'I live for this game, so I was disappointed and frustrated. And my frustrations I will never ever hide!'

Hansen clearly wears his heart on his sleeve, so when he inevitably makes errors it must be hard for him to recuperate. 'When you play the game, you don't really feel what's around you. But it also comes during the week, during your life. How do you learn from your mistakes? How do you want to get on with it? If you are full of confidence during the week and you train well, then okay, you can make a mistake, but you are still full of confidence and you know that you can bounce back. That comes during the way you train and during the way that you approach every game. Mistakes? They happen for everybody, but if you go into the game full of confidence and focussed, then you are going to forget it quickly and move on to the next section.'

Hansen amazingly provided an assist in Reina-style for Michiel Kramer in the 85th minute of the match between ADO and Vitesse Arnhem, but it was his encounters against PSV Eindhoven that left the most feeling. 'When you play against a player like Memphis Depay, if you give him space then he is going to punish you. He has really good qualities, you can see that. Don't give him any space, I would say.' That PSV side also contained Liverpool midfielder Georginio Wijnaldum, although the Dutchman had departed for Newcastle a month earlier when Hansen incredibly won ADO's Goal of the Season award in August 2015.

'That's one of these things that you cannot really explain. It's just timing, the right time, at the right moment. These things are sometimes in your life. This one second can change a lot of things. It can be a penalty stop in the right moment, at the right time. Here, it was a back-heel in the right moment, at the right time,' laughs Hansen.

So was it just pure instinct or did Hansen regularly perform such tricks in training? 'No, I played a lot of indoor football when I was young, where I used my feet a lot, but this was just trying to direct it to the goal. I could feel that I had hit it really good, but I think I had about 20 players still in front of me before the ball could go in. It just went, perfect! That was crazy! The thought was that the game is not finished yet, that we have not won yet. There was more a feeling that if PSV score now this goal is not going to be as good as it really was. That was more the thought, "Okay, we need to get the win now and then my goal can be as good as it was."'

Hansen joined FC Ingolstadt 04 in the summer of 2016, who had been managed by now-Southampton boss Ralph Hasenhuttl for the three previous years. 'I had two really good seasons in Holland, and I had a couple of options from Germany. It was a little bit the same story as Liverpool, they showed so much initiative from the start. They invited me down to see the club and I spoke with a lot of people in and around the club. They showed me the city and we talked about the situation. How it would be if I came here. I knew that it would be 50/50 fight if I came. So, I thought, Germany, Bundesliga. I spent a lot of time in Germany when I was young with Brondby. The German league has always been really attractive for me to play in and when I heard the situation that there was a good chance I would play and that we would see during the pre-season. I'm a fighter. I'm a competition man. Competition for me is okay, as long as it's fair and I felt it was a fair competition here, so I thought why not? There was a good chance I could get some games in the Bundesliga,' adds Hansen.

Ingolstadt is the newest major city in Germany but has a real village vibe. It's situated 44 miles north of Munich and has much heritage due to its medieval defensive wall and the Kreuztor gates. The Illuminati were formed there in the 18th century, while it's also the site of the Audi headquarters. By the central train station, an elderly man tries to force a cassette into the car stereo of his old Toyota Yaris. In the square, ten senior gentlemen sit around the beer market drinking pints, which isn't that unusual except that it's 9.50am on a Wednesday. Ingolstadt were only formed in their present state in 2004, when ESV Ingolstadt and MTV Ingolstadt merged together. They started their first campaign in the Oberliga Bayern, which is the fourth tier and the highest amateur level. In 2015, they were incredibly promoted to the Bundesliga.

'For me personally, it has been a great ride from going back to the second division in Denmark to build yourself all the way back up to the highest level in Europe again. Not every road to success is straight forward. I spoke with [Daniel] Agger about this. He is one of these guys who was counted as nobody, got his chance in the first team with Brondby and went straight to success. But he had all these twists and turns before he made his career.' Agger is six years older than Hansen, but they both left Brondby to move to the north-west of England in the same year. The centre-back didn't make his club debut until he was 19 but made his international bow a year later and then moved to Anfield.

Ingolstadt's training ground is situated next to the Audi Sportpark arena and all the players have the latest Audis with the number plates IN FC. The reception area, which is situated upstairs, has four girls working in the ticket office. When it's lunchtime, they lock the door and queue up in the cafeteria. It's a completely different atmosphere to the ones encountered in England. They finished 11th in their first season in the topflight but were unfortunately relegated in the year that Hansen played there in 2017.

The Bundesliga saw Hansen pit his wits against some of Europe's top strikers and wingers, but which was the most difficult opponent in his season in the country? '[Arjen] Robben or [Robert] Lewandowski. These two guys; you really have to keep an eye on them all of the time because they move so much. It's one of these two guys. [Pierre-Emerick] Aubameyang, we had him under control in the game in Dortmund. For me, Lewandowski causes a lot more trouble.'

Ingolstadt's relegation meant that the stopper spent the 2017/18 season on loan back in the Netherlands. 'At Heerenveen, it was a little bit special because it was at the last minute. I wanted to play at the highest level possible and of course Ingolstadt went down to the second Bundesliga. I got the chance to stay in a better league and I had to make a decision in four hours. I spoke very quickly with my family and we decided to try and do that.'

Hansen spent four months at SC Heerenveen, but as their keeper Warner Hahn returned to full fitness he was allowed to return to Ingolstadt. 'Then, in the pre-season for the second part of the season he injured his shoulder again and they wanted me to come back and finish the season there. We reached the play-offs for Europe, so it was a good season. I'm happy that I went there to keep playing at a good level.'

Martin Odegaard was among his team-mates at the Abe Lenstra Stadium. The Norwegian signed for Real Madrid at the age of 16 in 2015 and is still owned by the club. He spent his first two years playing for the Real Madrid Castilla, but training with the first team as it was written into his contract. His involvement became something of a power battle between president Florentino Perez and managers Carlo Ancelotti and Zinedine Zidane, with the coaches believing he didn't merit a place in the squad at that time. He is currently on loan at Real Sociedad and attracting praise for his performances in La Liga.

'He is a fantastic kid that is really professional and down to earth,' says Hansen on the young prodigy. 'He was always the last to leave the gym, he was always on time, he was always polite and had a great attitude. He just wanted to get better. You have to meet the person before you can get an idea of what they are like, as I only read about him. He has got a big future ahead of him.'

Hansen was on holiday with his family, when he received a phone call from his agent. Basel's goalkeeper Tomas Vaclik had left for Sevilla and the Swiss club were in need of a replacement. 'There were only four days before the season started and I again had to make a quick decision. I thought whether I should do this or not, then I looked at Basel and the type of club it is. I thought, I have to go! It was a little bit hectic, but it was the right step to make.'

Basel is a very multicultural city with lots of Scandinavians living in the vicinity. The club has an excellent structure and facilities, which has helped the likes of Mohamed Salah and Xherdan Shaqiri in their development to become top players. 'It's a very respected club in Europe. A lot of good players have come through playing at Basel. It's a club that usually plays in Europe. There has been a lot of focus on the club and that's one of the reasons why I came here.'

I spoke to Hansen on two occasions, 18 months apart. However, that period seems to have enabled him to take stock on what's truly important in his life. He hadn't played regularly for six months but was still positive about his circumstances. 'It's tough, but you sometimes have to accept that other people are performing. That's when you have to say, "There's nothing I can do about that!" I just have to do my work, be sharp and if my chance comes then I have to catch it. That's what I do on the training pitch, then off it you have to stay positive and try push the guys in the right direction.

'I'm a dad of three beautiful kids and that also takes up some of my attention. I have to take everything into account now. You have to respect your family life. I can't keep moving my kids around and others. I'm trying to settle. Of course, I want to be playing football all the time and in football it can change in a split second. There can be an offer from a different club, or I can stay here. At the moment, I'm just focusing on what I can control. If a good club comes and says, "Martin we would like you to come here and compete for the first spot or be the number one." I know myself; I rarely say no, if I have an opportunity to play football.' Hansen didn't say no and he moved to Strømsgodset Toppfotball in Norway at the start of the 2019/20 campaign. In January 2020, the now 30-year-old made the transfer back to Germany with Hannover 96.

His time at Liverpool may not have ended in the ideal way, but the goalkeeper hasn't ruled out a move back to England one day. 'England has a big place in my heart because I spent a lot of time there and I learnt a lot of things about football. I got to know a lot of people there also. My wife also has a weakness for England and for sure it's my aim to maybe play one day again in England,' confesses Hansen. 'I went straight from Brondby to Liverpool in the early days, now I have had to work my way around. There are ups and downs, and sometimes you have to take a few steps back to hit the road. It's something I'm really proud of today. That no matter what people have said, or they don't count on me, I know that I can make the highest level and I'm not done yet.'

Chapter 13

Peter Gulacsi, *Hungary, Hull and Red Bull*

'IT'S NOT maybe how people imagine,' says Peter Gulacsi on how he left his hometown club Budapesti Vasutas Sport Club to join the more traditional Hungarian giants of MTK Budapest. 'We just went and asked if I could join the club. You laugh, as this isn't the way things work in England.' That wasn't the only non-traditional method that formed his transfer to MTK. 'A funny story, I had some kind of contract with my old club and I had to pay 20 balls for them to let me go.' Does the RB Leipzig goalkeeper think he's worth more than 20 balls now? 'Maybe 20,000,' he replies. It was just a gesture of goodwill rather than a prediction of his actual worth at that age, but it's still a peculiar transaction to take place between two football clubs with so much money in the game.

Gulacsi grew up in Zuglo, which is the 14th district of Budapest. He lived there with his father Gabor and mother Agnes along with his two sisters. 'It's the closest green area to the centre of Budapest. We had a nice garden, where I could play in my free time. It's just five to ten minutes from the city centre by car. Both of my parents were educated people and I had a very nice childhood. Studying was always the number one priority.'

Gulacsi was a hyperactive child by his own admission and with his whole family so into football, then it seemed like a natural fit to give it a try. 'My whole family was interested in football; my grandparents, my dad, my mom even loved watching football, but no one played football. They said, "Okay, he's an active kid, so let's try it." I fell in love. As I said, studying was always the priority until I was 15 and then I went to an academy. To finish high school and get my A levels was something I had to do and was expected of myself, but football just slowly became more and more important in my life.'

The OTP Bank Liga is the Hungarian national championship and the four most successful clubs in the country all reside from Budapest. Ferencvaros, MTK Budapest, Ujpest and Budapest Honved share 87 league titles between them. But Gulacsi and his family didn't support any particular club or even focus on one league in Europe. 'Everybody in Hungary follows the national team and then in my childhood it became more possible to watch foreign leagues,' he adds. 'First it was the Premier League, then you could watch the Spanish and Italian leagues. It was just something that we did on the weekend. As I can remember, on a Saturday I always watched the whole Premier League games and then the Bundesliga highlights. On a Sunday, from three o'clock it was Serie A games. It was something I always did on weekends and my parents as well. There are a lot of possibilities in Hungary, but we just loved football as a family.'

Gulacsi lived just 100 metres away from BVSC's ground, so he would walk to training each day. He was at the club for eight years before he was sold for 20 balls. 'At 13, a lot of players left to go to bigger clubs because they had more possibilities to become a professional player. We made the decision with my parents that now was the time to make a change and try to see if I could make it or not. It was an important part of my life, but it was more like a family club. With good friendships and relationships. We were also successful, not all the time, but in the youth leagues we were always doing okay. We were not the best though, of course. MTK and Ferencvaros were the two best clubs in Budapest – if not the whole of Hungary – at that age. We took a chance.'

It was less of a chance and more of a natural progression. He already knew the coach and the majority of the players after playing against them on numerous occasions. MTK didn't develop players until they were 13, so they just picked them up from different clubs. Gulacsi was now at one of the powerhouses in Hungary and he had to travel further afield into the capital. 'It's a beautiful city and it's really historic,' he says. 'It's in a very good condition. How it looks is very similar to Prague, maybe not as popular as Prague. But it's really beautiful, with the Danube River in the middle. We have over two million people living in Budapest, so it's a really big city. In recent years, it's become more and more international in terms of shopping and restaurants. The quality of life is quite high especially compared to the other regions in Hungary. Budapest is a big European city now.'

Another footballer born in Budapest was the iconic Real Madrid forward Ferenc Puskas, so his status must be a constant reminder for each hopeful player? 'For us younger generation, not that much anymore. Of course, his legend is still in Hungarian football. Unfortunately, we couldn't live up to that kind of quality in recent times, which is why he is still well remembered. If we had a fantastic team now – I'm not saying people would forget, but maybe it would be easier to focus on the present a little more. Hungarian football is not on the same level as it was in the generation of Puskas and he is a big legend in Hungary. I have of course seen videos, but football has changed a lot since then. You still have to remember and respect him. We just want to do our thing now and if not at that level, we can at least reach something that people will remember.'

After four years at MTK, an unexpected opportunity arose. Gulacsi was now third-choice goalkeeper and would play for the second team. That summer, MTK and Liverpool formed a three-year relationship, where every year one player had the chance to go to Merseyside on loan. The two clubs had previously had transfer dealings when Krisztian Nemeth and Andras Simon made permanent moves to England. 'I had a big decision to make, I had just been promoted to the first team and I had the opportunity to spend a ten-day trial at Liverpool. When you see the facilities and spend ten days in that world, then it's quite obvious where you want to be. It was the first ten days of pre-season training, so a lot of the international players weren't there and it's why the first-team and second team were training together. It was kind of a mixed group. It was a great opportunity to play with some first team players and the goalkeeping coach. When I came back to Hungary after the ten days, I was really desperate to go to Liverpool. When that opportunity came, I said, "Yes!" straight away.'

Gulacsi was already close friends with Nemeth and Simon following their time together in the MTK academy and with the Hungarian national youth teams. The three of them would naturally socialise off the pitch, but it was also important to integrate with the rest of the squad. 'In the beginning it's easier, but you have to be careful not to be just a Hungarian group inside of a club. When you do it clever and pay attention to mix with the team and the others, then it's not a problem. It cannot just be three of you hanging around and not with the rest of the team. We payed attention and I think it worked well. After a few years it changed, Krisztian and Andras left and it was a different situation.'

Nemeth and Gulacsi still keep in touch, with their partners close friends. The former was a promising striker in Liverpool's reserve team and was tipped for an outstanding career due to his finishing ability. He scored five goals in his first three appearances for the second string and was the Premier Reserve League North top scorer in that 2007/08 campaign. Nemeth left the club in 2010 and his path has taken him to Greece, Netherlands, Qatar, USA and now Slovakia with DAC Dunajska Streda. 'After that first season everyone predicted him to be a top player,' says Gulacsi. 'It's just a shame with injuries and maybe not the right moves after, it just didn't go the way that people expected. He had some difficulties, a really good half season in Holland and a good season in the MLS.'

Gulacsi had already adapted to living away from his family in the final two years at MTK, but this was in an environment that he already knew. Now he was moving to a new country and city, although he admits it assisted his personality development. 'It was not easy; I made a decision to live with a family and not to rent an apartment straight away. It was a good decision because they were a lovely family and I was very lucky to have them, and they helped me settle in my first year in Liverpool, until I got to know the city. I literally didn't have to do anything, just play football. They were always there for me and came to watch me all the time. It was a good middle step to becoming more independent. After one year, I was ready to move to an apartment and look after myself. At the age of 17, it was a clever decision. You have to grow up straight away. You have to look after yourself and be strong mentally. It was a big challenge, but I think it helped me get where I am today.'

Liverpool had just lost to Milan in Athens when Gulacsi reached the club. It was their second Champions League Final in three years after victory in Istanbul. 'The time when I arrived at Liverpool, the club was among the best in the world. Not just because of the two Champions League finals, but Rafa Benitez and the squad that we had. This was a world-class environment to be in. The club managed to maintain that for a couple of years. We came a few points short from Manchester United [for the league], another semi-final ... At that time, we had Xabi Alonso, [Javier] Mascherano, Fernando Torres, Stevie [Gerrard]. The squad was absolutely fantastic.'

The reserve side wasn't bad either, with many of the players going on to have decent careers within the game. 'Mikel San Jose, he still plays at Bilbao and has played a few times for Spain. That season Damien Plessis was a big part of things. I think everybody expected him to be a top player. Emiliano Insua is playing for LA Galaxy now and has been in the Argentina squad, So, there were a few big players. From the British guys, Jay Spearing was a main player and Stephen Darby. They played many times for the first team, but unfortunately, they couldn't make it or stay at the top level of the Premier League. They were fantastic players. It was not easy for them. The reserves had just won the treble, and everybody was talking about the next generation. The quality of the first-team squad was on a level that meant it was really difficult for young players to get into the first team. We had such an unbelievable squad, with every position having two or three international players.'

Rafael Benitez was the reason that Liverpool were such a force during this period with the Spanish manager raising expectations at L4. Gulacsi had the occasional conversation with Benitez, but his own standing within the squad meant that he didn't have that much interaction. 'I saw from his work that he is a top manager. I think at that time; he was tactically among the best in the world. We could play against any team and we were always ready and always had a plan to beat them. Wherever he has been, he has been successful. As a group, we had a lot of tactical training with 11 v 11, where we would prepare for situations that we may face at the weekend. This was around nine years ago, and I don't think it was as typical. Tactics are getting more important in football all the time and at that time, I think that made the difference for that Liverpool team. We always had a plan; we were well prepared for our opponents and we knew what their strengths were and what we could expect at the weekend. Maybe tactical sessions are not the most interesting for players, as everyone likes small games and shooting, but Rafa knew what the team needed. It was really impressive, when you are playing every three days and rotating the squad to keep the players fresh. They were always prepared for games.'

Gulacsi had a closer relationship with the goalkeeping coach Xavi Valero, who had only just joined himself. Valero was credited by Torres for his assistance in helping him score goals from one-on-one situations with different goalkeepers. 'He was one of Rafa's right-hand men and Rafa trusted him 100 per cent. If Xavi would have said I was playing at the weekend, then I would have played because he had that much trust in him. I still keep in touch with Xavi. He has always followed my career. He is always giving me advice and commenting on my game, he is a workaholic. I was really lucky to have him at Liverpool. When I arrived there, I was a 17-year-old Hungarian goalkeeper and I still had many things [to learn] such as technically and physically and we worked on those things to help me improve a lot in the three years that I spent with him.'

Liverpool exercised their option to buy Gulacsi at the end of that 2007/08 season, with the Hungarian signing for £225,000. It was much the same for the next five months, but then in February 2009 he had his first taste of first-team football. A reserve team game against Manchester United illustrated his competence at this grade. The next day in training Valero asked Gulacsi how he felt after 18 months at Liverpool. 'I said, "I feel good at the reserve level. I had some games where I thought some improvement was possible, but I was getting there. I was really comfortable at this level." I think when he heard the word "comfortable", that's when he made his mind up. They already knew that there was a possibility to go to Hereford, but they didn't want to discuss with me until they knew how I felt about my game.'

Gulacsi had to go to Benitez's office and then Valero called him to confirm the plan. 'Peter, we want you to go on loan to Hereford United,' said the goalkeeping coach. 'It's a three-month experience and we think that you can benefit from it a lot. It's the next step.' Gulacsi was taken aback. 'In this moment I was in shock because I had been in this safe environment, with fantastic pitches, training with the first team and playing for the reserves,' he confesses. 'It's almost the perfect scenario for a young player. Then, to hear that I had to pack up that afternoon and then in two days I would be playing for Hereford against Yeovil Town. I had no idea what to do. I could see that they both thought I would really benefit. I said, "Of course, I will go!" On my way back to my apartment, I thought what am I going to do now? I got home, packed quickly, took my boots and gloves from the training ground. I was in a taxi – as I didn't have a driving licence at this time – on the way to Hereford, which is a three-hour drive from Liverpool. I arrived at the hotel and then that was it. In one day.'

Gulacsi snaps his fingers. 'I was in another club. I didn't really think about it. At the end, it was such a fantastic experience. Hereford at that time were in the bottom three and we stayed in the bottom three of League One. It wasn't the most successful time and I think that we won three of the first four games and then we never won again for the last 15 games and got relegated. But as a young keeper, I was voted Player of the Month a couple of times. I had so much to do and they were competitive games. League One is not a bad level, it's a different kind of football from the Premier League. As a goalkeeper, I still faced shots, headers, crosses – the same situations. Compared to the reserve league, it was a completely different environment to play in – good stadiums, with 5,000 to 10,000 people. I'm happy I did it.'

Liverpool saw how Gulacsi dealt with the experience and he was offered a new deal. It was a little surprising given the precarious financial position that the club was in. Owners George Gillett and Tom Hicks had placed huge debts on the club and players now needed to be sold or they faced the prospect of administration. 'It's always different what you see as a young player. I think everybody was aware of the situation. The transfer fees that clubs pay today are not comparable with that time, but when you are losing players like Mascherano and Alonso for between €20m and €25m. It's sad to see. In the time of Rafa, he only had the money that he made to spend. It's a very difficult situation for a manager, when you want to compete with Chelsea for example or Manchester United. It's not possible to compete with them with no money. It's very frustrating, when you look at the squad that we had at this time – it was probably one of the best in the world. With three or four more players at the same quality, then we would have been on the level as some of the clubs that I have mentioned.'

Midfielder Alberto Aquilani was among the new recruits in the summer of 2009 having joined from Roma. 'He came to fill the space from Xabi. We had just finished second in the league behind United and expectations were to play on the same level,' says Gulacsi. 'To fill the space of Xabi Alonso is not easy and he is a different style of player. Xabi moved to Bayern Munich at around 33 and was one of the best in the league with his passing. This is how he is. He was a fantastic player. It was not easy for Alberto, he was trying, and he is a very nice guy, but the expectations towards him were on the same level as Xabi Alonso. He is a different type of player and it was difficult to live up to the expectations.'

Despite the evident problems off the pitch, one midfielder that always hit the required standard and beyond was captain Steven Gerrard. 'I always stayed out on Fridays [after training] and had five penalties from Stevie. I think I can count on one hand the amount that I saved in five years. He is just a legend. His qualities as a football player everybody knows – his shooting technique, you can't describe it. The only player that I saw on that same level was Xabi. When they both played in the same midfield, as an opponent you give them one second, then they would change the game with a 40-yard ball, and you have no chance to defend that. As a person and captain, he is such a big idol for everybody. His work rate and passion were just everything that Liverpool was about.'

In April 2010, Gulacsi joined Tranmere Rovers on an emergency seven-day loan deal, which was later extended. John Achterberg was Liverpool's academy and reserve goalkeeping coach and is now the first-team goalkeeper coach for Jürgen Klopp's men. He had previously made over 350 appearances at Tranmere in an 11-year spell. 'John told me about the physio at Tranmere, as if he was some kind of legend. I was like, "I have come from Hungary, I don't know Tranmere Rovers' history!" I went there and again they were in the relegation zone, we had five games to go and had to win four out of five. I went there on the Thursday, trained some set plays on the Friday and then played on the Saturday.'

Gulacsi then witnessed first hand what Achterberg had been trying to tell him. 'The coach runs on to the pitch to treat the players. I had no idea what was happening. I only found out after the game, that he had been the physio at the club for 15–20 years and then the owner sacked the manager and wanted someone that would feel the importance of staying in the league. So, he put the physio as manager.' Les Parry was given the role at Tranmere after they sacked former Reds legend John Barnes and his assistant Jason McAteer in October 2009, and he also continued to be their physiotherapist for the rest of the season. 'We managed to stay up at the end; we played Stockport on the last day of the season and we had 6,000 Tranmere fans away from home invading the pitch after the game. They were taking the crossbar, the net and it was a proper football experience.'

Gulacsi was showing vast progress but his path to being the first-choice goalkeeper was blocked by the extremely talented and reliable Pepe Reina. 'Pepe is a great guy. From my first day in the club, he was unbelievably friendly. He loves joking around, and I think we got on very well. I had so much respect for him. Just to train with him! When you watch someone on the television playing in the Premier League, then the next day you are training with them, it's a great experience. He is not the same type of goalkeeper as I am because my physical attributes are different to his. He is very quick, a little smaller, but still very strong and explosive. He has a different style. He has more technical things, coming from Spain, it's probably one of the best technical goalkeeping countries in the world.

'He was very gifted. Watching his speed in training was fantastic. Also, his role in the club, inside the team, he was a real leader in the team. It was such a close relationship between him and Xavi [Valero]. They both had respect for each other. If Pepe had an idea, then they would try to do it or the other way around. That's how they improved. You could see the level that Pepe played under Rafa; at that time I think he was in the three best goalkeepers in the world.'

Benitez and his managerial team, including Valero, left just a week after the conclusion of the 2009/10 season. The result would have devastating effects on Reina's form. 'For sure, it affected him because he got used to his way of working from Spain to England. He had the goalkeeping coach from Valencia [Jose Ochotorena], then three years with Xavi. That was the way that he was used to. This role in the team and having coaches that understood him was important. With Roy [Hodgson] and Mike Kelly, it was a different environment. They are also good coaches and were unbelievably successful at other clubs, but it was something new for everybody especially for Pepe and his style. The changes didn't help him. I'm also a goalkeeper and I know how difficult it is to change maybe a style of play or training. It didn't help him.'

The next six months were extremely turbulent at Liverpool with Roy Hodgson at the helm. 'He came from Fulham which was a different kind of club,' Gulacsi continues. 'After Rafa, it was a difficult situation for him. Already, under Rafa in the final season, it wasn't what people expected. We had finished seventh but were close to getting in the Champions League. Everyone was used to getting in the Champions League and fighting for the title. It wasn't an easy situation for Hodgson, then we played Europa League which for the club was also something new to play on Thursdays. It was a challenge. We lost quite a few really good players and it didn't go the way that people expected or wanted.

The atmosphere in the changing room was still the same. People were desperate to be successful.'

In January 2011, the public will of the supporters came to fruition and Kenny Dalglish returned to replace Hodgson after a 20-year hiatus. 'Kenny came in at the right time. It was important to bring someone in who was so much-loved and respected by the fans and inside of the club. I think it was a clever move. That was probably the closest that I came to play. I had other times, when I was number two because of injuries. Under Kenny, I was half a season the number two goalkeeper. When you're so close, then you are desperate to get a game.'

It was, ironically, against Hodgson's West Bromwich Albion that Gulacsi felt he was going to make an appearance as Pepe Reina gave away a penalty in the 88th minute. 'I was already taking off my top and getting ready, when I realised that we had already made three subs, so there was no chance and then he was only given a yellow card anyway,' laughs Gulacsi. 'I was fully focused and living the games; unfortunately because we were fighting for top four, there was no chance for me to get any games. Pepe also had the record for not missing any games, which he was happy to carry on. In six seasons, he didn't miss one Premier League game which was fantastic. It was still a great experience to be number two on matchdays. Just to be that involved in the team.'

Another reason for the turnaround in fortune was the signing of a striker called Luis Suarez. 'Luis came in and straight away he performed at the level of Fernando before,' adds Gulacsi. 'It was a great move for Liverpool. He was scoring straight away, and his work rate and passion were so impressive, not just his goals. The amount of goals and kind of goals that he scored; people will always remember him in Liverpool. He was a guy who couldn't lose a single training game or competition, he was desperate to win everything. He would cheat, he would kick you, he would smash you, he would do anything just to win. That's the passion that he has. This passion has got him into trouble often, but without this passion he wouldn't be who he is.'

That summer Liverpool signed Doni from Roma and Gulacsi moved out on loan once again. 'Hull City seemed like the perfect opportunity,' he confesses. 'It didn't go the way that I planned it to go and that was down to me. I had already played around 40 games in League One, but the Championship is a big step forward. Maybe, mentally I wasn't ready for it. It's a very tough league. As a young player – especially a young goalkeeper – to survive there, you have to be mentally really strong. We didn't start the season the way we wanted, we lost to Blackpool, then beat Ipswich and then lost a Yorkshire derby to Leeds 4-1, where I made a mistake.'

Manager Nigel Pearson was immediately under pressure and then when the goalkeeper suffered a minor injury, he decided to make a change. Hull lost their next game to Crystal Palace, but then won 1-0 for the following three matches against Reading, Peterborough United and Portsmouth. 'It was not easy for me to get back in goal and I missed around ten games. Adriano Basso was playing and then Pearson left for Leicester City, then Nick Barmby became manager and I got my place back. From that moment, I was ready, and I knew what it was about. I played solidly. Unfortunately, I had an injury just after Christmas. My medial ligament meant that I missed two months; at that time we signed Vito Mannone from Arsenal, who made a club record of six clean sheets in his first six games.' Gulacsi's injury and Mannone's form meant the Hungarian never really had chance to recover his place. 'It was a big experience and a lot to learn because I realised that when I got my next chance at the top level to be a number one keeper that I knew what to do different. I wasn't ready mentally and it was something to learn.'

Martin Hansen was a fellow goalkeeper at the same time as Gulacsi and he saw something different in the Hungarian's character. 'Peter is just a quiet hard-working guy,' says Hansen.

'An unbelievable talent, I think he was one of the reserve players who you thought can reach a really high level because he was a really good goalkeeper. He had a good mentality, no matter how disappointing a message could be for him or how shit a training session was, you wouldn't see it with him. I think mentally he was maybe killing himself at home, I don't know, but he never showed weakness. It's a very strong thing to have. Maybe, you have a bad training [session] or you are told that you are not training with the first team, even though you were supposed to or whatever. He didn't show that they can break his neck.'

Reina's dip in form and the variety of goalkeeping options at Liverpool must have given Gulacsi some hope that he could one day break into the team. 'I believed, but I had to be realistic,' he says. 'I was more of a number three and then I was number two, when Brad Jones had to go to France for his son's therapy. As a number three it can happen to get a chance and I was always hoping for it. I was realistic and knew my situation, even though I wished for more and I gave my best. It didn't really help me that there were so many changes after Rafa. My development under Rafa and Xavi was an impressive one, I went twice on loan to League One and I think at the time that they left it was the right time to get a season-long loan maybe outside of the UK and go to be a number one keeper. But because of the changes, that didn't happen. I had to start at zero again and then prove myself again and again. We had Roy Hodgson, Kenny and then Brendan Rodgers. It was not easy, but I of course believed in myself that I would get a chance. Then, when the chance came, I wasn't there. I was on loan at Hull, Pepe got a red card and then Doni got a red card. Brad played against Blackburn and then an FA Cup semi-final.'

Back at Anfield, Rodgers arrived from Swansea City with a fresh ethos on football and he told Gulacsi that he would have a fair chance to be the back-up goalkeeper. 'I had to battle with Brad Jones for the number two spot, which means that there's a chance to play maybe in the Europa League, but for sure in the FA Cup or in the League Cup,' says Gulacsi. 'I decided to stay and take the chance. In the end, Brad became number two, probably because of his experience. The style of play of Brendan Rodgers suited me really well, but Brad had that little bit of experience that I didn't have. Pepe was injured quite a lot, so I managed to sit on the bench 15–20 times. It wasn't a bad season for me, but still I didn't play. I played for the reserves and I wanted more.'

Gulacsi was now 23 and he made a decision with his agent that it was time to take the situation into his own hands. 'I still had one year left on my contract, and we said to them that we want to make a decision; I either leave or be number two keeper and start playing. Because of my lack of experience, the club said that they couldn't guarantee that I would be number two, so we decided to look for another opportunity.'

As the Hungarian under-21 national team goalkeeper and captain, it was natural for scouts to watch him in action. Red Bull Salzburg were just one of the clubs monitoring his ability. 'They have a fantastic scouting system,' admits Gulacsi. 'The players we have now at Leipzig and at Salzburg show that we scout young talent, who don't get the opportunity to play at the top level. At that time, the club were looking for a goalkeeper who has international experience, who has trained a lot in a top environment. So, he knows how to play for an offensive team that has control in games and maybe has only one or two saves to make in a game, as was the case with Liverpool. Who also has the motivation to go to Austria because for keepers in top clubs, it's not everyone's dream to go to play in the Austrian league, as they feel that they are already in England or Germany, so why would they leave?

'For me, it was exactly the opposite. I saw a fantastic chance to be at a top club in a country that is fighting for titles and playing internationally. To be a number one goalkeeper because that was my priority, where I'm not just going to be sitting on the bench. They never guaranteed that I would be the number one goalkeeper because no club will do that in the world, but they told me that I would get a chance. I spent three days' trial in Salzburg, because I was only playing for the reserves and the national team, so they didn't really get that much chance to scout me that often to make a decision straight away. I spent three days there, trained three or four times and had some tests. They said they wanted to sign me, and I was very happy, then it was down to the two clubs and my agent to make a deal. It was a massive change from England to Austria, not so much in football terms, but in life. It is a completely different culture. We spent two beautiful years in Austria, me and my wife. We were very happy that this happened, not just because of the club itself, but the country and city were fantastic.'

Red Bull purchased Salzburg in 2005 and the club has won ten league titles since. They finished runners-up in Roger Schmidt's first campaign in 2012/13, with the coach and sporting director Ralf Rangnick playing vital roles in implementing the philosophy which has brought them success. 'Yeah, Roger was important,' says Gulacsi. 'I didn't know him that much before I went to the club, but from the first day I felt that he was a very brave coach, who really liked my style of play. They were looking for a type of goalkeeper that was used to playing for an offensive team, playing high and clearing the balls outside of the box. At Salzburg and Leipzig, we play a very offensive and brave pressing game, where the defensive line is quite often around the middle line. As a goalkeeper, you have to play high and take risks, you have to defend the space behind the defence. From the first day on, I think Roger really liked my style of play and was very happy with me. But he was the type of coach that never said those things, it would only show that he was happy when I played again the next week. He would criticise me for every single goal, he was always fighting with the goalkeeper coach to try to find a better way to defend those kinds of situations.'

Schmidt would obsess over every detail in a bid to gain a competitive advantage. 'He would come to me three days after I conceded the goal and say, "I was thinking yesterday, maybe if you did this!" Then, the goalkeeper coach would be like, "No! No!" He was a very similar personality to Xavi [Valero] in that case, he was somebody that was always thinking what you can do better? How can we improve you? How can you be even better? What solutions do we have for these kinds of situations? I like to work with these kinds of people, as he didn't give me a feeling of, "Oh! He's not happy with me!" It gives you a feeling that he wants more from me. It was with the whole squad. That's why we were so successful as a team, as he gave a feeling to every single player and you could never really be satisfied with yourself because he was pushing you all the time.'

Schmidt and Rangnick also had a huge influence on the development of Liverpool winger Sadio Mané. 'You could see straight away that he was going to be a top player,' says Gulacsi, who spent one season with the Senegalese forward. 'I'm not surprised that he is now one of the favourites at Liverpool. We played some friendly games against Bayern and he was just leaving defenders behind him. That speed that he has in the first couple of metres is just unlearnable. It's something that he was born with and it's just natural.'

Mané is shy and friendly behind closed doors. 'He had the right people around him which is important for those kinds of players that come from difficult situations and become a star so quickly. He is a very nice guy.'

Gulacsi moved to RB Leipzig in 2015, where he was coached by Southampton manager Ralph Hasenhuttl. 'I think he has a very good way to deal with players. On the first day, he brought a very good atmosphere to the team and when you have a young squad like we have, then it's very important how you manage the players. We don't have big stars, who don't need talking to because they just do their own thing and have enough confidence and experience. The young players always need that little bit of care and I think that he does that really well. He always knows when and how to speak to people. On the footballing side, tactically he is very well prepared, and they work a lot on how to make us better and how to prepare for opponents. That's the whole point of RB Leipzig, we have a fantastic philosophy of football and personality. It's always important for our sporting director to not just bring in players that are not just good footballers, but also fit really well into the personality of the team.'

The principles on the pitch behind RB Leipzig are to be admired and could act as a blueprint for many other clubs in Europe. However, the break from the traditional 50+1 fan ownership model in Germany has led them to become the most despised team in the country from a neutral perspective. 'As a player, I don't think that it has that much influence on us,' admits Gulacsi. 'It's more towards our fans. They have more difficulty, when things happen away from home. It's really sad. Us players just go out on the pitch; we don't have influence on what happens outside. I think that it is slowly getting better, and people are getting used to our presence in the top league. It's a shame for our fans when something happens because without fans football is not the same sport. That's why it's sad when our fans have to think about travelling away because that's what makes away games so special, when you have your own fans there.'

Leipzig were only founded in 2009, when Red Bull GmbH purchased the playing rights of a fifth-tier club called SSV Markranstadt. In 2016 they were promoted to the Bundesliga, a year after Gulacsi had moved to the Saxony side. Their first campaign in the top flight exceeded expectations and they were level on points with Bayern Munich after the opening 15 games. They had won 11 of them and lost just once. 'In football, you can just get into that flow sometimes. You just have to keep the momentum going, we didn't really think about it too much. Once you start analysing it, then you maybe jinx it. We just enjoyed every moment of it. When you have that feeling that you can compete at the highest level and it wasn't down to luck because in all the games we won, we were better than our opponent. We just had so much confidence in the team. We already knew about the quality that we had, but you just don't know if that will be enough in a top league. When we realised that our quality would be enough in this league, then our confidence just exploded, and it just keeps on going. That first push in that season has helped everything go so much quicker at the club.'

Leipzig finished runners-up that season and qualified for the Champions League. They regressed to sixth in 2017/18, although there was no doubting the individual talent of a number of their players. Naby Keïta was one who showed significant progress to earn a move to Liverpool as he became one of the best box-to-box midfielders in Germany. Timo Werner was another and the former Stuttgart striker netted 50 league goals in three seasons. 'He has fantastic speed, so he doesn't just have to stay on the offside line,' Gulacsi says about the man who agreed a move to Chelsea in the summer of 2020, having also been heavily linked with Liverpool. 'He can beat defenders that are one or two metres at a disadvantage, that's why he is very dangerous. His speed is very difficult to defend especially how our game is, as we win balls sometimes in the opponent's half and they are a little bit open. Timo is all the time in the right position, so that he is ready to receive the last pass and he is a fantastic finisher. He was a very important player for us.'

Leipzig's closest chance of silverware to date came in the 2019 DFB Cup Final, when they lost 3-0 to Bayern. Robert Lewandowski scored twice, and the Polish forward has been a constant thorn in their side. 'You can't really tell what his biggest strength is. He is good with his head; his finishing is fantastic and his positioning. He is maybe not the quickest, but he is still very quick. He is a fantastic striker. He has been the best opponent.'

I met Gulacsi at the RB-Training Center Cottaweg, which is only a ten-minute stroll across the Jahnallee bridge to where they play their home games. It's extremely quiet as the shot-stopper poses for pictures in front of a future Volkswagen car. He smiles politely and tells them that he likes it, but the reality is he isn't keen on the colour. Gulacsi is content with life at the Red Bull Arena. The club now have former Hoffenheim boss Julian Nagelsmann in charge and are competing regularly at the top end of the Bundesliga. In his private life, Gulacsi has a baby daughter, Domi, with his wife Diana, who works as a wedding planner.

'I left Liverpool as a 23-year-old goalkeeper with no games and now I'm number one for my country and playing for a club who is among the best in Germany and playing in the Champions League. I don't think that you can wish for much more than that. I just try to improve day on day and to stay on this level for as long as possible. I have worked hard for it and I went the harder way for it, but everything I have achieved is down to work. I just want to go the same way. I'm very happy here in Leipzig. It was my big dream to be a number one keeper in a club in a top league, which I am now, and I just want to keep going. You never know what will happen. I never say never, but I'm feeling really good here.'

Chapter 14

Danny Ward, *Wales,*
Huddersfield and Karius

WHILE SITTING on his settee at home, relaxing and watching television, Danny Ward's phone started to ring. 'Listen, you're not going to Wrexham tomorrow, you're going up to Liverpool, you're signing there,' said the caller. Ward sat bemused for a moment; he hadn't even played for Wrexham's first team and here he was being told he was about to join the six-time champions of Europe. 'I thought to myself, "What's going on there! That was a bit of a strange phone call,"' says Ward. It was his agent on the other end of the line, but the content of the conversation was still perplexing. 'It was a surprise. I had a couple of sniffs off other clubs in the year leading up to that and there was interest but nothing concrete.'

Wrexham wanted to keep the 18-year-old but they had just come out of administration. Just nine months previously they had received a £200,000 tax bill from HMRC, so the £100,000 on offer for a youngster who had never played for them was always going to be too much to turn down. At the time they were competing for the Conference title, although they lost out by five points for the one automatic promotion place to Jamie Vardy's Fleetwood Town.

Ward had been at both Liverpool and Manchester United's youth systems as a kid, but he returned to his place of birth at the age of 14. 'To come back to my hometown club was a bit of a culture shock, but at the same time you know the area and you know what the club means to people even at a young age. It was a sobering experience and I think it was one that I cherish especially in my younger age because it makes you appreciate everything a lot more,' he says.

Wrexham's Racecourse Ground is recognised as the oldest international stadium in the world, after it hosted Wales's first match in 1877. It holds less than 11,000 spectators and is in need of modernisation, with one of the stands considered to be derelict. The facilities at the two most successful clubs in English football are naturally better than a non-league side struggling to maintain their finances and Ward knew even as a teenager that he would have to work hard on a daily basis. 'I was lucky enough to be picked up again by Liverpool and you see the different levels, it helps you appreciate things a hell of a lot.'

As a child he travelled with his family to Old Trafford, where he would watch and admire Peter Schmeichel but mainly Ruud van Nistelrooy. 'My dad was a big Manchester United fan, so we used to go and watch every now and then; whenever we did, he would score. When you're a kid and someone is scoring goals or doing fancy tricks you seem to be attracted to them more on the pitch. He was one of my heroes. I wanted to [be a striker] when I was a young lad. I remember I was in my first proper game at my local club, I must have only been six or seven and we were playing the year above. We were playing the Saturday morning, but on the Friday night I had injured half the team just from pure enthusiasm. I wasn't dirty or anything, I was obviously a bit bigger and ganglier than every other kid. We had to call the game off because we had no players. The following week, the manager said to my old man, "Do you mind if we give your lad a go in goal, otherwise we are not going to have a team to put out." I didn't really look back from there since,' laughs Ward.

A former Liverpool striker had helped Ward on his way at Wrexham. Dean Saunders scored 23 goals in all competitions and was the Reds' leading scorer in his single season before he left for Aston Villa. 'It was tough love with Dean Saunders. In a weird way as a player when you get that bit of tough love, you don't really see if the manager likes you or not. It's a difficult situation, but then obviously looking back – even though I didn't play a first-team game for Wrexham – he obviously thought very highly of me and the way he was with me has eventually moulded me into the person I am off the pitch as well as on the pitch which is great, so I was lucky enough to work with him.'

Wrexham also saw Ward train alongside Mathias Pogba, whose brother Paul continues to divide opinions and is never too far away from the spotlight. 'In terms of Pog, if only he was like Paul then I think Wrexham would have been in the Premier League by now,' jokes Ward. 'He was a good lad. He's a very big lad, a big presence. He wasn't a bad dancer actually, so he might give his brother a run for his money.'

Ward joined Liverpool in 2012 and he remembers the strong competition of Pepe Reina, Brad Jones and Peter Gulacsi that were ahead of him in the pecking order for the number one jersey. 'When I first signed, I had a couple of days over a month at Melwood and it's just a way of settling in. You get introduced to some big personalities especially Pepe, who is a real character. At that I think he was going through a bit of a tough spell himself and maybe his form had dipped a little bit on the pitch, but when you see him behind the scenes, the way he trains and the way he works hard, you always know that he's a top-class goalkeeper. It's no fluke that he is where he is now and he has medals from World Cups and European Championships, which is brilliant, and he deserves it because of the hard work that he does regardless of what people see on the pitch. I was lucky enough to see behind the scenes.

'I didn't see as much of Brad when I first came because of the tragedy of what happened with his family and his young boy.'

Jones had lost his six-year-old son Luca in November 2011 after a year-long battle with leukaemia. The Liverpool players wore black armbands in a sign of respect in the 2-1 victory over Chelsea that season. 'It was heartbreaking and affected everyone at the football club I think, it was a real sobering experience for everyone, none so more than Brad. He came back and started playing a few reserve games just to get fit. Something like that will affect anyone in any walk of life and Brad to be fair was amazing especially when he came back in. The mental strength that he showed was absolutely amazing. You have a real respect for the man because of what he has been through. He wasn't so much overlooked, which is a horrible word, but he was always kind of in the background.'

Jones spent nine years with Middlesbrough before he moved to Liverpool. In 2016, he joined Feyenoord and his 17 clean sheets helped them to win their first Eredivisie title in 18 years. Jones's height and his time in England meant he was good at taking crosses and relieving pressure on the Feyenoord defence. His assistant manager was Jean-Paul van Gastel and he regards the Australian as one of his favourite-ever goalkeepers. 'He was very important,' recalls Van Gastel. 'He was one of the older guys and he was used to being in squads in England. He was a winner. For the young guys in the dressing room, he was very important because everyone listened. He had the power that everyone listened to him.'

Van Gastel noticed that Jones was not only a nice guy but also had a strong work ethic. 'He was hard working, always busy working on his body – on the pitch and in the gym. You could have a good pint with him and enjoy life. He made a very good impression on me. He was very professional.'

Ward was also clearly impressed with him from his time at Liverpool. 'People didn't get as much chance to see him in a Liverpool shirt, as much as he would have liked, I know that for a fact but behind the scenes he was probably the most professional player that I have ever been around. His work rate was phenomenal.'

Gulacsi was another keeper who Ward learnt from and had great admiration for. 'Pete was a character as well. He was a funny guy Pete; I spent more time with him in the reserves. Again, it's no fluke where he is because he works hard. Having ability is probably about 40 per cent of it, another half is your attitude and the rest of it is working hard. If you don't have that work rate and that desire to push yourself every day, then you won't reach the top level.'

As well as the goalkeepers, Liverpool's attacking options were also of a high standard with Luis Suarez, Philippe Coutinho and Mohamed Salah all around in Ward's tenure. 'At the time when we had Luis, I think we didn't really appreciate him as much, we kind of took it for granted especially the boys training around him all the time. What he did in training was magical sometimes. I remember him getting the ball with his back to the by-line, in line with the goal that I was in and somehow he managed to whip the ball over as if it was going over two crossbars and all of a sudden it drops in the stanchion in the far corner. You just stand there in amazement.'

Coutinho impressed and adapted easily to Jürgen Klopp's philosophy. 'He really matured into that star man role. He has undoubted ability and his work rate as well. The counter-pressing and the real high energy game, it comes from the front players and I think Phil took to it like a duck to water,' said Ward. The talented Brazilian moved on to Barcelona in January 2018, but he has rarely been missed with Liverpool's attacking trio of Roberto Firmino, Sadio Mané and, of course, Salah.

'I think he is right up there,' says Ward about the Egyptian. 'He got some unfair criticism the one year,' he adds about the 2018/19 campaign. 'Just because he didn't go out and score a thousand goals or something like he did in the season before. Having that season has put a little bit of pressure on him and I think he has handled it really well. I think he has had another fantastic season and it just highlights how big a season he did in his first year. Also, the other boys around him are chipping in. People like Sadio have had amazing seasons and you see them from a different angle when you look from afar like I have done this season. You appreciate how good Mo is 100 per cent.' Salah and Mané both finished the 2018/19 season as top scorers in the Premier League with 22 goals alongside Arsenal's Pierre-Emerick Aubameyang. They both scored more than 15 goals each in Liverpool's title triumph a year later.

Ward also played with some extremely talented players who hoped to reach similar heights but for whatever reason failed to fulfil their potential. Mario Balotelli, Iago Aspas and Christian Benteke were just a few who didn't acclimatise to Liverpool life, a fact which bewildered Ward. 'I think Mario wasn't really a surprise just because obviously everyone knows the way Mario is. It was more frustration because you could see in training that he had everything, he had the presence, he was strong, could hold the ball up, was quick and had probably the most powerful shot I have ever seen in my life. Sometimes you would just close your eyes when he was driving it and just hoped it would hit me somewhere.'

Regarding Aspas, 'I didn't see him practising corners too much down at Melwood,' said Ward, in reference to the infamous time the Spaniard's corner set up a counter-attack for Chelsea during the title challenge of 2013/14. Aspas had illustrated many of the same characteristics which had made Suarez such a force and regular observers of La Liga knew there was a quality player waiting to be unleashed. 'He struggled a bit with maybe the culture of British football as it's a bit more physical and Iago is only quite slight. He definitely had the ability, everyone at the club knew it otherwise we wouldn't have paid the money that we did. These things happen in football; it didn't work out for him at Liverpool and he has gone back home to Celta Vigo and he has been flying. Then, he scores on his debut for Spain, it just shows that football is a funny world – it might not work out somewhere and then you go somewhere else and things seem to click for you.'

Benteke was phenomenal for Aston Villa with 42 goals in 89 appearances across three years. 'Christian was along the same lines as Iago, sometimes you go to a club and these things don't work out. He was a lovely fella around the training ground, and he has got real quality, but it just didn't work out for him. That's football and hopefully it works out for him elsewhere.'

Ward's first taste of regular football came in 2015/16 with Aberdeen and he certainly feels that the Scottish Premier League is under-rated. 'I think it doesn't get the credit that it should. It's a strange league because people compare it to down here in England, but there's some real talent up there and tough teams to play against. It's the same as any other league, you have different styles of play. Teams have to work on their budgets and at the moment Celtic are miles ahead in that respect because of the Champions League and the rich history they have got.

'I absolutely loved my time up there. The Scottish people were great, they made me feel really welcome and you actually feel part of the city when you are there. People down here automatically put the standard of the football down there, but it was very good. I think it was invaluable at that point to get a regular run of games and to see what it was like to be a number one. I can only thank everyone at Aberdeen especially Derek McInnes because he took a bit of a punt on me. He had only seen me play under-21s football at that time and a couple of games at Morecambe from the season before, but fair play to him. I like to think that I repaid him in the time that I was up there.'

Ward kept 13 clean sheets for the Dons and his form impressed Brendan Rodgers, so much so that his loan spell was cut short in the January. However, he had to bide his time before making his Liverpool debut against Bournemouth, when he had to produce several saves in a 2-1 victory. 'It was quite strange coming back from Aberdeen – from playing every week and then having that transition to being back on the bench working towards a chance with the first team. The flip reverse I had for six months was trying to keep people from having the shirt that I was wearing, but it was another challenge. When the manager finally decided to give me a chance it was amazing. I didn't feel out of place, which is something I was more pleased about regardless of the result. It felt not comfortable, but you felt confident with the players that you have around you. When you have Lucas Leiva and Kolo Toure with so much experience in front of you it can calm anyone.'

In the summer of 2016, Wales competed in their first major tournament in 58 years and only their second in the country's entire footballing history. Wayne Hennessey had started all ten of their qualifying matches for the European Championships, conceding only four goals, but the first-choice goalkeeper suffered a back spasm in the build-up to the opening game in France. Ward had previously made two substitute appearances at international level so the fixture in Bordeaux against Slovakia was his full debut. 'It was amazing, the whole thing seemed to go by in a flash. From that first game, which obviously some of the memories of that will always be with me and my family. It was probably one of the most special moments of my life. It was unexpected, but so special.'

Their performances united a nation and drew admiring glances from a number of underperforming footballing powerhouses including England. 'When you are there, you are in this bubble. You get a game and then a day when all the families are there, you sit and have some food, catch up and find out what's happening back home,' adds Ward. 'Then, you obviously see the social media aspect of it with the Wales fans taking over France. We were in amazement and you don't appreciate it fully until you are back on that bus going around Cardiff and there are thousands of people welcoming the football team home. For that period of time especially, it was football over rugby which is a big thing in Wales. The experience was amazing and the fact you got to spend it with special people like that. People always go on about team spirit, togetherness and Wales have got it. We are a real brotherhood and to live in each other's pockets for the length of time that we did, which was 24/7, it was amazing that there were no little irritations. It was amazing, really special.'

That unity was exactly the image that Nicky Wire, James Dean Bradfield and Sean Moore had when writing the official Wales song 'Stronger Together' for the tournament. 'Do you know what?' says Ward. 'One thing I will take from the Euros. Every morning, me, Wayne Hennessey and Owain Fon Williams would go into the gym. We would go on different training facilities such as on the bike. Wayne would say, "Right then lads, come on!" and he put the Manic Street Preachers song on. Before anyone else got there the three of us would just be screaming our heads off singing it because even though we were having a bit of a laugh and a joke, it's actually quite a good song. We learnt all the lyrics, it's brilliant.' Is it the Welsh 'Three Lions'? 'It will be for me especially because we did so well. It's another reminder of the tournament itself.'

Chris Coleman's men not only exceeded expectations in France but gave Wales their proudest moment in football. So what did Ward put the success down to? 'Having Gareth Bale!' quips the 27-year-old. 'It was a mixture, we had some really good players obviously Gareth speaks for himself, Aaron Ramsey, Joe Allen, Ashley Williams, all through the spine of the team. I think even the players that don't get a mention [often], the Mr Consistents like Chris Gunter, Neil Taylor, Joe Ledley and big Wayne in goal. Everyone was putting a shift in and it was all about the team, it was never about each person trying to make themselves look good or worrying. We all knew that we were in it together regardless and that was probably what was our biggest strength.'

The hard work ethic installed within the squad helped them to overachieve, but it certainly helps when you have a world-class superstar that plays for Real Madrid. 'The guy is built like a racehorse,' says Ward on Bale. 'He's quick and on his day, you can't stop him regardless, the only way to bring him down is to try to tackle him and that's if you can get near to him to do that. From a goalkeeping point of view, he's so consistent, he has got an absolute hammer of a left foot and the movement he gets on the ball and the accuracy is frightening. Sometimes you might have one in 20 that go in the top bin from maybe a normal player and it's done all sort of crazy movements. But with Gareth he's so consistent it's a surprise when one doesn't hit the target.'

Ward then spent a season on loan at Huddersfield Town, with Klopp's friend and former Borussia Dortmund reserve team manager David Wagner in command. 'I really enjoyed it, again coming to a new league is a challenge. The Championship is such a hard league, there are so many big teams and so many games. They all want to get promoted and if you look across the board you can pick out maybe 15 teams that could realistically go up. We had an amazing start.'

Wagner's philosophy was very much in line with Klopp's way of thinking, as he demanded his players to press together and for his defence to play higher up the field. The two coaches are close away from football, with Wagner performing the function of best man at Klopp's wedding. 'I don't think it's so much that they work the same, it's just the continental approach,' says Ward. 'We trained in the afternoons a lot more and we had double sessions if we had a full week leading up to a game. The manager [Wagner] had his way of doing things which is fine because all the boys were buying into it.

'The same at Liverpool, the manager [Klopp] came in and changed the training times a little bit. The general style of play was quite similar; try to keep the ball, play fast attacking football and get your flair players on the ball. At the same time, when you lose it the instant reaction is to win the ball back. That's not just one or two players, who could get played around, that's the whole team. The keeper being a sweeper, the back four squeezing in, the midfielders getting about making sure they are in the right positions and the forward players doing their bit for the team. The attacking players get a lot of credit for the creative play because they are very talented boys, but at the same time I don't think they get enough credit for the high pressing and the sacrificing of themselves for the team.'

This style of football means that the goalkeeper has a different tactical responsibility and therefore some are better suited to playing as a sweeper-keeper. 'If you are going to go and press a team, you can't leave a massive gap between yourself and the back four. In a low block, when you are under the cosh a bit you can't be too high because the quality of the players means they can score from anywhere if you are stood on the edge of your box and the rest of the team are in a low block. There are always little things you can pick up, different starting positions from different areas that the ball is on the pitch. If someone puts it down the channel, then it's making a decision. If you are in the right place, then you are able to make a quick decision. Most of the time it's the right one, you either come to clear your lines or let it come into your box and stay at home. I will see where the next one is, where's the striker? Is he going to cross the ball? Is he going to drive in? You try and be proactive as a footballer especially as a goalkeeper. You have to concentrate for so long, but sometimes things aren't in your control and you have to react off what's going on in front of you.'

Huddersfield were promoted to the Premier League at the end of that season after beating Reading in the play-off final. Ward saved two penalties in the shoot-out after extra time to go with another penalty stop in the semi-final game with Sheffield Wednesday. 'It was probably – bar playing the first game of the Euros for Wales – the best experience I have had in football. The whole day. Everyone dreams about playing at Wembley and to finish it off in that fashion is the best possible way you could as a goalkeeper; a clean sheet and to save a penalty that helps your team get promoted to the Premier League. The pressure is massive, as everyone labels it the richest game in football. It was special.'

With Loris Karius and Simon Mignolet fighting it out for the number one spot at Anfield, it was expected that Ward would stay with the Terriers for another year. Huddersfield still required a goalkeeper and Ward needed playing time at the highest level, but Klopp had other ideas. 'I thought it would have been better for myself personally – I think it would have been better for all parties. The club at the time had their reasons for it. At the end of the day, I was a Liverpool player and Liverpool's needs come first.'

Ward's return to Merseyside and several high-profile errors from Karius and Mignolet in the first part of the campaign led to many supporters to question Klopp's decision not to use the Welshman. 'It was very frustrating. I look back after being there for a number of years, I maybe didn't get as many opportunities as I would have liked, but thankfully when I did get them, I felt like I did quite well. It might have endeared me to Liverpool fans a little bit more. That last season when we came so close with the whole Kiev experience, it was tough looking back.'

Liverpool reached the Champions League Final in 2018 and, despite the difficulties in travelling to the Ukraine, the capital city was a sea of red. The defeat to Real Madrid was naturally hard to take for fans, but the experience en route to the game was one that will never be forgotten. In the match, Ward's international team-mate Bale scored a ridiculous overhead kick, although Karius's mistakes probably stand out more for the Kop faithful. 'Me and Loris are the exact same age, born on the same day and in the same year. People forget that at the time it happened for a goalkeeper, he was such a young lad. It must have felt like he had the weight of the world on his shoulders after that.'

Karius stood desolate on the pitch at the end of the game as Los Blancos began to celebrate their 13th European title. Ward was the first to console the German in a moment that didn't go unnoticed. 'I just put myself in his shoes, if that was me it would have felt like the loneliest place in the world. As a goalkeeper, the 18-yard box alone in 90 minutes can feel like a lonely place, but after something as high profile as that. The way the game went, must have felt like he was all on his own. I thought it was only right to go over and console him because at the end of the day, we have been through a lot together.'

Ward's relationship with both Karius and Mignolet was extremely positive throughout, despite the rivalry for the first-team spot. 'The thing with goalkeepers is you spend so much time in each other's company on the [training] pitch, you are constantly trying to push each other and it's a healthy competition. If you see one of the boys doing a bit extra in the gym or on the pitch, then you think if they are doing that then, I have got to do that and more. The other boys had the same sort of mentality and it pushed us on and nearly brought us a Champions League.'

The introduction of Alisson Becker in 2018 was a major contributing factor in Liverpool going one step further and claiming the trophy a year later. It was a world-record fee for a goalkeeper at that time and Ward knew instantly that he wasn't going to get his opportunity, so a day later he left for Leicester City. 'We were just getting ready to play Blackburn in pre-season and I played a couple of halves beforehand. I missed the Burnley game, then the manager said I would be playing against Blackburn. The day before I had a phone call to say a bid had been accepted. I came in the next day and I was like, "Well! I'm obviously not going to play tonight because I have got to get myself down to Leicester." I spoke with the manager and a few of the boys, then I came down.' Ward would obviously have loved to have played on a more regular basis, but he has no regrets about spending time under the tutelage of Klopp. 'I loved my time working with Jurgen. The way he got the boys playing, the way he made you feel, even squad players felt that love. I feel quite lucky to have worked with someone of that sort of calibre.'

He knew that he would likely be back-up to Kasper Schmeichel for the Foxes, but he would at least get more action. He made his debut in a 4-0 win over Fleetwood Town in the second round of the EFL Cup in the August and then was the penalty hero again in the next two rounds against Wolverhampton Wanderers and

Southampton. So, how did Ward get so proficient at stopping shots from 12 yards? 'It's not the 12 yards that's the issue, it's the rest of the 90 minutes I think,' he laughs. 'I don't know. I think it's a bit of luck to be honest. I have been a bit fortunate that in the last few years it's one penalty shoot-out that I've lost and the rest we have managed to come through. It's not just me, the lads have still got to put the ball in the back of the net as well. I just try and keep them out and fortunately I have been able to do that on quite a few occasions in the last few years.'

Tragedy struck Leicester City on the 27 October 2018 when their owner Vichai Srivaddhanaprabha died in a helicopter crash outside the club's King Power Stadium following their Saturday evening match with West Ham United. The Thai billionaire was one of five people aboard the aircraft. He had created a real family atmosphere since taking ownership in 2010. 'It was really difficult for everyone and for obviously different reasons as well,' admits Ward. 'There have been players and people around this place that have been here for the whole journey with the boss and to see them. The new boys arrived last summer, and we spent a lot of time around him. In pre-season he came and made himself known to all the boys. He was a special guy. It was really hard for everyone to take, not just in Leicester but in world football. It was such a tragedy and a shock.'

Claude Puel was sacked as Leicester manager in February 2019 and replaced with Ward's former Liverpool boss Rodgers. 'I'm loving it,' confesses Ward. 'It's a fantastic club and has a real family feel about it, not just between the players with the great spirit in the training room, but also around the place. Not just the coaching staff and the media people, but everyone – the people in laundry to the people in the canteen and at the ground. I'm definitely loving it.' Rodgers almost won the Premier League with Liverpool and Ward witnessed the run-in first hand. 'Going so close to the league was no fluke; all right we had quality players, the likes of Luis and Stevie, but the manager at that time moulded the team together. We were desperately unlucky, and we just fell short at the end which was heartbreaking for everyone.'

The competitive friendship that Ward now enjoys with Schmeichel and Eldin Jakupovic at Leicester is similar to the one that he had with his colleagues at Liverpool, although there are differences. 'With Kasper, Eldin and even the young boys as well, we all train as one big unit. Which was a bit different after Liverpool with Melwood and the first team away [from the younger keepers]. You might come across some of the young boys, who come up for a few days training. There's a real goalkeepers' union about this place and you get to see the under-18s. We try and give them little pointers; it's brilliant not just for us as senior keepers, but for the young lads as well.'

Monaco finished second in France's Ligue One in 2017/18 to follow up their title-winning campaign the year prior. The club's ability to sign players for cheap and then sell them on for a vast profit has been admired across Europe. Manchester City, Liverpool and Chelsea have been among the clubs to pick off the talent and Leicester joined them with the acquisition of Rachid Ghezzal in August 2018 and then signing Youri Tielemans in the 2019 winter transfer window. 'I think Rachid has got a lot of quality. It's sometimes difficult for boys from foreign countries to come in and adapt to the Premier League straight away. It might take some more time than others. We see what he's about every day in training and we know how good he is. He has the world at his feet, when he is running at people with that left foot.' Ghezzal spent the 2019/20 season on loan at Fiorentina in Italy having struggled to acclimatise at Leicester. 'Youri has been the complete opposite and he has taken to the league like a duck to water. That happens, it can go either way, but you can't write people off. He has been fantastic; I think that in sync with the manager coming in has really helped us, with the way that he wants to play. Youri can play as a number six, as a number eight, or further up the pitch. He can make the final pass and move around. I think he has been absolutely brilliant for us.'

Chapter 15

John Achterberg,
Tranmere, Coaching and Alisson

'THERE WERE some great times and then some not so good,' explains John Achterberg about his time as a goalkeeper across the water. 'We had some really good periods in the cup and things like that, but it's not good when you get relegated.'

Achterberg is originally from Utrecht, Netherlands, a beautiful city and often under-rated part of the country. It regularly gets overlooked by visitors in comparison to the more notorious Amsterdam and Rotterdam. The Liverpool goalkeeper coach played for five years in his homeland with NAC Breda and FC Eindhoven, but that isn't where he is describing. Achterberg had 12 years on Merseyside as a player with Tranmere Rovers. He arrived on the Wirral at the age of 27 and 22 years later he is still there. Achterberg is testament to the idea that Liverpool as a city can really get under your skin and it can easily be embraced, although he has certainly been fortunate for it to work out that way.

John Aldridge was his first manager at Prenton Park, but a dispute over his contract almost saw Achterberg leave in 2000. He was even dropped by Aldridge for that year's League Cup Final against Leicester City. The issue was resolved and Achterberg was restored to the team the next season as they enjoyed another good cup run, when among other results they defeated Everton 3-0 in the FA Cup. They also beat Southampton 4-3 after trailing 3-0 at half-time, although goals from Danny Murphy, Michael Owen, Steven Gerrard and Robbie Fowler saw them knocked out by Liverpool at the quarter-final stage.

Their league form wasn't so good, and they were relegated into the Second Division. Tranmere remained there for the rest of Achterberg's playing career, during which time he worked with Dave Watson, Roy Mathias, Brian Little, Ronnie Moore, John Barnes and Les Parry. With over a decade of service and a variety of ups and downs, then Achterberg is surely a legend of the club. 'I think that's for other people to decide, to be honest,' he says modestly. He did have a variety of opportunities to leave the north-west throughout, but ultimately he didn't because his family were always happy in the area.

The last 11 years have been spent coaching Liverpool's goalkeepers, which has also given him a mixture of emotions. 'I was 38, I had been player-coach at Tranmere for the last three years,' says Achterberg. 'I always had the idea that I would do this after playing.' It was Rafael Benitez and Xavi Valero that offered him the opportunity to join Liverpool. 'I had a few meetings with them, and they asked me to coach the reserves and to try and help the academy to improve. I didn't have to think too long about it because it was the natural next step.'

Achterberg worked with a number of young goalkeepers in this time including Peter Gulacsi, Martin Hansen, Dean Bouzanis and Charles Itandje. 'I would just talk to them about my experiences as a player,' he says. 'They obviously had some good qualities and I tried to develop them by creating sessions to improve their individual needs.' His philosophy of playing on the front foot and teaching goalkeepers to work in an attacking way is the reason that he was brought to Anfield by Benitez and also why he has been successful in recent years with Jürgen Klopp as manager.

'You try to help them to reach their level, and hopefully you give them the right instructions. You are there to help everyone. You want them to get better and hopefully help them in their career.'

The role of coaching goalkeepers beneath the first-team squad is about nurturing the talent and preparing them mentally for the challenges to come. It's perhaps harder than teaching outfield players because the opportunities at clubs the size of Liverpool are less likely. There can only be one goalkeeper on the pitch, while the scrutiny and responsibility are far greater. The relationship between coach and player is often much more personable, as a cycle of evolution is created.

In 2011, Achterberg was promoted to the first team by Kenny Dalglish, where he worked with Pepe Reina, Brad Jones and Doni. 'The level was good,' confirms Achterberg. 'Pepe had big experience and done really well before I started. It was good to work with them, but also to learn to deal with that level of goalkeeper. You just give your thinking and try to help. I gave my experience, but Pepe, of course, had huge experience and Brad had played in the Championship. Still, I hope that I gave them some things to think about and some help in their way of playing.'

Achterberg knew that he had to adapt his teaching style as he was no longer shaping future footballers but instead modifying seasoned professionals. 'That is your job, no? You are there to assist, try to improve, to see things, to discuss with them and show them which video to help them to reach an even better level.'

In Brendan Rodgers's second season he signed Simon Mignolet from Sunderland and without any European football to contend with, the Reds went from seventh to runners-up and narrowly missed out on the league title by just two points.

'Some people say that he [Mignolet] didn't improve in the period he was here, but if you look at the games before he came to us then he improved a lot,' confesses Achterberg. 'Simon would probably tell you himself that he improved a lot since he came from Sunderland to Liverpool. I know people were not positive about him all the time, but Simon also played a lot of good games. In the end, it was decided to get a new goalkeeper and that's how it works in football. I think all the goalkeepers have improved. If you work with them day-in day-out, you can see them closely. You can see that they have improved and made steps.'

Mignolet was just 21 when he arrived at Sunderland and he had to compete with Craig Gordon for the number one spot. He played in more games than the Scottish international in their two years together before Gordon left for Celtic. The Belgian was praised for his good performances by fellow goalkeepers and managers at the Black Cats, but the surveillance on his every move was much more limited. Rodgers wanted a goalkeeper that was comfortable in possession and he had seen enough of Mignolet to convince him he could progress further.

'He improved in everything,' admits Achterberg. 'In his crosses he improved a lot and in his playing. I know people made comments, but his shot-stopping was already good. He has improved in all aspects, I would say. He obviously got more experience from playing in big games and under pressure. You are learning every aspect, in order to deal with situations. All that stuff you work on day-to-day in training.'

Klopp is the fifth manager that Achterberg has worked with at Liverpool and although each has had their own tactical ideas, the goalkeeping coach insists that his job hasn't altered that drastically since he first arrived. 'The role hasn't changed too much because my thinking of a goalkeeper fits within the way Liverpool want to play,' he says. 'So, you want a goalkeeper who can play a high line, who can sweep up behind, who can come for crosses, can launch a quick counter-attack to relaunch the game fast, can play with his feet for build-up play. They are all aspects that you want. That's the profile of the club and that's how you want to teach the goalkeepers from the academy through to the first team.

'That's what you look for in a goalkeeper, if you are looking to buy one. Are they good all-round? Because if you teach goalkeepers to be good all-round, then they can play in any team. If you play in a really defensive team it's different. If you play for Burnley, you may spend the 90 minutes on the 18-yard box behind the defence. It asks different questions of goalkeepers. We have a team that plays in the opponent's half, so that means the goalkeeper has to cover a lot more space behind the defence. So, it's a different way of goalkeeping and you try to teach that. You have to find a goalkeeper that works and plays in the same way.'

Klopp's style of football has been more organised and systematic in its approach than previous coaches. The German boss makes no secret of his huge faith and belief in his fellow management team, which means he can focus solely on his own task in hand. 'He gives us the responsibility to make the sessions and how we work the goalkeepers. Obviously, we talk about the goalkeepers, but he trusts the way I work and how I think. He can see what we do, so he knows how we think. He trusts me in what I do!'

Liverpool are now much more than the 'gegenpressing' machine of Klopp's early years at Anfield. They now have a mixture of skills at their disposal which allows them to combat various teams' approaches towards them. 'You prepare for what's going to happen in the next game and what the opponents do,' confesses Achterberg. 'You try to make sessions to show this.' The coach will show his players footage of future opposition and explain to them how they attack, how they press and the individual strengths and weaknesses of their players. 'What they do with corners! What they do on free kicks! Do they press the goalkeeper! You prepare them beforehand and use the information to make training improve! It's a whole cycle, you have to look at everything.'

Loris Karius joined Liverpool in 2016 after five years with one of Klopp's old clubs, Mainz. He was deemed to be better suited to working with a higher defensive line, but a few high-profile mistakes saw the pundits assemble to ambush. 'Hopefully you sign the best goalkeeper that you can sign,' Achterberg explains.

'That's what you do. If you sign a goalkeeper with potential, then you hope you can turn that potential into the best. But there is never a guarantee in football! You try to help and try to improve and that's how it is!'

After a period where both Mignolet and Karius were rotated, the former Manchester City academy player displayed some consistency at the start of 2018. Liverpool lost just four games from 22 in all competitions when Karius was between the posts. The perception of him was beginning to change but then Liverpool met Real Madrid in the Champions League Final. Sergio Ramos collided with Karius just moments before his attempted throw-out was intercepted by Karim Benzema for the opening goal. There was little he could do about Bale's acrobatic finish to give Madrid a 2-1 lead, but the fumble for the third was a catastrophic moment for the youngster. 'You have to try and stay positive,' says Achterberg on how he assisted Karius to deal with the situation. 'There are too many people that think too negative and that doesn't help. I tried to be positive and spoke to him, it's the only way I think and feel. For any goalkeeper that I work with, I want them to do well and I want them to be the best. I don't want them to make any mistakes, but that's not always how it works.'

Five days after the final in Kiev, Karius was diagnosed with 'visual spatial dysfunction' by a team of medical experts at the Massachusetts General Hospital in Boston, USA. The condition hampers someone's ability to process visual information about where are objects are in space. For many, who had already made their own minds up about the incident, they were unwilling to reassess. It was rather unfairly seen as an excuse.

'He is a good goalkeeper,' insists Achterberg. 'He is good in speed reactions and pretty good at game reading. Obviously, there are always things that can be better and improved, that's with everyone. Things happened that we never wanted to happen and then we got another goalkeeper in and Loris went out on loan. That's football.' Achterberg watched Karius regularly in his time in Turkey with Besiktas and maintains regular contact with the German.

The third goalkeeper at Liverpool in this time was hoping he might get more opportunities. 'Danny Ward was a really good goalkeeper,' admits Achterberg. 'We sold him for £12m. He did really well in the games that he played. Obviously, the decision was made to sell him. He needed to go and play. He thought he was going to be number one at Leicester, but [Kasper] Schmeichel signed a new contract. He was doing really well with us. It's good to see boys making the right choices and he improved a lot.'

The criticism following the Champions League Final didn't just stop with Karius and others on the pitch as the search for someone to blame intensified. Achterberg was now a target from a section of the supporters and some fan-owned media outlets. It's extremely rare that the goalkeeping coach has his judgement called into question, although it perhaps emphasises the huge spotlight shining on the best sides in world. Klopp was quick to defend Achterberg and rightly stated that 'people in pubs' don't see the work that's put in behind the scenes.

'You can see how I dealt with it, if you followed it?' says Achterberg turning the question back on to me. I quickly scramble through my notes to see if I had missed a huge fall out that I was blissfully unaware about. 'I didn't really react to it,' he confirms, putting me at ease. 'It's easy to react if someone is negative, but you have to be stable in your way of thinking. If I was not doing my job, then I wouldn't have been in the job. You have to work hard, but you have to be good at the job. That's not being big headed, but you have to know what you are talking about.'

Having had a playing career for over 16 years, Achterberg wasn't averse to negative opinions from supporters and journalists. 'It might affect the kids more, but you have to switch off from it. Everyone has opinions, it's a way of life. Whether it's the hairdresser or another job. Liverpool is one of the biggest clubs, if not the biggest club, in the world. We have massive support, so people have opinions. They are entitled to them and something isn't right, then they will criticise, whether it's me, any player or any staff member. That's how it is! You have to be calm with that because that's part of your job. You have to ignore it and not let it affect you.'

Liverpool were on the hunt for yet another goalkeeper, but real life isn't *Football Manager*. The transaction is often quite complicated. 'Everyone wants to have the best goalkeeper in the world, but there can only be one,' says Achterberg. 'Obviously, we are Liverpool and we want the best. But so, do ten to 15 other clubs! When everyone was really negative about the goalkeepers, that's fair enough, but I would say, "Do you know how many top clubs there are in the world? I can give you ten to 15 top clubs, but can you give me ten to 15 top goalkeepers?" No one can!'

I suggest that Achterberg is like a protective dad over his players. 'That's your job, as well, to protect,' he admits. 'You need to always stay calm; no one is perfect. We want the perfect goalkeeper and the best goalkeeper. We have one of the best now in the world, if not the best. That's the truth. He is improving all the time and doing better.'

Liverpool's purchase of Alisson was a culmination of events that all worked out simultaneously. 'Can you buy the best goalkeeper in the world? Is there an option to buy the best goalkeeper in the world? Do you want to spend the money on the best goalkeeper in the world? It's all about availability, does a club want to sell their best player? Can the club afford it? Does everyone agree with the solution? That's how it works. That's not just with the goalkeeper, that's with every player. You have to make decisions.'

Alisson joined Liverpool in July 2018 for a then-world-record fee for a goalkeeper. Regular observers of Roma in Serie A and the Champions League knew the Reds were getting a phenomenal athlete. 'I think Ali fits within the style we want and is probably the best in the world at this moment,' admits Achterberg. 'The way we play, I think he is the best. That's also for other people to decide and he has to keep showing that every day, here in training and in games. He needs to keep wanting to get better and motivated. To keep producing his best day-in day-out. I don't think it's possible to find a better goalkeeper.'

The improvement to Liverpool's defence was clear and his commanding presence was obvious almost immediately. 'He has a really good speed reaction and power, which helps. He reads the game really well and is on the front foot. He has a great mind and is very resolute in his decision-making. He can change speed to resolve problems.'

Alisson's confidence in his own capabilities means he can make up for errors made by his team-mates. If he receives a short back-pass, his starting position and pace ensures that he can quickly cover the ground to diffuse the situation. 'He worked in Italy, where they work a lot in lower tempo, but more in technical ways of catching. In England, we work more in physical, speed, power, reactions and being positional in the right places. We defend the goal as high as they can, to close the angles in every position, that's what we try to do in our way. He is really good and calm in mind, under pressure, it doesn't matter if it's a final or a friendly game he just stays calm and makes calm decisions. He is making good decisions with his distribution. He always finds a solution and the players trust him.'

Alisson's adaption to the Premier League has been exceptional, although there were some slight reservations at first due to his courage and assertion in possession. Opponents will close down the goalkeeper far quicker than many other leagues, which means the thought process and decision-making has to be far more advanced. This partially explains why two players who were so proficient at Barcelona in Victor Valdes and Claudio Bravo struggled to adjust. They won countless trophies at the Camp Nou between them, but their time in Manchester at United and City respectively has seen them surprisingly fail to make an equal impact.

Alisson's Cruyff turn against Leicester City in only his fourth game saw Kelechi Iheanacho dispossess him before laying it back for Rachid Ghezzal to pull a goal back. Liverpool held on for a 2-1 victory, with Klopp explaining to the press afterwards that his outfield players were as much to blame for not providing suitable passing options. 'I didn't kill him over it,' says Achterberg. 'I spoke to him to say, "There may be an issue sometimes, if you do that." In football, there are times that if a striker runs at you at 100mph, then if you kicked it, you would hit the striker, so you have to find a different solution. 1) Kick the ball over to the sidelines to avoid hitting him and giving a throw-in away or 2) Cruyff turn him to free yourself. It's a decision as a goalkeeper that you have to make. I did it in the past myself. You learn from your mistakes and he has done that.'

There's no debate over who is Liverpool's top goalkeeper anymore. The pecking order is firmly established, but the club still needs proficient back-up players. 'It was clear that Ali was going to be the number one and Si [Mignolet] the number two, I was really happy with that situation. Because I also felt that Si was at a good level and could help us through games. Si decided that he wanted to play and left, then we looked at the goalkeepers that were available and Adri [Adrián] was one who was possible to get. He was on a free transfer.'

When Alisson was injured at the start of the 2019/20 campaign, then former West Ham United keeper Adrián had to deputise. He made his first start for Klopp's men in the UEFA Super Cup in Istanbul just nine days after he signed for the club. 'He did pretty good to be honest for a goalkeeper that had to adapt to the way we work within little time,' Achterberg says. 'Sometimes you call it the honeymoon period, when someone comes in new and straight away shows what he can do. For us, he did unbelievably well. I don't think we lost a game for a long while when he was in goal. He put us in a really good place and done well in that scenario.'

Liverpool won the Champions League in 2019 and then the Premier League for the first time in 30 years just 12 months later. The impact of Alisson as the final piece in Klopp's trophy-winning jigsaw cannot be understated. As a goalkeeping coach is it better to work with someone that has the full repertoire of skills or is it more advantageous to teach a goalkeeper who has greater growth potential? 'It's easier,' responds Achterberg, as he chooses to have the fully equipped keeper. 'Because there's less criticism from the outside. I don't find it a problem, as you just keep working, but that's still the case. You trust what he does, so that helps you as a coach. You expect him to make good solutions. Every game I feel tension because I always hope that it all goes okay, and everything is perfect. In that way, it doesn't change too much. It's great to work with him, but the main thing is we have to keep improving and keep him hungry. We want him to stay as the best for a long time and we want to win.'